Fun for a Fiver in London

Ben West has written for many newspapers and magazines including the *Guardian*, the *Independent*, the *Daily Telegraph*, *The Times*, the *Daily Mail*, the *Evening Standard* and *Reader's Digest*. He was chief property writer of the *Daily Express* and the *Sunday Express* from 1999–2001. He has appeared on numerous radio and television programmes and his work has been translated into foreign languages as varied as Korean, Czechoslovakian and Polish. He recently completed a play that generated considerable interest in a dire pub theatre in a grim suburb of London.

Also available in Pan Books by Ben West

Fun for a Fiver in Amsterdam

Ben West

Fun for a Fiver in London

PAN BOOKS

First published 2002 by Pan Books
an imprint of Pan Macmillan Ltd
Pan Macmillan, 20 New Wharf Road, London N1 9RR
Basingstoke and Oxford
Associated companies throughout the world
www.panmacmillan.com

ISBN 0 330 48606 3

A CIP catalogue record for this book is available from
the British Library.

Typeset by SetSystems Ltd, Saffron Walden, Essex
Printed and bound in Great Britain by
Mackays of Chatham plc, Chatham, Kent

Contents

Introduction

The person who said that the best things in life are free has clearly never driven a factory-fresh Ferrari. But that doesn't mean to say that obtaining something without paying much or anything for it isn't gratifying. Especially when the basic art of existing can be prohibitive at the best of times.

Whatever your age and interests, whether you are a Londoner wishing to discover more of this great city, a cash-strapped parent with children to entertain, or a visitor to the capital who, after shelling out for transport, board and lodgings doesn't wish to also have to travel the expensive tourist trails that so many end up on, this book is for you.

The many suggestions contained in this book counterbalance the charge frequently made about London – that it is exceptionally expensive. Everything included here – at the time of writing – costs under £5 for adult admission and many things included are free.

Many people know *vaguely* of a handful of things that are cheap or free in London. This guide clearly and concisely explains when, where and how they can obtain a wealth of them, and answers questions such as 'Do you have to turn up early to get an acceptable view?', 'Does something cost £5 only at a certain time?', 'Do you have to apply first for tickets?'

In the same way that it makes sense to discover your own country before expensively jet-setting around the world (how many people from southern England see the Yorkshire Dales, Durham or the Scottish islands before booking their first flight to Spain?) equally does it not make sense to experience the abundance of cheap and free things on offer in the capital before spending a small fortune on London leisure?

And it is a small fortune. A couple of adults visiting, say, the London Dungeon, Rock Circus, Madame Tussaud's and the Tower of London – often invariably after a lengthy queue – would receive little change from £85.

Splashing out for expensive admission tickets to a well-known tourist attraction is no guarantee of satisfaction. How often have you paid a visit to one of London's most popular tourist attractions, at considerable expense, and discovered that there seemed to be no restriction on numbers admitted, or that you were herded round like cattle, pushed onwards by the crowd if you dared pause at any of the exhibits?

It is surprising how badly designed many attractions are, the most common problems being sharp edges at toddler level around display cases, just waiting to cause an accident, and bad signposting and inadequate facilities for those in wheelchairs, those otherwise disabled or those with push-chairs. Paying a big admission charge on top of such trials hardly pacifies the harassed visitor.

You can experience many of London's wonders most

adequately without paying much or anything for the privilege. For instance, you can obtain a better sense of the excellence of Tower Bridge by walking over the bridge at car level for free rather than by paying £6.25 adult admission for the tour of the bridge, which lasts over an hour and includes a walk across the upper walkways. These are so enclosed by glass and metal, you might as well be looking out from any old office building.

Theme parks are especially expensive to visit. Their phenomenal success is difficult to understand when you consider what they offer. If you've been to one you'll be aware of the yells and screams, becoming louder the nearer you get to the entrance gates. These are not due to the thrills of the rollercoasters and other terrifying rides, but are the reactions of visitors on discovering the admission charges.

For example, Chessington World of Adventures currently charges around £20 for an adult and £16 for a child, and a family of four would pay out over £60 before buying any drinks or food. Incredibly, some of the attractions require further expenditure. And there's no prior warning that, because so many people have been admitted, half an hour or even an hour's wait for the more popular rides is not unusual. On busy days – most weekends and school holidays – many visitors therefore only experience the less exceptional attractions, such as fairground rides, the playground and zoo – at an exceptionally high cost.

A number of these famous but pricey stops on the well-worn tourist trail could well be located in any city in the world, having no particular relevance to London. Many of the cheap or free events and venues on offer in London, and contained in this book, explain the capital, its rich history and people far more effectively than the obvious, expensive tourist spots. For example, an hour in the public gallery of the Old Bailey can effortlessly reveal aspects of the British character and past and present in a way that Rock Circus and the like never could.

Boundaries of the Book

London covers a large area and it can be difficult to decide on its boundaries. Some people define the place as anywhere with an 020 7 or 020 8 telephone code; others would say that anywhere with a London north, south, east and west postcode counts as being part of the capital. Then there's the 32 boroughs that make up Greater London to consider, or you could define the place as the area within the M25 or that covered by the A–Z street map. Whatever definition you subscribe to, I trust that on the whole the entries in this book represent your idea of London.

Geography hasn't been the only matter to cause problems during the compilation of this book. For example, £5 would buy you an afternoon of coffees or a couple of drinks in many cafes and bars in London, but of course it would be impractical to include them all here. Likewise, you can buy an adult admission cinema ticket for £5 or under at many cinemas in town, but including them all is outside the scope of this book.

This book is primarily concerned with discovering those things you can enjoy in London that are free or inexpensive and which are unique, rare or stand out from the crowd. For this reason, many more theatres are included than cinemas, for example. Venues where you can enjoy a good theatrical performance for less than £5 for an adult ticket are rare; cinemas showing the same old Hollywood fare are not.

A Few More Points About This Book

The book is arranged alphabetically by subject but there is also a regional index so you can easily plan a visit to a number of attractions when going to a particular area. There are also some suggested itineraries for a good day out.

Every endeavour has been made to ensure details were correct when going to press. Nevertheless, obviously policies and prices change so check details such as opening times and admission charges before setting out. Many places may be closed or alter opening times on particular days, especially around Christmas and on bank holidays.

Some of the places listed are administered by trusts, charities and associations that do not charge admission fees, but would welcome a voluntary donation to help keep the establishment open to the public.

If any books mentioned in the text are not in print, they should be obtainable from your local library.

When visiting open spaces and nature reserves, visitors should keep to any marked paths to avoid causing any damage or disturbance.

The nearest overground rail station and/or underground

station is included for many entries, although sometimes a further walk or bus ride may be necessary.

The published London telephone numbers do not include the prefix 020, which is required when dialling from outside London.

Any comments or suggestions of things to include in future editions of this book would be welcomed. Please write to: Ben West, *Fun For A Fiver in London*, Pan Books, 20 New Wharf Road, London N1 9RR.

Animal and Bird Enclosures in Parks

Admission is *free* unless otherwise stated.
For further animal encounters see *City Farms* p. 64.

Battersea Park Children's Zoo Battersea Park, Queenstown Road, SW8 (8871 7540) *Open: Apr–Sept daily 10am–5pm; Oct–Mar Sat, Sun 11am–3pm. Adults £1.80, children, concessions 90p. Sloane Square underground/Battersea Park/Queenstown Road rail.* A little zoo with animals that include monkeys and meerkats, ponies and pigs, a llama and goats. Elsewhere in the park is a deer enclosure.

Clissold Park Green Lanes, N16 (8800 1021) *Finsbury Park underground/rail.* Fallow deer, rabbits, waterfowl and tropical birds including a peacock and a mynah bird.

Golders Hill Park North End Road, NW11 (8455 5183) *Golders Green underground.* Antelope, fallow deer, wallabies, pygmy goats and aviaries with a good variety of exotic birds including cranes, magpies, flamingoes and pheasants.

Greenwich Park Maze Hill, SE10 (8858 2608) *Greenwich/Maze Hill rail.* A herd of deer roam a 13-acre enclosure and the central pond has a good variety of wildfowl.

Holland Park Illchester Place, Kensington, W8 (7602 9483) *Holland Park underground.* Muscovy ducks, peacocks, bantams and other birds.

Horniman Gardens 100 London Road, Forest Hill, SE23 (8699 1872) *Forest Hill rail.* A little children's zoo with small animals.

Maryon Wilson Park Thorntree Road, SE7 (8854 0446) *Charlton/*

Woolwich Dockyard rail. A deer park and children's zoo with goats, ponies, sheep, rabbits, chickens and donkeys.

Plashet Zoo Plashet Park, Plashet Grove, Shrewsbury Road, Forest Gate, E7 (8503 5994) *Open summer Tues–Sun 10am–5pm; winter Tues–Sun 10am–4pm. East Ham underground.* A small zoo with ponies, pygmy goats, llamas, wallabies, butterflies and various birds.

St James's Park The Mall, SW1 (7930 1793) *St James's Park underground.* On the island and lake in the centre of the park there are over 30 types of bird including pelicans, moorhens and various types of geese and ducks. In addition, many other bird varieties fly in and out.

Trent Country Park Cockfosters Road, Barnet, Herts (8449 8706) *Cockfosters underground.* In Pets Corner there is a variety of animals such as sheep, pigs, rabbits and chickens.

Victoria Park Victoria Park Road, E9 (8985 1957) *Mile End underground.* Fallow deer and pygmy goats on the eastern side of the park.

Annual Events:
Festivals and Festivities

Admission at all events is *free* unless otherwise stated.

JANUARY

New Year's Day London Parade *Starts at Parliament Square at noon and ends at Berkeley Square in Mayfair around 2.45pm. Westminster underground.* An estimated 700,000 to 1 million people attend this huge procession which passes through

Whitehall, Cockspur Street, Lower Regent Street, Piccadilly Circus, Piccadilly, Berkeley Street and Berkeley Square. There are various floats and horse-drawn carriages carrying the mayors of Westminster and the London boroughs. Also a fair and aerial displays. If you think you'd fit into the procession and could offer some form of street entertainment, you can participate for free. Telephone the organisers for details on 8566 8586.

Charles I Commemoration Whitehall, SW1 (7836 3205) *Last Sunday in January, 11.30am. Charing Cross underground/rail.* In 1649 Charles I was removed from the Banqueting House, Whitehall, and executed at the scaffold. To commemorate this, members of the King's Army in 17th-century garb, parade from St James's Palace down the Mall, through Horse Guards to the Banqueting House and on to King Charles's statue in Trafalgar Square. They lay a wreath at the Banqueting House and then return.

Chinese New Year Festival Around Gerrard and Lisle Streets and Newport Place, Soho, W1 (7439 3822) *In late January or early February, on the nearest Sunday to the date of the Chinese New Year, at around 11am–5pm. Leicester Square underground.* The high point of the Chinese calendar means London's Chinatown comes alive with music, colourful dancers, stalls, performers and decorations on windows and balconies. Dragon and lion dancers entertain the crowds.

FEBRUARY

Clowns' Service Holy Trinity Church, Beechwood Road, Dalston, E8 (7254 5062) *First Sunday in February. Dalston Junction rail.* Members of the Clowns' International Club attend a special church service here in full costume, laying a wreath on a memorial to Grimaldi, originator of the clown. A clown show follows in the church hall, which is particularly popular with children.

Lincoln's Inn Fields Pancake Day Races Lincoln's Inn, WC2 *Shrove Tuesday (the day before Lent), races begin 11am. Holborn underground. Also* **Great Spitalfields Pancake Day Races** Spitalfields Market, Brushfield Street, E1 (7375 0441) *Shrove Tuesday, from noon. Liverpool Street underground/rail.* Of interest to all tossers, pancake day marks the beginning of Lent when fat and meat were prohibited and therefore used up in savoury pancakes. On this day races are held throughout the country, where the competitors run while tossing pancakes in frying pans. Not as yet an Olympic event, sadly.

MARCH

International Women's Week *Greenwich, early March.* A week packed with events for women, held all over the London Borough of Greenwich. It includes health, fitness, sports events and coaching, talks, poetry, presentations, dance classes, exhibitions and more. Look out for leaflets in the borough earlier in the year.

Chelsea Antiques Fair Chelsea Old Town Hall, King's Road, SW3 (01444 482514) *Around a week in mid-March. Adults £5, under-18s free. Sloane Square underground.* Loads of antiques to browse.

Spring Equinox Druid Ceremony Tower Hill Terrace, EC3. *Held in March: details from the Druid Order (8659 4879). Tower Hill underground.* This hour-long ceremony is one of the ancient rituals of the Order of Druids, who wear white hooded gowns. It celebrates spring, the season of renewal.

Oranges and Lemons Service Church of St Clement Danes, Strand, WC2 (7242 8282) *Held in March/April. Aldwych underground.* 'Oranges and lemons, say the bells of St Clements . . .' goes the nursery rhyme. After a special service, children from St Clement Danes School are given an orange and a lemon to celebrate the day these fruits first appeared in London.

Holi Festival Roe Green Park, Kingsbury Road, NW9 (8900 5659) *Kingsbury underground.* A Hindu celebration held in March.

Head of the River Race *On the Thames from Mortlake, SW14, to Putney, SW6. Last Saturday in March. Mortlake rail (start of race)/Putney Bridge underground (end).* Although less well known than the Oxford and Cambridge Boat Race, this is probably more fun as over 400 crews of eight-oared boats, starting at 10-second intervals, compete to be fastest. The best views are from Chiswick Bridge, Hammersmith Bridge or from Putney Bridge at the end of the race.

APRIL

Oxford and Cambridge Boat Race *On the Thames from Putney, SW6 to Mortlake, SW14 (7611 3500). Saturday in April. Putney Bridge underground.* This annual clash between the rowing teams of Oxford and Cambridge universities, lasting under 20 minutes, has been held on the Thames since 1849. The two boats are cheered on by large crowds on the riverbanks and bridges along the four-mile, 374-yard course, even though few get a particularly good view.

Tyburn Walk *From the Old Bailey (the Central Criminal Court), Newgate Street, EC4 to Tyburn Convent, 8 Hyde Park Place, W2. Last Sunday in April at 3pm. St Paul's underground.* A silent procession led by a Catholic bishop takes around two hours to walk the three miles from the site of Newgate Prison (the Old Bailey) to a special service at Tyburn Convent. The Walk is held in memory of Catholics martyred at Tyburn Gallows during the 16th and 17th centuries.

Easter Show Battersea Park, SW11 (8871 7530) *Easter Sunday, parade begins around 3pm. Battersea Park rail.* Large crowds arrive for a carnival of sideshows, a fair, concerts, stalls, children's competitions, a children's theatre, a steel band and various stalls.

Kite Festival Blackheath, SE3 *Easter Sunday and Monday. Blackheath rail.* A dazzling collection of stunt kites.

London Harness Horse Parade Battersea Park, Queenstown Road, SW8 (01733 234451) *Easter Monday from around 9am onwards. Battersea Park rail.* The parade in the park, first held in 1885, features horse-drawn carriages competing for rosettes and brass badges, and side shows.

London Marathon *From Greenwich Park, Blackheath, SE3, to Buckingham Palace, SW1, via the Isle of Dogs and Victoria Embankment (7620 4117). A Sunday in April, 9am. Greenwich/Blackheath/Maze Hill rail (start), Embankment underground (end).* Crowds of over 500,000 line the whole 26-mile route of this, the world's largest road race. There are over 35,000 participants (many raising money for charity) including celebrities, the disabled and those in fancy dress.

The international record breakers take a little over two hours to complete the course, but the funrunners ensure it is an all-day event.

MAY

Canalway Cavalcade Little Venice, W2 *May Day weekend Sat–Mon. Warwick Avenue underground.* Around 30,000 visitors enjoy this pageant which encompasses 150 decorated boats, canoeing displays, boat handling competitions, raft races, folk music, Morris dancers, jazz and brass bands, a trade and craft show, theatre, children's activities, teddy bears' picnics and other attractions. The Sunday evening sees an illuminated procession of boats.

Highbury Festival Highbury Fields, N5 *First two weeks of May. Highbury and Islington underground.* Musical events and other entertainments, art exhibitions and an all-day jazz extravaganza on the Bank Holiday Monday.

Museums Week *A week in May, usually starting on the third Saturday.* Many museums put on special events.

Watch This Space Theatre Square and Terraces, National Theatre, SE1 (7452 3327) *May–Sept Tues–Sat, lunchtimes and evenings. Waterloo/Embankment underground.* A festival of riverside events with street theatre, acrobatics, comedy, music, mime and magic from all over the world.

May Fayre and Puppet Festival St Paul's Church Garden, Covent Garden, WC2 (7375 0441) *Held on nearest Sunday to 9 May. Covent Garden underground.* Celebrating the first Punch and Judy show, reported by diarist Samuel Pepys on 9 May

---

1662, in the doorway of the church. There's a procession and entertainments, a parade from 10.30am and a service in the church from 11.30am.

Chestnut Sunday Bushy Park, Hampton Court Road, Middlesex, TW12 (8979 1586) *Second Sunday in May from noon to 7pm. Hampton Wick rail.* An event dating from Victorian times with a parade including veteran bicycles such as Penny Farthings and carriages passing along the mile-long Chestnut Avenue. The trees are in bloom, but of the 1,300 trees curiously only a fifth are chestnuts. There are also other entertainments including Victorian bands, Victorian re-enactment groups and horse displays.

Covent Garden Festival of Opera and the Musical Arts *Two-week festival in May (7369 1793). Covent Garden underground.* The festival typically includes a parade, mini-operas, choral and theatrical works, celebrity interviews and an opera troupe performing in Covent Garden shops and bars during lunchtimes and in the evening.

Victoria Embankment Gardens Summer Entertainments Villiers Street, WC2 (7375 0441) *May–July. Charing Cross underground/ rail.* The festival begins with weekend festivals celebrating dance and music, mime, poetry and the like, and has lunchtime and evening performances of street theatre, mime, music, opera and other attractions towards the end.

Camley Street Natural Park Festival Camley Street Natural Park, 12 Camley Street, NW1 (7833 2311) *Held on a Sunday in late May. King's Cross underground/Camden Road rail.* A community gathering with music and dancing.

Whitestone Pond Summer Open Air Art Exhibition Whitestone Pond, Heath Street, NW3 *May–Aug, Sat, Sun 11am–6.30pm. Hampstead underground.* Paintings, prints, pottery and other crafts are all on display.

Oak Apple Day Royal Hospital Chelsea, Royal Hospital Road, SW3 (7730 5282) *29 May. Sloane Square underground.* The Chelsea Pensioners honour their founder, Charles II, on the anniversary of his escape after the Battle of Worcester in 1651, when he hid in an oak tree. In the ceremony, his statue is decorated with oak leaves.

Family Fun Days The Albany Centre, Douglas Way, SE8 (8692 0231) *One day a month from May to August. New Cross underground/ rail.* Entertainment for children including music, clowns and a bouncy castle.

Broadgate Arena Summer Entertainments Broadgate Centre, Eldon Street, EC2 (7588 6565) *May–Sept Mon–Fri 12.30–2pm. Liverpool Street underground/rail.* This outdoor site is used for a variety of imaginative events including music, dance and theatre. There could be anything from fashion shows, riding displays and Elvis impersonators to pageantry and jousting, aerobics masterclasses and karate. Music ranges from blues to classical, folk and reggae. There are even giant chess and draughts sets available if you fancy a game. The Arena also hosts events at Halloween, Christmas and on Burns Night.

JUNE

Not the Royal Academy Llewellyn Alexander Gallery, 124–126 The Cut, SE1 (7620 1322) *Early June to early September, Mon– Sat 10am–7.30pm. Waterloo underground/rail.* What happens to the 13,000 paintings not hung at the Royal Academy Summer Exhibition? Not the Royal Academy organises a constantly changing exhibition of the best. This event has been held since 1991, echoing the 19th-century 'Salon des Refuses', when Manet and Sargent rebelled against the French Academy and mounted their own Paris exhibition.

Beating the Retreat Horse Guards Parade, SW1 (7414 2271) *Early/mid June. Charing Cross underground/rail.* These impressive military displays of marching and drilling bands are held over a couple of days.

Trooping the Colour Buckingham Palace to Horse Guards Parade, SW1 (7414 2479) *Second Saturday in June, 10.40am. St James's Park underground.* To celebrate her official birthday on 11 June, the Queen leaves Buckingham Palace at 10.40am in an open carriage, going down the Mall to meet the Brigade of Guards and the Household Cavalry at Horse Guards Parade at 11am. After the Queen returns to the Palace at around noon there is an RAF flypast down the Mall, the national anthem is played, and there is a gun salute fired in Green Park. Attending the event is not free but you can watch the procession down the Mall, and free tickets are available by ballot for the first rehearsal. For tickets write with a stamped addressed envelope to the Brigade Major (Trooping the Colour), Household Division, Horse Guards, Whitehall, SW1.

Spitalfields Festival Christchurch, Commercial Street, E1 (7377 1362) *June. Liverpool Street underground/rail, Aldgate East underground.* A lively celebration of music from the 17th to the 20th century with, typically, lunchtime and evening concerts, music theatre, art exhibitions, educational and visual art events and even live relays of concerts free to the Old Spitalfields Market.

Covent Garden Flower Festival Covent Garden Market, WC2 (7836 9136) *Last week in June. Covent Garden underground.* Street performances and fashion shows augment the floral displays.

Dulwich Country Fayre Dulwich Park, College Road, SE22 (7525 3735) *A Saturday and Sunday in June, 11am–6pm. North/ West Dulwich rail.* Magic, circus skills workshops, police dog demonstrations, riding displays, a cycle circuit, bandstand and other attractions.

Brent Countryside Day Fryent Country Park, Fryent Way, Kingsbury, NW9 (8900 5659) *A Sunday in June. Wembley Park underground.* This country festival offers family entertainment in the form of farm animals, sheepdog trials, nature walks and other events.

Cycle Promenade Day Richmond Park, Holly Lodge, Richmond, Surrey (8948 3209) *A Sunday in early/mid June. Richmond underground/rail.* Various entertainments, a five-mile easy-to-follow route and free cycle checks to promote cycling.

Stoke Newington Midsummer Festival *A week in mid-June (7254 3735). Stoke Newington rail.* A week of events in which local artists and performers perform in various Stoke Newington venues. The very varied attractions include music, dance, carnival, readings, guided walks, art exhibitions and workshops. The grand finale on the Sunday is the Church Street Festival Party with its opening procession, sports displays, dance, circus performance, a fayre and lots of music.

Tierra Latino Kennington Park, SE11. *Second weekend in June. Oval underground*. Live Latin American bands, dancing, funfair and stalls selling ethnic food.

Knollys Red Rose Rent *Seething Lane, EC3 to Mansion House, EC2 (7481 2928) Around 24 June. Bank underground*. At around 10.45am various robed dignitaries from All Hallows-by-the-Tower Church walk from Seething Lane to the Lord Mayor of London's official residence, Mansion House at Walbrook, EC4, to present the Lord Mayor and his wife with roses to commemorate the Mayor fining Sir Robert Knollys for building a footbridge in Seething Lane in 1381.

Lesbian and Gay Pride Festival Victoria Park, Victoria Park Road, E9 *Third Saturday in June. Bethnal Green underground*. An increasingly huge event with a turnout of around 150,000 with half of that taking part in the march. There are many events, including live music and cabaret.

City of London Festival *Venues around the City (7638 8891). Lasts three weeks from late June*. Includes 20 to 30 events that could range from classical, jazz and pop to operetta, opera and theatre in some of the square mile's most beautiful churches, squares and other venues.

Greenwich Park Family Day Greenwich Park, SE10. (8858 2608) *A Saturday in late June/early July from noon to 5pm. Greenwich/Maze Hill rail*. Lots of fun events for all the family, which could include steam engine rides, archery displays, farm animals, bands, clowns and gymnastic displays.

Deptford Festival *Various venues in Deptford, SE8 (8692 4446), Around late June to late July*. A month-long festival with a greatly varied programme including a carnival procession.

JULY

Greenwich and Docklands International Festival *Venues around Greenwich and Docklands (8305 1818). Greenwich rail / Cutty Sark DLR.* Many of this arts festival's events are free including the opening night celebrations which include a firework display, live music and street theatre at Cutty Sark Gardens, SE10. There are often a number of free exhibitions, workshops and classes, children's events, poetry and music. During the festival, in nearby SE3 there's Blackheath Village Fayre, which has increasingly abandoned its olde worlde feel to become a small modern fair plus jumble sale. It also includes displays such as police dogs jumping through hoops of fire, and trapeze artists.

Croydon Summer Festival *Two weeks in July (8760 5400). Croydon rail.* Typically music, a fair, street theatre, circus performers and a firework finale.

Hackney Show Hackney Downs, Downs Road, E5 (8356 7315). *First Saturday in July noon–8pm. Hackney Central rail.* Over 40,000 people attend this fun, family event. There's music, comedy, variety entertainment, a dog show, film tent, a children's play area, stalls and sideshows.

Bexley Festival *First two weeks of July at various Bexley venues (8308 4836).* Includes international street theatre and cycle races in the town centre, the opportunity to try sports and water activities such as waterskiing, windsurfing and sailing in Danson Park, a regatta, a rugby festival, and live music.

Catford Arts Festival St Dunstan's College, Stanstead Road, SE6. *Early July. Catford / Catford Bridge rail.* Although many of the events are not free, there are workshops and demonstrations

---

covering such subjects as silk-screen printing, doll making and pottery, and there are several visual art events.

Shell LSO Music Scholarship Final Barbican Concert Hall, Silk Street, EC2 (7638 8891) *Barbican/Moorgate underground*. In early July four young musicians play classical music alongside the London Symphony Orchestra to compete in this prestigious event. Apply early for tickets and for more information telephone 7588 1116.

Paddington Performance Festival Paddington Recreation Ground, Grantully Road, W9 (7375 0441) *First Sunday in July, noon–6pm. Maida Vale underground*. A celebration of performing arts. Clowns, jugglers, stilt walkers, acrobats, trapeze artists, unicyclists and other circus acts merge with lots of music, workshops and games.

Coin Street Festival Gabriel's Wharf, 56 Upper Ground, SE1 (7401 3610) *Takes place on various days from early July to early September. Waterloo/Charing Cross underground/rail*. Gabriel's Wharf, a workplace for about 20 craft and designer artists, holds a festival with, typically, live music and dance from around the world, a children's carnival procession, collectors' cars, street theatre, children's workshops and possibly even an open-air circus. From Tues–Sun 11am–6pm throughout the year the craftspeople can be seen making sculpture, jewellery, ceramics, fashion items, etc.

Doggett's Coat and Badge Race London Bridge, SE1 to Albert Bridge, SW11 (7626 3531). *A day in late July. London Bridge underground*. Thomas Doggett, an 18th-century Irish comedian left a legacy for this half-hour race (the oldest rowing event in the world) to commemorate the anniversary of George I's accession to the throne. It involves six Thames watermen racing for four and a half miles against the tide. The winner receives a distinctive scarlet uniform and a silver badge.

Clerkenwell Festival Clerkenwell Green, EC1 (7253 6644) *A week-long festival from mid-July, ending on first Sunday after 16 July. Farringdon/Barbican underground.* Street entertainment, stalls, music, children's activities and processions.

Swan Upping *Takes place on the Thames (Sunbury-on-Thames to Pangbourne, Berkshire). Mon–Fri third week in July, 9.30am–5pm. (7236 1863).* The swans on the Thames are owned by the Queen, the Dyers' Company and the Vintners' Company – two City livery companies. This extraordinary 300-year old ceremony, in which boats manned by colourfully dressed oarsmen search for swans for five days, establishes who owns the cygnets and marks their beaks accordingly.

Vintners' Company Procession Upper Thames Street, EC4 (7236 1863) *On the second Wednesday in July. Blackfriars underground.* Dressed in traditional costume, members of the Vintners' Company proceed from Vintners' Hall in Upper Thames Street to the Church of St James's, Garlickhythe, to celebrate the election of their newly sworn-in master. The Company's wine porters head the party sweeping the road with birch brooms to clear the way.

Disability Arts Day Victoria Embankment Gardens, Villiers Street, WC2 (7375 0441) *Late July. Charing Cross rail/underground.* Features a cabaret show.

Jazz on the Streets Midsummer Festival *Central London spaces including Marble Arch, Soho Square, Golden Square, South Moulton Street, Covent Garden Piazza, Carnaby Street, W1.*

Last week of July. (8211 0976) Covent Garden/Picadilly under-ground. Ten or more live jazz events from morning until night.

Cart Marking Guildhall Yard, EC2 (7489 8287) *A day in late July. Moorgate underground/rail.* This registration ceremony of horses and carts evolved after increasing concern for traffic congestion – not today, but in the 17th century.

Shri Vallabh Nidhi UK Asian Festival Roundwood Park, Harlesden Road, NW10 *Willesden Green underground.* Held in July or August, this is a Hindu celebration lasting a week or more.

AUGUST

Riding Horse Parade Rotten Row, Hyde Park, W1 *First Sunday in August around 1pm. Hyde Park Corner underground.* Over 50 horses and their riders compete in various events.

Portabello Festival Portabello Road, W11 (8964 4419) *Around the first two weeks of August. Ladbroke Grove underground.* Music, performance and street theatre.

Ealing Summer Festival Walpole Park, Mattock Lane, Ealing (8579 5436). *First two weeks of August. Ealing Broadway underground.* An arts and music festival with jazz and other music per-formances, storytelling for children, a food fair etc.

Festival of Summer Walks *Call 7339 8500 for details.* A variety of guided walks all around the capital organised by the Ramblers' Association in mid/late August.

Children's Festival Calthorpe Project Community Garden, 258–274 Gray's Inn Road, WC1 (7837 8019) *A Sunday in mid- to late-August. King's Cross underground/rail.* Various events for under- and over-8s which have included such things as play areas, art workshops, karaoke, trapeze workshops and children's bands.

Kids' Week *Around the last week of August. Ring 0870 0732000 for details.* A huge entertainment extravaganza in which about 25 West End theatres allow children to see their shows for FREE, although adults have to pay. There are also many free theatre workshops and activities. A number of West End restaurants offer children free meals during the week if accompanied by an adult.

Notting Hill Carnival *August bank holiday Sunday and Monday, 10am–late. Takes place on the streets around Ladbroke Grove and Notting Hill, W10, W11 (8964 0544). Ladbroke Grove/ Notting Hill Gate underground.* Established in 1965, this is possibly Europe's biggest outdoor festival with over a million people attending. There are several live music stages and sound systems with calypso, house, rap, ragga, Caribbean soca and reggae music, as well as dancing, costume parades and a procession. It's a riot of colour and sounds with great atmosphere and wonderful food, but it gets extremely crowded.

SEPTEMBER

Hay's Galleria Oyster and Seafood Fair Tooley Street, SE1 (7940 7770). *Usually the first Fri–Sun in September, 11am–7pm. London Bridge underground.* There's everything from live music and comedy on a fish theme, fish cookery demonstrations and a chance to sample a variety of seafood. FREE except some food samples.

Brick Lane Festival Brick Lane and Allen Gardens, E1 (7655 0906)

First Sunday in September, 1pm–7pm. Liverpool Street/Shore-ditch underground. A wide variety of live music and dance from around the world, including steel bands, samba and salsa music. There are also craft and food stalls, children's entertainment, street theatre and rickshaw rides.

Limehouse Festival *Various venues around Limehouse, E14. Limehouse DLR.* Dependent upon the tide, this weekend event is usually held in September or October and has attractions ranging from Chinese dragons, vintage boats, narrow boats and sailing barges, theatre, arts, dance, environmental displays, children's activities, live music, street entertainers and various stalls.

Autumn Equinox Druid Ceremony Primrose Hill, NW3 *Held in September: details from the Druid Order (8659 4879). Camden Town underground.* This is an ancient ritual by the Order of Druids, celebrating autumn, the season of harvest.

Chinatown Festival Gerrard Street, W1 and Newport Place, WC1 (7287 1118) *Leicester Square underground.* Quite like the Chinese New Year Festival but smaller. There are stalls and entertainments including dancing dragons.

Thames Festival *A weekend in mid-September (7928 8998). Waterloo underground/rail.* Arts events with a funfair, music, costumes, fireworks and a river procession in the vicinity of Waterloo and Blackfriars Bridges.

Chelsea Antiques Fair Chelsea Old Town Hall, King's Road, SW3 (01444 482514) *Around a week in mid-September. Adults £5, under-18s FREE. Sloane Square underground.* Loads of antiques to browse through.

Covent Garden Market Festival of Street Theatre Covent

Garden, WC2 (7836 9136) *Two weeks in September. Covent Garden underground.* A celebration with various acts including puppeteers, acrobats and stilt-walkers.

Angel Canal Festival City Road Basin, N1 (7267 9100) *A Sunday in early September, 11am–6pm. Angel underground.* A community festival with stalls, music, boat trips and Punch and Judy.

Queen's Park Entertainment Day Queen's Park, Kingswood Avenue, NW6 (8969 5661) *Generally second Sunday in September. Queen's Park underground.* The community puts on music, games and other entertainments as well as stalls at this well-attended event.

Slough Canal Day Bloom Park, off Middle Green Road, Slough (7286 6101) *Usually second Sunday in September. Slough rail.* Various entertainments including Shire horse rides, morris dancing, clog dancing, music, stalls, story telling and bouncy castles.

Battle of Britain Week *Around 15 September. Westminster underground.* A series of events including an RAF fly-past over London, memorials, and on the Sunday, remembrance services at Westminster Abbey and other churches.

Great River Race *Takes place on a Saturday in mid-September, beginning between 10am and 2pm depending upon the tide (8398 9057).* Around 250 oared and paddled boats race the 22 miles from Ham House in Richmond, Surrey to Island Gardens, the Isle of Dogs, E14. It is quite spectacular to watch as such a great variety of boats take part including old passenger barges, Hawaiian war canoes, Irish curraghs, Chinese dragon boats and (replica) Viking longships. Many

---

of the boats are 100–150 years old. The start of the race is staggered and it takes nearly two hours for all the boats to leave, and over five hours from the first boat leaving to the last finishing. The race can be seen all along the Thames, but it's most fun to view from the start or finish.

Horseman's Sunday Church of St John and St Michael, Hyde Park Crescent, W2 (7262 1732) *Third Sunday in September: morris dancing at 11am, service at 11.30am. Paddington underground.* Originating when a riding stables protested when faced with closure in 1969, at the front of the church the vicar blesses over 100 horses in a 30-minute service. The horses head for Hyde Park, and around 1.30pm show jumping takes place in the north of Kensington Gardens.

Open House Days *A weekend towards the end of September (0900 160 0061).* In this festival, which celebrates London's architecture, the public are welcome to visit over 500 buildings of particular architectural significance or cultural interest for FREE that they would normally not have access to. In the past, buildings as wide ranging as court-houses, a modern monastery, ITN's headquarters and a nuclear bunker have taken part in the scheme. Get a programme and book early as many venues get booked up rapidly.

OCTOBER

Raising of the Thames Barrier Unity Way, Woolwich, SE18 (8305 4188) *Usually in early October. Charlton rail.* This is the best time to see this feat of modern engineering, installed in 1982. You can watch the ten huge metal gates being raised or dropped against the high tide from the riverbank as a commentary provides background to what is happening. There's a pleasant riverside walk and a children's play area.

Punch and Judy Festival Covent Garden Piazza, WC2 (7836 9136) *Usually first Sunday in October. Covent Garden underground.* A collection of the traditional ferocious and untamed puppets, both from the UK and other parts of Europe.

Costermonger's Pearly Kings and Queens Harvest Festival St Martin-in-the-Fields, Trafalgar Square, WC2 (7766 1100) *First Sunday afternoon in October. Charing Cross underground/rail.* Costermongers sold fruit and vegetables on London's streets, and their representatives, over 100 cockney Pearly Kings and Queens in their traditional costumes covered with pearl buttons, gather for a harvest thanksgiving, bringing fruit and vegetables for the poor and old.

Harvest of the Sea Thanksgiving St Mary-at-Hill, Eastcheap, EC3 *Second Sunday in October, service 11am. Monument underground.* Grateful fish dealers bring their catches to this special service.

Southwark Festival *Mid-October to early November. Venues include Guy's Hospital, Southwark Cathedral, Hay's Galleria, Borough Market,* SE1 *(7403 7400). London Bridge underground/rail.* Lots of free events including lunchtime classical concerts, a family fun day, visual arts, street theatre and a food fair. There is a spectacular fireworks display on the last day.

Shakespeare in Spitalfields Spitalfields Market, E1 (7375 0441) *Late October. Liverpool Street underground/rail.* Talented thespians perform Shakespeare.

Trafalgar Day Parade Trafalgar Square, WC2 (7928 8978) *Sunday nearest to 21 October at 11am. Charing Cross underground/rail.*

There is a parade made up of hundreds of sea cadets and marching bands, and a commemoration service for Nelson's 1805 victory with wreaths laid at the base of Nelson's column.

State Opening of Parliament House of Lords, Palace of Westminster, SW1 (7219 4272) *Late October or early/mid November, or when a new government comes to power. The Queen arrives at Parliament at 11am. Westminster underground.* The public cannot attend the official ceremony where the Queen officially reopens Parliament after the summer recess (but can watch it on television) but can see her arrive and depart in a state coach, along with the Household Cavalry. There are gun salutes to mark the occasion at Hyde Park, W2 (Hyde Park Corner underground) or Green Park, SW1 (Green Park underground) at noon and the Tower of London, EC3 at 1pm (Tower Hill underground).

NOVEMBER

Bonfire Night *5 November* All over Britain firework displays with huge bonfires (not all free) are held in parks and open spaces to commemorate the failure of Guy Fawkes' 1605 Gunpowder Plot to blow up Parliament. There are usually good displays at Alexandra Palace, Battersea Park, Blackheath Common, Crystal Palace, Highbury Fields, Primrose Hill and Ravenscourt Park.

London to Brighton Veteran Car Run *First Sunday in November, beginning around 7.30am at Serpentine Road, Hyde Park, W2 (01753 681736). Hyde Park Corner underground.* This, the oldest competitive motoring event, first held in 1896, celebrates the end of the requirement for a man with a red flag to walk in front of the car. Crowds cheer the magnificent pre-1905 cars with an average speed of around 20mph all along the route, via Westminster Bridge, the A23 and to Brighton. The first cars arrive at around 10.30am.

Admission of the Lord Mayor Elect Guildhall, Gresham Street, EC2 (7606 3030) *Second Friday in November. Bank/St Paul's underground.* Apply to the Keeper's Office for a ticket to see this 20-minute silent ceremony where the retiring Lord Mayor hands over the insignia to the new one.

Lord Mayor's Show The City of London (7606 3030) *Second Saturday in November, 9am–5pm. Bank/Temple underground.* At around 11am the new Lord Mayor travels in an 18th-century gilded coach from Mansion House in the City to the Royal Courts of Justice in the Strand to swear solemn vows, returning by about 2.15pm. The streets of the City are taken over by a procession of about 120 floats, 20 marching bands and street dancing. It all ends with fireworks from a barge on the Thames between Waterloo and Blackfriars bridges.

Remembrance Sunday Ceremony The Cenotaph, Whitehall, SW1. *Second Sunday in November, 10.30am. Westminster underground.* Crowds gather to pay one minute's silent tribute to Commonwealth citizens who lost their lives in the two world wars. Buglers of the Royal Marines sound The Last Post, and the Queen, other members of the Royal Family, the Prime Minister and further representatives of Government and the Services lay wreaths. The Bishop of London then takes the Service of Remembrance.

DECEMBER

For Christmas events, see *Christmas* p. 54.

New Year's Eve Celebrations Trafalgar Square, W1. *From 9pm, 31 December. Charing Cross underground/rail.* A huge party to see in the New Year, with Auld Lang Syne sung by a choir of thousands. Not for those who particularly cherish their space, and the widespread drunkenness can be quite threatening. The all-important midnight chime of Big Ben is invariably drowned out by the deafening revelry, but at least public transport home is FREE this night.

Watchnight Service St Paul's Cathedral, Ludgate Hill, EC4 (7236 4128) *New Year's Eve, 11.30pm. St Paul's underground.* A particularly well-attended service.

Art Galleries and Exhibitions
Entrance is *free* unless otherwise stated.

Africa Centre 38 King Street, WC2 (7836 1973) *Open: gallery Mon—Fri 9.30am—5.30pm; Sat 11am—4pm. Covent Garden underground.* The gallery has pictures and crafts by African artists.

Agnew Galleries 43 Old Bond Street, W1 (7629 6176) *Admission charge for some exhibitions. Open Mon—Fri 9.30am—5.30pm. Bond Street underground.* Established 1860, there are exhibitions on such things as 18th-century drawings, watercolours and Old Masters. Many works can be seen here before they end up at museums.

Anthony Wilkinson Gallery 242 Cambridge Heath Road, E2 (8980

2662) *Open Thurs—Sat 11am—6pm; Sun noon—6pm. Bethnal Green underground.* Minimalist.

The Approach Approach Tavern, 47 Approach Road, E2 (8980 2321) *Open Thurs—Sun noon—6pm. Bethnal Green underground.* Modern British.

Architectural Association 34–36 Bedford Square, WC1 (7887 4000) *Open Mon—Fri 10am—7pm; Sat 10am—3pm. Tottenham Court Road underground.* A gallery with absorbing architectural exhibitions.

Architecture Foundation The Economist Building, 30 Bury Street, SW1 (7839 9389) *Open Tues, Wed, Fri noon—6pm; Thurs, Sat, Sun 2—6pm. Green Park underground.* This campagning charity has regular exhibitions looking at modern architecture and how to improve our cities and towns.

Association of Photographers Gallery 81 Leonard Street, EC2 (7739 3631) *Open Mon—Fri 9.30am—6pm. Barbican underground.* Striking images used in today's newspapers and magazines.

Austin-Desmond and Phipps Pied Bull Yard, 15a Bloomsbury Square, WC1 (7242 4443) *Open Mon—Fri 10am—5.30pm. Holborn underground.* Principally modern British painting is shown at this commercial exhibition space.

Bankside Gallery 48 Hopton Street, SE1 (7928 7521) *Open Tues 10am—8pm; Wed—Fri 10am—5pm; Sat, Sun 1—5pm. Adults £3.50, children under 16, concessions £2. Southwark underground.* Home of the Royal Watercolour Society and Royal Society of Printer-Paintmakers.

Barbican Art Gallery Silk Street, EC2 (7382 7105) *Open Mon–Sat 9am–11pm; Sun noon–11pm. Barbican underground*. This, the world's largest arts centre under one roof, houses various exhibitions in the Concourse Gallery and the foyer galleries, with displays in the libraries too.

Battersea Arts Centre (BAC) 176 Lavender Hill, SW11 (7223 2223) *Open 10am–6pm; Tues–Sat 10am–10pm; Sun noon–10pm. Clapham Junction rail*. Contemporary works.

Blackheath Gallery 34a Tranquil Vale, SE3 (8852 1802) *Open Mon–Sat 10am–5pm. Blackheath rail*. Always an impressive selection at this small established gallery.

Bloomsbury Workshop 12 Galen Place, off Bury Place, WC1 (7405 0632) *Open Mon–Fri 10am–5.30pm. Holborn underground*. There's a gallery displaying paintings, prints, sculptures and sketches by the Bloomsbury Group.

British Cartoon Centre 7 Brunswick Centre, Bernard Street, WC1 (7278 7172) *Opening times vary. Russell Square underground*. As well as exhibitions, there are workshops covering cartoons, comics and animation.

Brixton Artists' Collective 35 Brixton Station Road, SW9 (7733 6957) *Open Mon, Tues, Thurs, Fri 11am–6pm; Sat 10am–5pm. Brixton underground*. A stimulating series of exhibitions mostly by local artists.

The Bull Arts Centre 68 High Street, Barnet, Herts (8449 0048) *Open Mon–Fri 10am–5.30pm; Sat, Sun noon–5.30pm. High Barnet underground*. Local, contemporary art including installations, sculpture, photography and painting.

Camden Arts Centre Arkwright Road, NW3 (7435 2643)

Open Tues–Thurs 11am–7pm; Fri–Sun 11am–5pm. Finchley Road underground. Three gallery spaces focusing on contemporary art.

Camerawork 121 Roman Road, E2 (8980 6256) *Open Tues–Sat 1–6pm. Bethnal Green underground.* Unconventional, challenging exhibitions of contemporary photography.

Chelsea College of Art and Design Manresa Road, SW3 (7514 7750) *Sloane Square underground.* End of term exhibitions and occasionally smaller ones at other times, consisting of painting, sculpture, ceramics, graphics and interior design.

Chisenhale Gallery 64–84 Chisenhale Road, E3 (8981 4518) *Open Wed–Sun 1–6pm. Bethnal Green/Mile End underground.* Innovative contemporary art in this huge (31 x 12 metres), stark exhibition space boasting no natural light, just lots of concrete and plain white walls.

Cockpit Arts Studio Cockpit Yard, Northington Street, WC1 (7916 1080) *Open Mon–Wed, Fri 10am–6pm. Holborn underground.* Make an appointment to see one of around 80 craftspeople working here. A huge choice including ceramics, glass, woodwork, metalwork, jewellery and textiles.

Contemporary Applied Arts 2 Percy Street, W1 (7436 2344) *Open Mon–Sat 10.30am–5.30pm. Goodge Street underground.* Ceramics, glass, metal, textiles, furniture, wood, pottery, jewellery and other exhibits.

Courtauld Gallery Somerset House, The Strand, WC2 (7873 2526) *Open Mon–Sat 10am–6pm; Sun noon–6pm. Adults £4, concessions £3, FREE to under-18s. Covent Garden/Temple underground.* An impressive collection of Impressionist/post-Impressionist masterpieces.

Crafts Council 44a Pentonville Road, N1 (7278 7700) *Open Tues–Sat 11am–5.30pm; Sun 2–5.30pm. Angel underground.* This is the national body for promoting crafts, and the gallery is a showcase for contemporary pottery, printing, textiles, etc. There's a reference library and general crafts information service.

Delfina Project Space 51 Southwark Street, SE1 (7357 6600) *Open Wed–Sun 11am–6pm. London Bridge underground/rail.* Modern British contemporary works.

Drill Hall Arts Centre 16 Chenies Street, WC1 (7637 8270) *Exhibitions can be seen 6–11pm when shows are playing. Goodge Street underground.* Art exhibition space in the bar area.

Dulwich Picture Gallery Gallery Road, Dulwich Village, SE21 (8693 5254) *Open Tues–Fri 10am–5pm; Sat, Sun 11am–5pm. Adults £4, £3 OAPs, FREE to other concessions. FREE for all, Fridays. West/North Dulwich rail.* Recently sumptuously refurbished, an excellent introduction to baroque art with a famous collection of 17th- and 18th-century Old Masters including works by Rubens, Rembrandt, Canaletto, Gainsborough and Van Dyck. Regular temporary exhibitions, workshops and children's events. Also holds FREE four-day courses, 'Art for the Unemployed'.

Eagle 159 Farringdon Road, EC1 (7833 2674) *Open Wed–Fri 11am–6pm; Sat 11am–4pm. Farringdon underground/rail.* An impressive art space above a popular pub boasting great food.

England and Co. 14 Needham Road, W11 (7221 0417) *Open Tues–Sat 11am–6pm. Notting Hill Gate underground.* A small, unpretentious commercial gallery.

Estorick Collection of Modern Italian Art 39a Canonbury Square, N1 (7704 9522) *Open Wed—Sat 11am—6pm; Sun noon—5pm. Adults £3.50, concessions £2.50, FREE to under-16s. Highbury and Islington underground/rail.* Modigliani, surrealist de Chirico and futurists Balla and Boccioni are among the distinguished artists displayed here.

Flowers East 199–205 Richmond Road, E8 (8985 3333) *Open Tues—Sun 10am—6pm. Bethnal Green underground.* A wide range of mainly British modern artists.

Frith Street Galleries 60 Frith Street, W1 (7494 1550) *Open Tues—Fri 10am—6pm; Sat 11am—4pm. Tottenham Court Road underground.* Modern British artists displayed in an attractive wood-panelled public gallery.

Gabriel's Wharf 56 Upper Ground, SE1 (7620 0544) *Open Tues—Sun 11am—6pm. Waterloo/Charing Cross underground.* About 20 craft and designer artists can be watched here making ceramics, sculptures, jewellery, fashion, etc. in their workshops. There are also market stalls.

The Gallery St John's, Smith Square, SW1 (7222 1061) *Open Mon—Fri 10am—5pm; Westminster underground.* A variety of exhibitions by contemporary artists.

Gallery Westland Place 13 Westland Place, N1 (7251 6456) *Open Mon—Sat 10am—6pm. Old Street underground/rail.* A wide range of European modern art.

Gilbert Collection Somerset House, The Strand, WC2 (7240 4080) *Open Mon—Sat 10am—6pm; Sun noon—6pm. Adults £4, concessions £3, FREE to under-18s. Covent Garden/Temple underground.* Displays of gold, silver and mosaic decorative arts.

Goethe-Institut Gallery 50 Princes Gate, Exhibition Road, SW7 (7411 3400) *Open Mon–Fri 10am–8pm; Sat 10.30am–12.30pm. South Kensington underground.* German artists and art collections.

Greenwich Printmakers 1a Greenwich Market, SE10 (8858 1569) *Open Tues–Sun 10am–5.30pm. Greenwich rail.* Loads of prints by local printmakers.

Greenwich Theatre Gallery Croom's Hill, SE10 (8858 7755) *Open daily 10am–10pm. Greenwich rail.* Exhibitions change with each theatre show.

Guildhall Art Gallery 1 Guildhall Yard, off Gresham Street, EC2 (7606 3030) *Open Mon–Sat 10am–5pm; Sun noon–4pm. Adults £2.50, concessions £1, FREE to under-16s, FREE to all on Fridays. Bank underground/DLR.* A selection of the Corporation of London's collection of paintings including cityscapes and portraits of former mayors.

Hales Gallery 70 Deptford High Street, SE8 (8694 1194) *Open Mon–Sat 9am–5pm. Deptford rail/Deptford Bridge DLR.* Contemporary art.

Hamilton Gallery 13 Carlos Place, W1 (7499 9493) *Open Mon–Fri 10am–6pm; Sat 11am–5pm. Bond Street underground.* This is the place to go to see work by the top photographers including Helmut Newton, Irving Penn and David Bailey.

Harrow Arts Centre Uxbridge Road, Hatch End, HA5 (8428 0124) *Open Mon–Fri, and some Sats 9am–11pm. Pinner underground.* Modern works from the locality and elsewhere.

Hayward Gallery Belvedere Road, SE1 (7960 4242) *Open during exhibitions Mon, Thurs–Sun 10am–6pm; Tues, Wed 10am–*

8pm. Admission prices vary. Embankment/Waterloo underground. Excellent exhibitions of both contemporary and classical art on the South Bank.

Heifer Gallery 3 Calabria Road, N5 (8226 7380) *Open Mon–Fri 10am–5pm. Highbury and Islington underground/rail.* Contemporary works.

Instituto Cervantes 22 Manchester Square, W1 (7935 0353) *Open Mon–Thurs 9.30am–6.30pm; Fri 9.30am–5pm. Marble Arch/ Bond Street underground.* Regular exhibitions by Spanish artists.

Institute of Contemporary Arts (ICA) The Mall, SW1 (7930 3647) *Open daily noon–7.30pm. Admission prices vary. Charing Cross underground/rail.* Top contemporary art.

Italian Cultural Institute 39 Belgrave Square, SW1 (7235 1461) *Open Mon–Fri 9.30am–5pm. Knightsbridge underground.* Regular exhibitions by Italian artists.

Iveagh Bequest, Kenwood Hampstead Lane, NW3 (8348 1286) *Open daily 10am–4pm Nov–Mar, 10am–6pm Apr–Sept, 10am–5pm Oct. Archway/Golders Green underground.* English Heritage's splendid neoclassical mansion remodelled in c.1765 by Robert Adam, sits on the edge of Hampstead Heath and contains one of England's most impressive collections of paintings including works by artists such as Rembrandt, Vermeer, Hals, Reynolds, Turner and Gainsborough. It also houses antique jewellery and furniture.

Jerwood Space 171 Union Street, SE1 (7654 0171) *Open Mon– Sat 10am–6pm; Sun noon–6pm. Southwark underground.* Three gallery spaces and a great cafe.

Kingston Museum and Art Gallery Wheatfield Way, Kingston, Surrey (8546 5386) *Open Mon, Tues, Thurs—Sat 10am—5pm. Kingston rail.* A variety of exhibitions including those by local artists.

Lauderdale House Community Arts Centre, Waterlow Park, Highgate Hill, N6 (8348 8716) *Open Tues—Fri 11am—4pm. Archway underground.* Three galleries with exibitions of paintings, photographs and occasionally sculptures by artists from around the world.

Leighton House 12 Holland Park Road, W14 (7602 3316) *Open Mon, Wed—Sat 11am—5.30pm. Garden open Apr—Sept 11am—5.30pm. High Street Kensington underground.* A permanent collection of paintings by Lord Leighton (1803—96) and his contemporaries including Millais and Burne-Jones as well as temporary exhibitions of modern and historic art, and sculptures in the garden. The striking Arab Hall contains spectacular Isnik tiles.

Lewisham Arthouse Gallery 140 Lewisham Way, SE14 (8694 9011) *Open Wed—Sun 11am—6pm; New Cross underground/rail.* As well as exhibitions of contemporary works there are classes and FREE Saturday morning children's workshops.

Lisson Gallery 67 Lisson Street, NW1 (7724 2739) *Open Mon—Sat 10am—5pm. Edgeware Road underground.* A popular contemporary gallery, leaning towards abstracts.

Llewellyn Alexander Gallery 124–126 The Cut, SE1 (7620 1322) *Open Mon—Sat 10am—7.30pm. Waterloo underground/rail.* A highlight is the annual summer 'Not the Royal Academy' exhibition of works submitted but rejected by the Royal Academy Summer Exhibition (see page 17).

Lux Gallery Lux Centre, 2–4 Hoxton Square, N1 (7684 2785) *Open Tues–Sun noon–7pm. Old Street underground/rail.* Modern work displayed in this section of the Lux arts complex.

Lyric Theatre King Street, W6 (8741 2311) *Open 10am–6pm. Hammersmith underground.* Exhibitions in the foyer.

Mall Galleries The Mall, SW1 (7930 6844) *Open daily 10am–5pm. Charing Cross underground/rail. £2.50 admission, £1 concessions; Exhibitions are FREE to Westminster residents, and some are FREE to all. Occasional gallery tours.* One of the few London venues to show the work of well-established British artists alongside up and coming students and unknown painters.

Marble Hill House Richmond Road, Twickenham, Middlesex (8892 5115) *Open Oct–Mar Wed–Sun 10am–4pm; Apr–Sept daily 10am–6pm. Richmond rail/underground, St Margarets rail.* Georgian fine art.

Matt's Gallery 42–44 Copperfield Road, E3 (8983 1771) *Open during exhibitions Wed–Sun noon–6pm. Mile End underground.* Not a place of worship for those who follow Matt's cartoons each day in the *Daily Telegraph*, but a gallery displaying contemporary works in a wide spectrum of media by British and foreign artists that have often been specifically designed for the building.

Mayfair's commercial galleries, W1 *The galleries are typically open Mon–Fri 10.30am–5.30pm; Sat 10.30am–1pm unless otherwise stated. Some are closed in August. Green Park/Bond Street/Piccadilly Circus underground.* It's a good idea to treat the many private art galleries in the Cork Street, Bruton Street and Dering Street vicinity as one entity with many doors. They tend to concentrate upon established modern art, and even if their exhibitions don't stay in the mind, the names of these commercial London galleries certainly will. Anthony d'Offay, Annely Juda, Karsten Schubert . . . it seems a mandatory requirement before opening your own gallery that you possess an unusual, posh-sounding name. Don't be intimidated by the grand, stark rooms or possibly a disapproving stare from a member of staff. How do they know you're not a millionaire art buyer just because you're wearing tatty jeans and an old T-shirt? The galleries include:

Alan Cristea Gallery, 31 Cork Street (7439 1866) Prints and drawings.

Annely Juda Fine Art, 23 Dering Street (7629 7578) Modernist, abstract and expressionist work.

Anthony d'Offay, 9, 20, 21, 23 and 24 Dering Street (7499 4100) International, often avant-garde, contemporary artists including big names like Warhol and Lichtenstein.

Anthony Reynolds Gallery, 5 Dering Street (7491 0621) 20th-century British works.

Bernard Jacobson Gallery, 14a Clifford Street (7495 8575) Modern British art.

Fine Art Society, 148 New Bond Street (7629 5116) Mainly 19th- and 20th-century British works.

Gimpel Fils, 30 Davies Street (7493 2488) Modern art.

Jason and Rhodes, 4 New Burlington Place (7434 1768) Contemporary British art.

Marlborough Fine Art, 6 Albermarle Street (7629 5161) Shows here have included Freud, Bacon and Hockney.

Raab Gallery, 9 Cork Street (7734 6444) Specialises in large, dramatic canvasses.

Sadie Coles, 35 Heddon Street (7434 2227) Young British and American artists.

Stephen Friedman, 25 Old Burlington Street (7494 1434) International contemporary artists.

Waddington Galleries, 11 Cork Street (7437 8611) You can see work here ranging from up and coming newcomers to Matisse and Picasso.

White Cube, 44 Duke Street (7930 5373) Though small, it's seen the likes of Damien Hirst and Tracey Emin in recent years.

Morley College Gallery 61 Westminster Bridge Road, SE1 (7928 8501) *Open during exhibitions Mon–Fri 10am–6pm; Wed until 8pm. Lambeth North underground.* Modern British artists from the college and elsewhere.

Museum of Installation 175 Deptford High Street, SE8 (8692 8778) *Open Tues–Fri noon–5pm; Sat 2–5pm. Deptford rail.* Dedicated to installation art.

National Gallery Trafalgar Square, WC2 (7747 2885) *Open Mon–Sat 10am–6pm; Wed to 9pm; Sun 2–6pm; guided tours and lectures daily Mon–Sat. Admission charge for some exhibitions. Charing Cross underground/rail.* Much of the complete history of Western art can be found here. Around 2000 of the nation's gigantic collection of Western masterpieces from the 13th to 19th centuries are here including Constable, Turner, Monet, Michelangelo, Velazquez, van Eyck, van Gogh, da Vinci, Titian and Picasso. It's best to restrict yourself to a few galleries on each visit rather than try to trawl around the lot. There are regular temporary exhibitions. Children's quizzes are available. The Micro Gallery, the computer information centre in the Sainsbury Wing, can provide you with a personal printed-out tour map that highlights the pictures you most wish to see.

National Portrait Gallery 2 St Martin's Place, WC2 (7306 0055) *Open Mon—Wed, Sat, Sun 10am—6pm; Thurs, Fri 10am—9pm. Admission charge for some exhibitions. Charing Cross underground/rail.* Recently revamped and expanded, there is a wealth of paintings, drawings, engravings, sculptures, photographs and cartoons from the 16th century onwards. Most prominent figures in British history are represented here. Plenty of lectures and other events including occasional music recitals.

Open Air Art Exhibitions *Along the railings on the Piccadilly side of Green Park, W1 every weekend; Heath Street, Hampstead, NW3 at weekends June—August; along the railings on the Bayswater Road side of Hyde Park, W2 on Sundays.* Exhibitions by artists possessing a huge range of talents from good to atrocious.

The Orangery and The Ice House Holland Park, off Kensington High Street, W8 (7603 1123) *Open daily 11am—7pm during exhibitions. High Street Kensington underground.* All forms of work are shown at these galleries but check first as they are occasionally closed.

Orleans House Gallery Riverside, Twickenham, Middlesex. (8892 0221) *Open April—Sept Tue—Sat 1—5.30pm; Sun 2—5.30pm; Oct—Mar Tues—Sat 1—4.30pm; Sun 2—4.30pm. Richmond underground/St Margaret's rail.* This villa, designed by James Gibbs and built in 1710, has an opulently decorated baroque Octagon Room and is set in a beautiful woodland garden by the river. Varied exhibitions all year. Occasional free events including lectures.

Percy Miller Gallery 39 Snowfields, SE1 (7207 4578) *Open Tues–Fri 11am–6pm; Sat 11am–3pm. London Bridge underground/rail.* International contemporary artists.

Photofusion 17a Electric Lane, Brixton, SW9 (7738 5774) *Open Tues–Sat 10am–5.30pm. Brixton underground.* Contemporary documentary photography by photographers at home and abroad.

Photographer's Gallery 5 and 8 Great Newport Street, WC2 (7831 1772) *Open Tues–Sat 11am–7pm. Leicester Square underground.* Contemporary photography, particularly reportage.

Pitshanger Manor Museum and Gallery Walpole Park, Mattock Lane, Ealing, W5 (8567 1227) *Open Tues–Sat 10am–5pm. Ealing Broadway underground.* A display of Martinware pottery in this beautiful listed house set in a park, with an adjacent art gallery holding contemporary exhibitions.

Polish Cultural Institute 34 Portland Place, W1 (7636 6032) *Open Mon–Wed, Fri 10am–4pm; Thurs 10am–8pm. Regent's Park underground.* Regular exhibitions with a Polish theme.

The Pump House, Battersea Park, Albert Bridge Road, SW11 (7350 0523) *Open Apr–Sept Wed–Sun 11am–6pm; Oct–Mar Wed–Sun 11am–3pm. Battersea Park rail.* Contemporary works.

Purdy Hicks Gallery 65 Hopton Street, SE1 (7401 9229) *Open Mon–Fri 10am–5.30pm; Sat 10am–3pm. Southwark underground.* Mainly contemporary painting and photography.

Pym's Gallery 9 Mount Street, W1 (7629 2020) *Open Mon–Fri*

9.30am–6pm. Marble Arch underground. 19th- and-20th-century Irish art.

Ranger's House Chesterfield Walk, Blackheath, SE3 (8853 0035) *Open Apr–Sept daily 10am–6pm; Oct daily 10am–5pm; Nov–Mar Wed–Sun 10am–4pm. Adults £2.80, concessions £2.10, children over-5 £1.40. Blackheath or Greenwich rail.* A handsome 18th-century red-brick villa overlooking Greenwich Park with full-length Jacobean and Stuart portraits and other paintings.

Rebecca Hossack 35 Windmill Street, W1 (7436 4899) *Open Mon–Sat 10am–6pm. Tottenham Court Road underground.* A commercial gallery showing a stimulating selection of young artists.

RIBA Architecture Centre 66 Portland Place, W1 (7580 5533/7631 0460) *Open Mon, Wed, Fri 8am–7pm; Tues, Thurs 8am–9pm; Sat 9am–5pm. Oxford Circus underground.* Five gallery spaces explore architecture and design, and engineering and landscape design through models and drawings.

RIBA Heinz Gallery 21 Portman Square, W1 (7580 5533 ext. 4807) *Open Mon–Fri 11am–5pm; Sat 10am–1pm. Marble Arch underground.* Regular architectural exhibitions.

Riverside Studio Theatre Riverside Studios, Crisp Road, Hammersmith, W6 (8237 1000) *Open Mon–Sat 10.30am–11.30pm; Sun noon-11.30pm. Hammersmith underground.* Gallery space in the foyer showing a variety of artistic talents.

Royal Academy of Arts Burlington House, Piccadilly, W1 (7300 8000) *Open daily 10am–6pm. Green Park/Piccadilly Circus underground.* The Academy is housed in the huge Burlington House, a grand Palladian mansion, which would be even more impressive if they threw the ugly cars out of the central courtyard and installed some grass. Most Tuesdays to Fridays at 1pm there are tours of the 18th-century Private Rooms, where works by Royal Academicians are on display. You also get to see Michelangelo's Taddei Tondo, his only sculpture in Britain.

Royal College of Art Kensington Gore, SW7 (7590 4444) *Open Mon—Fri 10am—6pm during exhibitions. Gloucester Road/South Kensington underground.* Varied exhibitions of work in progress during the terms. There are degree shows in May and June.

Royal College of Music Portraits Department Prince Consort Road, SW7 (7589 3643) *Open Mon—Fri 10am—5.30pm by appointment only. South Kensington underground.* Music-related paintings, prints, photographs, engravings and statues.

Royal Festival Hall Galleries South Bank Centre, SE1 (7960 4242) *Open daily 10am—10.30pm. Waterloo underground/rail.* A mixture of styles in a variety of medias.

Royal National Theatre South Bank Centre, SE1 (7452 3400) *Open Mon—Sat 10am—11pm. Waterloo underground/rail.* Exhibitions throughout the foyers.

Saatchi Gallery 98a Boundary Road, NW8 (7624 8299) *Open during exhibitions only Thurs—Sun noon—6pm. Adults £5, children over 12, concessions £3. Swiss Cottage underground.* A large and exciting purpose-built gallery of contemporary art.

St Martins Gallery St Martin-in-the-Fields, Trafalgar Square, WC2 (7839 4342) *Open Mon—Sat 10am—8pm; Sun noon—6pm. Charing Cross underground/rail.* Artists, who are often present in the gallery, display their work against the ancient stone and brickwork of the church crypt.

Serpentine Gallery Kensington Gardens, W2 (7402 6075) *Open daily 10am–6pm. Lancaster Gate/South Kensington underground.* Innovative contemporary works in a wonderful location – a former tea pavilion within Kensington Gardens.

The Showroom 44 Bonner Road, E2 (8983 4115) *Open Wed– Sun 1–6pm. Bethnal Green underground.* An enterprising contemporary gallery.

South London Gallery 65 Peckham Road, SE5 (7703 9799) *Open during exhibitions Tue–Fri 11am–6pm; Thurs 11am–7pm; Sat, Sun 2–6pm. Peckham Rye/Queen's Road rail.* A centre for the arts since 1891, this has six exhibitions annually: often contemporary art including painting, photography, sculpture and video.

Special Photographers' Company 21 Kensington Park Road, W11 (7221 3489) *Open Mon–Fri 10am–6pm; Sat 11am–5pm. Notting Hill Gate underground.* A wide range of styles exhibited, from social documentary to fashion.

Stables Art Centre Gladstone Park, Dollis Hill Lane, NW10. (8452 8655) *Opening times vary. Dollis Hill underground.* A gallery displaying a wide range of contemporary artists.

The Studio 28 Beckenham Road, Beckenham, Kent (8663 0103) *Open Tues–Sat 11am–5.30pm. Clockhouse/Beckenham Junction rail.* The main gallery generally exhibits touring exhibitions, while the cafe bar shows local artists.

Tate Britain Millbank, SW1 (7887 8008) *Open daily 10am– 5.50pm. Pimlico underground.* Opened 1897, there are national collections of British paintings including works by Hogarth, Gainsborough, Reynolds, Constable, Blake, Sargent, and Pre-Raphaelites, and 20th-century painting and sculpture. The gallery's displays, covering the 16th century to the present, change annually. Plenty of events, lectures and films.

Tate Modern 25 Sumner Street, Bankside, SE1 (7887 8000) *Open Sun–Thurs 10am–6pm; Fri, Sat 10am–10pm. Southwark/ Blackfriars underground.* Although many visitors are more impressed by the magnificent building – the former Bankside Power Station – than its contents (international modern art from 1900 to now, including works by Mondrian to Matisse, Piccasso to Pollock), there are great views over the river and the infamous wobbly Millennium Footbridge over the Thames.

Todd Gallery 1–5 Needham Road, W11 (7792 1404) *Open Tues– Fri 11am–6pm; Sat 11am–4pm. Notting Hill Gate underground.* A large private gallery specialising in abstract works.

Tom Allen Arts Centre Grove Crescent Road, Stratford, E15 (8519 6818) *Open Mon–Sat (times vary) during various art events. Stratford underground/rail.* A small exhibition space showing work by artists countrywide.

Tricycle Theatre 269 Kilburn High Road, NW6 (7328 1000) *Open Mon–Sat 10am–11pm. Kilburn underground.* The gallery's exhibitions change regularly at this friendly theatre.

University College Art Collection Strang Print Room, South Cloisters, University College, Gower Street, WC1 (7679 2000 ext 2540) *Open during term time Wed–Fri 1–5pm. Goodge Street underground.* Temporary exhibitions of the collection, including prints, paintings, sculptures, photographs and books. Of particular note, there are Old Master etchings, engravings, early English mezzotints, works of the Slade School from the late 19th century (including some by Stanley Spencer and Augustus John) and a large number of drawings by Flaxman.

Wallace Collection Hertford House, Manchester Square, W1 (7935 0687) *Open Mon–Sat 10am–5pm; Sun noon–5pm. Bond Street underground.* Four generations of the Wallace family collected this remarkable assortment of arms and armour, furniture, clocks, porcelain, sculpture, and pictures, including ones by Titian, Gainsborough, Rembrandt and Rubens, and *The Laughing Cavalier* by Frans Hals. It has one of the best collections of 18th-century French paintings in the world. There's a new watercolour gallery and a glass-covered sculpture garden.

Wapping Project Wapping Hydraulic Power Station, Wapping Wall, E1 (7680 2080) *Open Tues–Sat noon–11pm; Sun noon–6pm. Wapping underground.* Recently opened, this big exhibition space includes work in electronic media.

Warwick Leadlay Gallery 5 Nelson Road, Greenwich SE10 (8858 0317) *Open Mon–Sat 9.30am–5.30pm; Sun 11am–5pm. Greenwich rail.* Regular small exhibitions.

Watermans Arts Centre 40 High Street, Brentford, TW8 (8847 5651) *Open Tues–Sat 11am–7pm; Sun noon–6pm. Gunnersbury underground/rail.* A variety of contemporary exhibitions.

Whitechapel Art Gallery 80 Whitechapel High Street, E1 (7522 7878) *Open Tues–Sun 11am–5pm; Wed until 8pm. Aldgate*

East underground. A lively programme of mainly 20th-century art exhibitions in this leading London art venue.

White Cube 2 48 Hoxton Square, N1 (7930 5373) *Open Tues–Sat 10am–6pm. Old Street underground/rail.* Big sister to its Duke Street W1 counterpart.

Woodlands Art Gallery 90 Mycenae Road, Blackheath, SE3 (8858 5847) *Open Mon, Tues, Thurs–Sat 11am–5pm; Sun 2–5pm. Westcombe Park rail.* Contemporary paintings, prints, sculpture, textiles ceramics, and photography by talented local artists displayed in a grand, if somewhat shabby Georgian villa. You can also explore the spacious, mature gardens, which are often gloriously empty.

Zelda Cheatle Gallery 99 Mount Street, W1 (7408 4448) *Open Tues–Sat 10.30am–6pm. Charing Cross underground/rail.* A distinguished small photographic gallery.

Auctions and Valuations

These auctioneers will value for FREE a wide range of antiques and other objects for you if you bring them along, and attending an auction (most have FREE admission) can be one of the best shows in town.

Bonhams and Brooks Montpelier Street, SW7 (7393 3900) *Open Mon–Fri 9am–4.30pm. Knightsbridge underground.*

Christie's 8 King Street, SW1 (7839 9060) *Open Mon 9am–4.45pm; Tues 9am–8pm; Wed–Fri 9am–4.45pm; Sun 2–4.30pm. Green Park underground.*

Phillips 101 New Bond Street, W1 (7629 6602) *Open Mon–Fri 8.30am–5pm. Bond Street underground.*

Sotheby's 34 New Bond Street, W1 (7293 5000) *Open Mon–Fri 9am–4.45pm. Bond Street underground.*

Bus Tours

At £1 within the central Zone 1 and 70p everywhere else for an adult (and 40p for children) London's buses represent very good value. Some routes provide great tours of the capital – far cheaper than the £12–£15 for a seat on one of the tourist bus sightseeing tours.

Some recommended bus routes:

8 Board a northbound no. 8 bus by Victoria Station on Buckingham Palace Road and it will take you by Green Park to Hyde Park Corner, on to Piccadilly and into Mayfair, Bond Street, Oxford Street, Holborn and the Old Bailey. The bus goes on to Cheapside, passing St Paul's Cathedral on your right, and then past the Bank of England and Spitalfields Market.

11 This takes you across London from west to east. You can start at the King's Road in Chelsea and ride past Victoria to Westminster Abbey. You then go to Trafalgar Square, down the Strand and Fleet Street to St Paul's Cathedral.

12 Board a southbound no. 12 bus in Praed Street, Paddington, and you will pass Marble Arch, go up Oxford and Regent Streets (the heart of the shopping district,) through

Trafalgar Square and its landmarks including Nelson's column and the National Gallery, past Downing Street via Whitehall, through Parliament Square and on to Lambeth Palace.

15 Catch an eastbound no. 15 at Piccadilly Circus and you'll pass Trafalgar Square, go down the Strand passing Charing Cross Station, the 200-year-old Adelphi Theatre and the Savoy Hotel with its art-nouveau facade. The bus trundles on past Aldwych to Fleet Street, past the historic four inns of court. Then it passes St Paul's Cathedral and Christopher Wren's 17th-century monument, Tower Bridge, the Tower of London and the East End. On Sundays get off at Aldgate for Petticoat Lane market.

53 Join the bus at Piccadilly Circus and you go through Trafalgar Square, Parliament Square and Westminster, on to Elephant and Castle and then to leafy Blackheath, Charlton and Woolwich.

73 Leaving Victoria, the no. 73 passes Park Lane and Hyde Park, Marble Arch, Oxford Circus, Euston, King's Cross, the Angel and Islington. You can go as far as Tottenham.

Christmas

Central London Christmas Lights *Lights are switched on from early- to mid-November until Twelfth Night in Oxford Street, Regent Street, South Molton Street, Covent Garden, Trafalgar Square, St Christopher's Place, Carnaby Street and Bond Street – all central London.* The lights along these streets help create a festive air, even though Christmas goods seem to be on sale the moment summer ends. There are also lights to admire or bemoan elsewhere in central London, such as at Knightsbridge, SW1 and Kensington High Street, W8.

Blackheath Christmas Lights *Blackheath Village, SE3, from early December. Blackheath rail.* The village almost looks like something out of a fairy-tale at night with its Christmas lights draping every shop. A celebrity resident, such as Laurence Llewelyn-Bowen, Jools Holland, Terry Waite or Danny Baker, generally formally turns on the lights in an afternoon ceremony on a Saturday early in December.

Santa Claus, Harrods *From mid-November, Harrods, Knightsbridge, SW1 (7730 1234). Knightsbridge underground.* Around 50,000 people visit, each child receiving a badge and a good quality book or toy for free – although at times the wait can make it seem as if you have been queuing from about Boxing Day the year before. The store's impressive Christmas window displays are also unveiled at this time. There's a real Christmas atmosphere in December if you walk along Walton Street, SW1, near Harrods as it gets dark, past the delicatessen, grocers, clothes, antiques and other beautifully laid out high-class shops.

Santa Claus, Selfridges *From mid-November, Oxford Street, W1 (7629 1234). Marble Arch/Bond Street underground.* Father Christmas has a grotto, although no free gifts. There's also a special Christmas Hall with dazzling decorations.

Santa Claus, Hamleys *From around 20 November, 188 Regent Street, W1 (7494 2000). Oxford Circus underground.* The rents at Hamleys are evidently too high to provide Santa with a grotto, so he walks around the store instead, chatting to the children.

Fortnum & Mason 181 Piccadilly, W1 (7734 8040) *Piccadilly Circus underground*. Fortnum & Mason has a Christmas department with a smart selection of wrapping paper, hampers, Christmas puddings and other seasonal foods, decorations and crackers.

London Christmas Parade *Held on a Sunday in late November. Begins Piccadilly, W1. Piccadilly Circus underground*. An American-style parade of floats, dancers, marching bands, clowns, jugglers, stilt walkers and cartoon characters makes its way from the Royal Academy of Arts to Piccadilly Circus, Regent Street, Oxford Street and then arrives at Marble Arch 90 minutes or so later.

Great Christmas Pudding Race Covent Garden, WC2 (7404 8760) *Usually first Saturday in December, 11.30am. Covent Garden underground*. Festivities last for much of the day, the highlight being celebrities and volunteers taking part in a relay race around the Piazza in fancy dress while carrying a pudding on a tray.

Broadgate Arena Broadgate Centre, Eldon Street, EC2 (7588 6565) *Liverpool Street underground/rail*. Stages Christmas events.

Trafalgar Square Christmas Tree Carol Concerts Trafalgar Square, WC2 *Early December. Charing Cross underground/rail*. Every year since 1947 the Norwegian government has given the citizens of London a large Christmas tree as an expression of gratitude for Britain's help in World War II. There are regular carol concerts around the tree until Christmas Eve, which can have a magical atmosphere.

Carol Concerts *St Bartholomew's, West Smithfield, EC1 (7606 5171); St Martin-in-the-Fields, Trafalgar Square, WC2 (7930*

1862); Southwark Cathedral, Montague Close, SE1 (7367 6700); Westminster Abbey, Dean's Yard, SW1 (7222 5152). Of the many carol services and other special church Christmas events taking place, those at these churches are particularly recommended.

Ice Skating Somerset House, The Strand, WC2 (7845 4600) *From mid-December to early January. Check for times and admission charges. Charing Cross/Covent Garden/Temple underground.*

Peter Pan Cup Swimming Race The Serpentine, Hyde Park, W2 (01753 544441) *December 25 around 8am. Lancaster Gate/ Knightsbridge underground.* Around 25 brave/mad swimmers participate in a small, festive race.

Churches and Cathedrals

Of the many churches in London, a number are architectural gems. There are 42 churches in the City of London alone, each worthy of a visit (and there were a mammoth 97 before the Fire of London in 1666). Here is a selection of these tranquil havens. Admission is FREE unless otherwise stated.

All Hallow-by-the-Tower Byward Street, EC3 *Tower Hill underground.* Despite only the red-brick tower escaping damage during the Blitz, preserved in the tiny crypt are some Roman paving, remains of Saxon crosses and an arch of a Saxon church built on this site in 675AD. Brass rubbings can be done here, for which a charge is made.

All Saints 7 Margaret Street, W1 *Oxford Circus underground.* Of the many churches built in the capital during the 19th century, this atmospheric building stands out for the variety of coloured bricks used for decorative effect and the granite, alabaster and marble in the interior.

Chelsea Old Church Cheyne Walk, SW3 *Sloane Square underground*. Dating from 1157 but extensively rebuilt since then, and containing a rich collection of monuments. Henry VIII is believed to have married wife no. 3, Jane Seymour, here soon after Anne Boleyn's execution.

Christ Church Commercial Street, E1 *Aldgate East underground*. The 75-metre triangular spire of this Hawksmoor church dominates Spitalfields.

London Oratory Thurloe Place, Brompton Road, SW3 *South Kensington underground*. Built in heavy Renaissance style in 1884 and boasting a nave that is 15 metres wide, this flamboyant Catholic church, known widely as the Brompton Oratory, has an interior rich in marble and mosaics.

St Alfege Greenwich High Road, SE10 *Greenwich rail*. This church is the third on the site. The first followed after the Archbishop of Canterbury Alfege was murdered by Viking raiders in 1012 and a second was built around 1210. This updated model, built in 1714, is one of the best examples of a Nicholas Hawksmoor church. Hawksmoor trained under Sir Christopher Wren. There are murals by James Thornhill, carvings by Grinling Gibbons and a memorial to General Woolfe, whose statue is in nearby Greenwich Park.

St Anne Limehouse, Commercial Road, E1 *Westferry/Limehouse DLR*. Hawksmoor, who designed this church, was a pupil of Christopher Wren, and was clearly influenced by his teacher. This Baroque church designed in 1712 has an immense tower and a magnificent organ built to commemorate the 1851 Great Exhibition.

St Anne and St Agnes Gresham Street, EC2 *St Paul's underground*. One of the churches rebuilt by Wren after the Great Fire of London of 1666 and restored after World War II. It has a spacious interior with a central vault and boasts elegant columns and various antiquities.

St Bartholomew-the-Great West Smithfield, EC1 *Barbican/Farringdon underground*. London's oldest parish church is the nearest thing the capital has to a Norman cathedral. Founded in 1123, the original remains include a half-timbered 13th-century gateway. Inside are huge Romanesque pillars. A rare survivor of the Great Fire, it featured in the film *Four Weddings and a Funeral*.

St Clement Danes Strand, WC2 *Charing Cross underground/rail*. A church has been here since the 9th century. It was rebuilt by Wren in the 1680s and then again after the World War II. It became the memorial church of the Royal Air Force and crests of hundreds of air squadrons are in the nave and aisles. The bells in the 38-metre tower could be the ones mentioned in the nursery rhyme 'Oranges and Lemons' (which is at least 500 years old), and play out that tune, although St Clement's Eastcheap, Clement's Lane, EC4 (Monument underground) another Wren church, with beautiful 17th-century woodwork, could also be the church referred to in the rhyme.

St Ethelreda Ely Place, EC1 *Chancery Lane underground*. Built in 1291, this is the oldest pre-Reformation Roman Catholic church in the capital. There's a huge vaulted undercroft with medieval roof timbers and a pre-Reformation model of Ely Place.

St George Bloomsbury Way, WC1 *Holborn/Tottenham Court Road underground.* The great Georgian church designer, Nicholas Hawksmoor, gave St George's a striking Corinthian portico supported by six columns and an unusual pyramid-style steeple crowned by a statue of George I in a Roman toga. Inside, the neoclassical design is enhanced by fine gilded plasterwork.

St George the Martyr Borough High Street, SE1 *Borough underground.* Rebuilt by architect John Price in 1736, this is a handsome church rich in historical and literary connections. Little Dorrit was married here in Dickens' novel. The churchyard, now a peaceful garden, was the site of the Marshalsea debtors' prison where Dickens' father was imprisoned, and a wall survives from this period.

St Giles Cripplegate Fore Street, EC2 *Barbican/Moorgate underground.* A Norman church originally stood on this site, where Oliver Cromwell was married in 1620 and the poet John Milton is buried.

St James's Piccadilly, W1 *Piccadilly Circus underground.* A busy Wren church with a splendid galleried interior and an altar, organ case and font carved by Grinling Gibbons. The spire, replaced in 1968, is made of fibreglass, of all things. There is a pretty paved memorial garden with a small outdoor craft market.

St Margaret's Westminster, Parliament Square, SW1 *Westminster underground.* Few visitors to Westminster Abbey also take time to discover its neighbour, St Margaret's, which is the official church of the House of Commons. It has many monuments and beautiful stained glass and has enjoyed a prestigious following: Chaucer and Caxton were parishioners, and Churchill, Milton and Pepys were married here. Sir Walter Raleigh is buried in the church.

St Martin-in-the-Fields Trafalgar Square, WC2 *Charing Cross underground/rail*. The fields have long gone, but James Gibbs' imposing church has a magnificent Corinthian portico and soaring steeple to admire and a spacious galleried interior with Grinling Gibbons woodwork, Venetian glass and a vaulted crypt. Brass rubbings can be done, for which a charge is made.

St Mary Abchurch Abchurch Lane, off Cannon Street, EC4 *Cannon Street underground/rail*. The quiet exterior of this impressive restored Wren church masks the magnificence of the interior with its marvellous painted dome and Grinling Gibbons limewood reredos.

St Mary-le-Bow Cheapside, EC2 *Bank underground*. Also known as Bow Church, this is the Wren-designed church standing out from drab office blocks in the area. To a true Cockney you have to be born within earshot of its 'Bow bells'. The bells sounded the wake-up call and evening curfew for the locality from the 14th to 19th centuries. Only the handsome tower and steeple survived World War II. The interior is unremarkable, but beneath the church there is an interesting Norman crypt, incorporating the walls of a Saxon church.

St Mary-le-Strand Strand, WC2 *Aldwych underground*. This church has stained-glass windows – stained by the traffic as well as by the creative urges of glaziers of long past –

marooned as it is on an island on one of London's busiest roads. Risk a visit at your peril. Recitals are invariably augmented by car horns. Designed by James Gibbs in 1717, it is a good example of the Baroque style.

St Paul's Cathedral St Paul's Churchyard, Ludgate Hill, EC4 (7236 4128) *Open Mon—Sat 8.30am—4pm; crypt, galleries, ambulatory Mon—Sat 10am—4pm. Guided tours 11am, 11.30am, 1.30pm; 2pm. Adults £5, concessions £4, children 6—16 £2.50, guided tours extra. St Paul's underground.* This Wren masterpiece is rich in decoration inside and out. The largest and most famous City church, it was rebuilt by Wren after the Great Fire. Its outstanding dome towers over the City and would dominate London's skyline if it wasn't for Canary Wharf. Like Canary Wharf, the cathedral was disliked by many when first built because it had no spire. The tombs of Lord Nelson and the Duke of Wellington are in the crypt. If you have the energy, climb the 627 steps to the top for a great view of the City.

St Paul's Church Bedford Street, Covent Garden, WC2 *Covent Garden underground.* Designed by Inigo Jones in 1633 and boasting a magnificent portico overlooking Covent Garden's piazza, this is known as 'the actor's church'. The interior features theatrical memorials. Eliza Dolittle met Professor Higgins here in Shaw's play *Pygmalion*, and in the film of the play, *My Fair Lady*.

Southwark Cathedral Montague Close, SE1 (7367 6700) *Open daily 8am—6pm. London Bridge underground/rail.* A fine Gothic building, London's oldest, with an interesting mix of architectures, some parts dating from the 13th century. It is a tranquil retreat and often overlooked by visitors to

London. By the entrance, under the railway arches, is Cafe Brood (1–6 Green Dragon Court, Bridge Arcade, SE1; 7357 8484) where you can get an excellent snack.

Westminster Abbey Dean's Yard, Parliament Square, SW1 (7222 5152) *Entrance FREE Wed 6–7.45pm; otherwise only nave and cloisters FREE. Open Mon, Tues, Thurs–Sat 7.30am–6pm; Wed 7.30am–7.45pm and between services on Sunday. The library is open May–Sept Wed 11am–3pm. Also College Garden open Apr–Sept Tues, Thurs 10.30am–6pm; Oct–Mar Tues, Thurs 10.30am–4pm. Nave and Royal Chapels adults £5, children 11–15 £2, concessions £3. Westminster underground.* This has been the British royal wedding, coronation and burial church since 1066. The magnificent architecture contains the tombs of many kings and queens and memorials to many famous and great people including Chaucer and Dickens. The herb and flower gardens in the 900-year-old College Garden, over an acre in size, are a restful retreat from the bustle of central London and amazingly tranquil considering the tourist-trap location. The Garden offers excellent views of the Palace of Westminster. Dean's Yard and the tranquil Cloisters are worth visiting (and here you can do brass rubbings, for which there is a charge) as is nearby Little Sanctuary, SW1, a secluded grassed square. It is best to visit the Abbey out of the tourist season or late morning midweek when it is quieter. There are nearly 30 services a week at the Abbey.

Westminster Cathedral Ashley Place, Victoria Street, SW1 (7834 7452) *Open daily 7am–7pm. Victoria underground/rail.* Head office of the Roman Catholic Church (UK division), the cathedral is an imposing building. It has a vast interior built in 1903 but in an early Christian Byzantine style, with the widest nave in England at 18 metres. There are Eric Gill sculptures, and columns and mosaics made from many types of marble. It is often forgotten, being off the usual tourist route yet is a magnificent, very un-English structure. There are great views of London from the tower (a £2 donation is requested to use the lift).

City Farms

For further animal encounters see *Animal and Bird Enclosures* p. 9.

In the last 20 years or so, city farms (on the defence in their own small way against urbanisation) have sprung up in the unlikeliest of places such as rubbish dumps, abandoned industrial sites and other unloved, forgotten wastelands. They are working farms, where the animals have to pay their way, but that doesn't stop them offering great recreational and educational opportunities, bringing the countryside and its activities to urban people. Many have regular events such as jumble sales, fun days, dog shows, barn dances, pig racing and sheep fairs.

They all have characters of their own. For example, Stepping Stones is a friendly, cosy little place where those running the farm are much in evidence, whereas Mudchute has more the appearance of abandoned, segregated fields with the livestock left alone and allowed to roam. Well, allowed to roam by London standards, anyway.

All the farms are run by volunteers, so if you would like a stronger taste of the countryside and would like to learn about animal care and some agriculture-related skills such as building and horticulture, get in touch with your nearest.

All offer FREE admission unless otherwise stated.

Brooks Farm Skelton's Lane Park, Skelton's Lane, E10 (8539 4278) *Open summer Tues–Sun 10.30am–5.30pm; winter Tues–Sun 9.30am–4.30pm. Leyton Midland rail.* Donkeys, pigs, sheep, cows, ducks and chickens.

College Farm 45 Fitzalan Road, Finchley, N3 (8349 0690) *Open daily 10am–6pm. Adults £1.50, under-16s 75p. Finchley Central underground.* Cattle, sheep, donkeys, a horse and all the other usual suspects are herded up here.

Coram's Fields 93 Guildford Street, WC1 (7837 6138) *Open Apr–Oct 9am–8pm, Nov–Apr 9am–dusk. Russell Square underground.* Although there are farm animals in residence, this couldn't really be called a farm, and is more a recreation area. Animals include goats, sheep, guinea pigs, rabbits, ducks and hens. There's also a children's playground. Adults are only admitted if accompanied by a child.

Dene City Farm 39 Windsor Avenue, Merton Abbey, SW19 (8543 5300) *Open Tues–Sun 9am–5pm. Morden Road rail.* Opened in late 1994 on a meadow in the National Trust's Morden Hall Park, there are the usual farm ingredients, including sheep, geese, chickens, calves and even the odd field.

Freightliners Farm Paradise Park, Sheringham Road, N7 (7609 0467) *Open Tues–Sun 9am–1pm; 2–4.30pm. Holloway Road underground/Highbury and Islington underground/rail.* A small, busy Islington farm – one of the oldest in the capital – with livestock including cows, geese, goats, ducks, pigs and bees.

Hackney City Farm 1a Goldsmith's Row, E2 (7729 6381) *Open Tues–Sun 10am–4.30pm. Bethnal Green underground.* Originally a brewery, this small, friendly farm of only 1.5 acres with goats, sheep, pigs, cows, hens, chickens, turkeys, rabbits, ducks, bees and a butterfly tunnel even manages to fit in a beautiful, peaceful flower garden.

Kentish Town City Farm 1 Cressfield Close, Grafton Road, NW5 (7916 5421) *Open Tues–Sun 9am–5.30pm. Chalk Farm/Kentish Town underground.* Five acres with horses, pigs, goats, rabbits, cows, sheep, ducks and chickens. Milking and feeding twice daily.

Mudchute Park and Farm Pier Street, E14 (7515 5901) *Open daily 9am–5pm. Mudchute/Crossharbour DLR.* London's largest city farm with a site covering 35 acres, this is a peaceful spot amongst the towering buildings of Docklands. There are sheep, goats, pigs, cattle, the odd llama, a pets' corner and the occasional horse and pony, as well as gardens, a riding arena (lunchtime pony rides are £1.50 – phone 7515 0747), study centre and cafe. An agricultural show is held in August.

Newham City Farm King George Avenue, E16 (7476 1170) *Open Tues–Sun 10am–5pm summer, 10am–4pm winter. Prince Regent DLR.* The east of the capital almost seems to have the monopoly on city farms. Despite the abundance of them in the area, Newham manages to enjoy over 50,000 visitors annually.

Spitalfields Community Farm Weaver Street, E1 (7247 8762) *Open Tues–Sun 9am–6pm summer, 10am–5pm winter. Shoreditch underground.* Though it's small, there's a good range of animals at this working farm, including goats, pigs, sheep, cows and donkeys.

Stepping Stones Farm Ben Johnson Road, E1 (7790 8204) *Open Tues–Sun 9.30am–6pm. Stepney Green underground*. Stepping Stones manages to evoke a real country farm atmosphere despite being overshadowed by tower blocks. Crammed into a relatively small space, as well as the usual cows, pigs, sheep, geese, chickens, rabbits and ducks, there's a wildlife pond, a play area with toys and books, a ferret, a donkey and guinea pigs.

Surrey Docks Farm Rotherhithe Street, SE16 (7231 1010) *Open Tues–Sun 10am–5pm (but check as often closed Fridays or for lunch 1–2pm). Surrey Quays/Rotherhithe underground*. By the Thames and dominated by Canary Wharf, there's a blacksmith's forge, a wind turbine, an orchard, wild area, vegetable garden, herb garden, riverside walk, duck pond and a room to observe their bees, in addition to the goats, pigs, donkeys, geese, turkeys and other animals – all in a farm of just two and a half acres. There are training projects for people with learning difficulties and various events through the year including a summer playscheme for the over-8s.

Thameside Park City Farm 40 Thames Road, Barking, Essex (8594 8449) *Open daily 10am–5pm. Barking underground/rail*. Goats, sheep, horses, chickens, ducks and geese.

Vauxhall City Farm 24 St Oswald's Place, SE11 (7582 4204) *Open Tues–Thurs, Sat, Sun 10.30am–5pm. Vauxhall underground*. Tiny but well stocked with animals.

Wellgate Community Farm Collier Row Road, Romford, Essex

(017087 47850) *Open Mon–Fri 9.30am–3.30pm; Sat, Sun 9.30am–12.30pm. Chadwell Heath rail.* Under two acres but with goats, sheep, pigs, geese, ducks, chickens, turkeys, rabbits and guinea pigs.

Cloakrooms

Why cart that heavy shopping and luggage around the capital? Leave it here for *free*:

Bank of England Museum Threadneedle Street, EC2 (entrance in Bartholomew Lane) (7601 5545) *Open Mon–Fri 10am–5pm; also Sun 11am–5pm from Easter to Sept. Bank underground.* Anything 'within reason' can be deposited.

The Barbican Centre Silk Street, EC2 (7638 4141) *Open Mon–Sat 9am–11pm; Sun noon–11pm. Barbican underground.* There is generally no problem leaving packages and bags.

British Museum Great Russell Street, WC1 (7636 1555) *Open Mon–Sat 10am–5pm; Sun 2.30–6pm. Goodge Street/Tottenham Court Road/Russell Square underground.* Coats, hats, umbrellas and small hand luggage may be deposited.

National Gallery Trafalgar Square, WC2 (7747 2885) *Open Mon–Sat 10am–6pm; Sun 2–6pm. Charing Cross underground/rail.* No packages or bags.

National Portrait Gallery 2 St Martin's Place, WC2 (7306 0055) *Open Mon–Sat 10am–6pm; Sun 2–6pm. Charing Cross underground/rail.* Small parcels, boxes, bags, umbrellas and walking sticks are acceptable, but suitcases and rucksacks are not.

Royal Festival Hall South Bank Centre, SE1 (7960 4242) *Open daily 10am—10.30pm. Waterloo underground/rail.* No restrictions.

Royal National Theatre South Bank Centre, SE1 (7452 3333) *Open Mon—Sat 10am—11pm. Waterloo underground/rail.* No restrictions.

Tate Gallery Millbank, SW1 (7887 8008) *Open Mon—Sat 10am—5.50pm; Sun 2—5.50pm. Pimlico underground.* 'Anything that's not alive is allowed . . .'

Cosmetics and Perfumes

Debenhams, DH Evans, John Lewis, Fenwick, Dickens and Jones, Selfridges Oxford Street, Regent Street W1 *Marble Arch/Bond Street/Oxford Circus underground;* **Harrods, Harvey Nichols** Knightsbridge, SW1 *Knightsbridge underground;* **Peter Jones** Sloane Square, SW1 *Sloane Square underground;* **Barkers of Kensington** Kensington High Street, W8 *High Street Kensington underground;* **Army and Navy** Victoria Street, SW1 *Victoria rail/underground.* Almost all of the big cosmetics companies (especially the more expensive brands) provide FREE samples of their products from time to time – whatever their consultants may say. How else are they going to get you hooked on to regularly buying their over-packaged, over-priced products?

The department stores stocking their goods often also provide FREE skincare and make-up consultations, FREE makeovers and occasional special events including product launches. It's worth getting on a cosmetic company's register (give your name and address to the beauty consultant) so that you hear of forthcoming promotional events where further samples are often given.

So, if one sales assistant has no samples – or is unwilling to give any – there are plenty of other outlets to try.

Most companies are quite forthcoming in offering samples although a short consultation may be necessary first. The samples usually last for at least a couple of weeks and are very handy for the handbag or travel bag.

If you like a dash of fragrance and are on the way to a party, a quick walk around the perfume counters won't go amiss. The use of several scents at the same time acts as a very effective insect repellent.

Cycling

Lee Valley Cycle Circuit Quartermile Lane, E15 (8534 6085) *Leyton underground. Open usually daily from around 9am to dusk, but can vary, so check first. Admission £2.20 (£1.10 for under-16s) if you bring your own bike, or £4.30 (£3.30 for under-16s) including bike hire.* There are impressive purpose-built tracks capable of challenging the most experienced biker as well as the novice, catering for mountain biking, road racing, time trialling, cyclo–cross and BMX. There are regular special events. On Saturdays 10am–noon there is a kids' club with tuition and competitions (£1 per session).

Herne Hill Cycle Stadium Burbage Road, SE24 (7737 4647) *Opening hours vary. Adults £4.15, children under-16 from*

£1.30. Herne Hill rail. Admission is sometimes FREE to spectators. The only velodrome in London. A variety of races are held.

London Bicycle Tour Company 1a Gabriel's Wharf, 56 Upper Ground, SE1 (7928 6838) *Waterloo underground/rail.* You can hire mountain, traditional and children's bikes from £2.50 per hour. Also rollerblade hire at £2.50 per hour.

Southwark Cyclists (7403 0329) Organises cycling events in and around the Southwark area.

Thames Cycle Route This route runs for around 45 miles from Dartford in the east to Hampton Court in the west. Call Sustrans on 0117 929 0888 for more details.

Dance

Age Exchange Reminiscence Centre 11 Blackheath Village, SE3 (8318 9105) *Blackheath rail.* Regular tea dances are held, admission £5, which includes a glass of wine.

Blackheath Halls 23 Lee Road, Blackheath, SE3 (8463 0100) *Blackheath rail.* Regular tea dances, admission around £5.

Chisenhale Dance Space 64–84 Chisenhale Road, Bow, E3 (8981 6617) *Bethnal Green/Mile End underground.* Contemporary dance events and workshops with admission FREE or under £5.

Cochrane Theatre , Southampton Row, WC1 (7242 7040) *Holborn underground.* Both contemporary and classical dance performances with tickets costing £4 upwards.

Dance Attic 368 North End Road, SW6 (7610 2055) *Fulham Broadway underground*. A variety of dance classes – including ballet, hip hop and flamenco – costing from £3 with £1.50 day membership.

Danceworks 16 Balderton Street, W1 (7629 6183) *Bond Street underground*. A varied programme of dance classes from £4 with from £1 membership.

Greenwich Dance Agency Borough Hall, Royal Hill, Greenwich SE10 (8293 9741) *Greenwich DLR/rail*. Many classes, dance events and tea dances cost £5 or under.

London Coliseum St Martin's Lane, WC2 (7632 8300) *Charing Cross underground/rail*. Spectacular dance productions tend to visit during the summer and winter. Although the Coliseum is often associated with high ticket prices, sometimes these are available for as little as £3.

Pineapple Dance Studio 7 Langley Street, Covent Garden, WC2 (7836 4004) *Covent Garden underground*. Dance classes cost from £4 with from £1 membership.

South Bank Centre Belvedere Road, SE1 (7960 4242) *Waterloo/ Embankment underground*. The Royal Festival Hall, Queen Elizabeth Hall and Purcell Room within the South Bank arts complex all put on dance performances with tickets starting at £5. In August the Centre organises and hosts *Blitz*, a month of FREE dance performances, workshops, lectures and other events.

Disabled Information

Artsline (7388 2227) This provides FREE information for the disabled on cultural and entertainment events and can forward FREE individual guides covering such things as restaurants and theatres. It only asks that you pay the cost of postage.

The British Sports Association for the Disabled (7490 4919) Gives advice and information on suitable sport activities for people with disabilities.

Greater London Association for Disabled People (GLAD) 336 Brixton Road, SW9 (7346 5800) *Open Mon–Fri 9am–5pm. Brixton underground.* You can collect a FREE *London Disability Guide* from them or they will post you a copy if you send them an SAE. The guide is available in large print, tape and braille formats.

London Transport's Unit for Disabled Passengers (7918 3312) Publishes a FREE guide, *Access to the Underground*.

Tripscope (8580 7021) Can help with general enquiries.

Drinks

I once met a man, clearly inebriated, who showed me a surprisingly complex map he had drawn up on the back of an old wine list. It showed the route he'd worked out (and took most weeks) linking a formidable number of off-licences that held Saturday afternoon wine tastings. Obviously, in the interests of public sobriety, it cannot be reproduced here. Nevertheless, the following off-licences and wine merchants have occasional, weekly or even daily tastings, which may include wines, beers, whiskies and even champagnes.

Majestic Wine Warehouses There is a most agreeable wine-tasting system in that 8–10 wines are on offer at the special wine-tasting counter every day throughout opening hours (Mon–Sat 10am–8pm; Sun 10am–6pm) and there are occasional themed tasting weekends too.

Oddbins There are usually tastings on Saturdays from 2–5pm; but on Friday afternoons in the City.

Wine Rack These generally have wine tastings on Saturdays and Sundays.

Nicolas The staff are happy for visitors to try their wines on Saturday afternoons.

Victoria Wines Branches have regular tastings, usually at least once a month, and these can vary from just one wine to a whole range of drinks.

Unwins A number of branches have regular tastings, usually on Saturdays.

Fashion

Harrods Knightsbridge, SW1 (7730 1234) *Knightsbridge underground.* Throughout the year FREE fashion workshops are held, often in association with magazines such as *Marie Claire, Harpers and Queen* and *Vogue.* Telephone for details.

Selfridges Oxford Street, W1 (7629 1234) *Oxford Circus underground*. Runs occasional FREE fashion shows with a complimentary drink.

Film and Video

Most first-run London cinemas showing the usual Hollywood fare regularly have adult tickets available at £5 or under, usually on Mondays and for daytime rather than evening screenings. The cinemas included here are in some way out of the ordinary.

Barbican Centre Silk Street, EC2 (7382 7000) *Opening times vary. Barbican underground*. Admission for some screenings at this arts complex costs under £5.

British Museum Great Russell Street, WC1 (7636 1555) *Open Mon–Sat 10am–5pm; Sun 2.30–6pm. Russell Square underground*. Regular FREE weekday film showings.

Instituto Cervantes 22 Manchester Square, W1 (7935 1518) *Open Mon–Thurs 9.30am–6.30pm; Fri 9.30am–5pm. Marble Arch/ Bond Street underground*. Telephone for details of FREE film shows put on by this institute created to promote Spanish culture.

National Gallery Trafalgar Square, WC2 (7747 2885) *Open Mon– Sat 10am–6pm; Sun 2–6pm. Charing Cross underground/rail*. Films with FREE admission on artists and schools of art on Mondays at 1pm.

Prince Charles Cinema Leicester Place, Leicester Square, WC2 (7734 9127) *Opening times vary. Leicester Square underground*.

Great value at £1.99–£3.50 a ticket, considering that this repertory cinema is located in the centre of town.

Riverside Studios Crisp Road, Hammersmith, W6 (8237 1111) *Opening times vary. Hammermith underground.* A repertory and arthouse cinema with tickets from £5.

Tate Britain Millbank, SW1 (7887 8000) *Open Mon–Sat 10am–5.50pm; Sun 2–5.50pm. Pimlico underground.* Regular FREE film showings each week.

Watermans Arts Centre 40 High Street, Brentford, Middlesex (8568 1176) *Opening times vary. Gunnersbury underground.* All tickets are under £5 at the cinema which has a good repertory programme.

Whitechapel Art Gallery Whitechapel High Street, E1 (7522 7878) *Open Tues–Sun 11am–5pm; Wed until 8pm. Aldgate East underground.* Regular FREE art-orientated film and video screenings.

Football

Arsenal Tour Arsenal Football Club, Highbury Stadium, Highbury Lane, N5 (7704 4100) *Tours by appointment at 11am or 2pm. Adults £4, children £2. Arsenal underground.* The tour of this art deco stadium includes visits to the museum, directors' areas, press rooms, board rooms and players' tunnels.

Millwall Football Club The Den, Zampa Road, SE16 (7232 1222) *South Bermondsey rail.* Request in writing to go on a FREE tour of the grounds, which lasts around an hour and a half.

West Ham United Green Street, Upton Park, E13 (8548 2748)

Upton Park underground. Ring to book a place on the tour, on the first Thursday of the month at 10am during the season.

Frequent Events
Pageantry can be seen daily in London.

Ceremony of the Keys Tower of London, EC3 (7709 0765) *Daily 9.45–10.05pm. Special pass required: write to the Resident Governor, Ceremony of the Keys, HM Tower of London, EC3N 4AB, enclosing a stamped self-addressed envelope and give at least two months' notice. Tower Hill underground.* A 700-year-old routine of locking up the Tower of London, home to the Crown Jewels, where the Sentry and the Chief Warder have an historic verbal exchange and the Last Post is sounded.

Changing of the Guard Buckingham Palace, SW1 *April–Aug daily 11.15am, Sept–Mar alternate days 11.15am. Can be cancelled in bad weather or during state visits. St James's Park underground.* This famous 40-minute ceremony, the changing of the sentries at the Palace, takes place inside the railings of the Palace and is London's most popular regular event so arrive in good time for a good view. The new guard leaves Wellington Barracks three minutes before the ceremony and, preceded by a band, marches down Birdcage Walk to the Palace.

Changing of the Guard Horse Guards, Horse Guards Parade, Whitehall, SW1 (7930 1793) *St James's Park / Charing Cross underground / rail.* Every day the mounted guard leaves Hyde Park Barracks at 10.28am (9.28am on Sundays) and goes via Hyde Park Corner and Constitution Hill to Horse Guards Parade at 11am (10am on Sundays) where the guard is changed. Seeing the immaculately attired guardsmen proceed through the park remains a memorable sight.

Gun Salutes *Details of these, and of other park events, are contained in the Park's Summer Entertainment Programme.* To obtain a copy, send an A4 SAE to The Old Police House, Hyde Park, London W2 2UH (7298 2000). Gun salutes take place in Green or Hyde Park at noon and at the Tower of London at 1pm on the following dates (or, if it is a Sunday, on the following day): 6 February (Accession Day), 21 April (the Queen's birthday), 2 June (Coronation Day), 10 June (the Duke of Edinburgh's birthday) and 4 August (the Queen Mother's birthday). There are also gun salutes to mark state visits (generally May and October), for Trooping the Colour (June) and the State Opening of Parliament (October or November).

Chelsea Cruise Eastern end of Carriage Drive North, Battersea Park, SW11. *Held on the last Saturday of every month. Queenstown Road rail.* Hundreds of owners of classic American cars, hot rods and motorbikes gather to celebrate car culture near the park's Peace Pagoda throughout the day.

Funfairs

Popular funfair sites include: **Alexandra Park** Muswell Hill, N22 *Wood Green underground;* **Battersea Park** Albert Bridge Road, SW11 *Sloane Square underground;* **Blackheath Common** SE3 *Blackheath rail;* **Hampstead Heath** NW3 *Hampstead underground.* Fairs are typically held on Good Friday to Easter

Monday and on Friday–Monday of the Spring (May) and August Bank Holiday weekends.

Gardening

Calthorpe Project Community Garden 258–274 Gray's Inn Road, WC1 (7837 8019) *King's Cross underground/rail*. This is useful if you have gardening skills but nowhere to practise them. The Project is happy for volunteers to help out in their acre of gardens. Regular helpers can look after their own section of garden single-handed.

Hackney City Farm 1a Goldsmith's Row, E2 (7729 6381) *Open Tues–Sun 10am–4.30pm. Bethnal Green underground*. Includes a large garden where volunteers can help plant and grow things and learn about propagating new plants, organic controls and companion planting.

Hampstead Heath, NW3 (8348 9930) *Hampstead underground*. From around May to September FREE horticultural clinics are held in the Flower Garden in Golders Hill Park on some weekend afternoons, and advice can be obtained on gardening topics.

Horniman Gardens 100 London Road, Forest Hill, SE23 (8699 2339) *Open 8am–dusk. Forest Hill rail*. Horticultural demonstrations are held about once a month on Wednesday afternoons from March to September and occasionally on Sunday afternoons too.

London Wildlife Garden Centre 28 Marsden Road, SE15 (7252 9186) *Open Tues, Wed, Thurs, Sun 11am–4pm. East Dulwich rail*. This London Wildlife Trust Centre promotes wildlife gardening and appreciation of wildlife in your garden. There are lots of gardening ideas, with a visitor centre, demonstration areas, a nursery, wildlife gardens with a pond, meadows and woods, and even beehives, a sensory/herb garden, a demonstration building with innovations that include plants on the roof for insulation and recycled newspapers in the walls. Events include four Open Days a year as well as talks, workshops, training programmes and clubs for 5 to 8-year-olds and 8 to 16-year-olds with environmental activities such as fossil hunting, tree planting and making nature films.

Greyhound Racing

An evening watching greyhound racing can be surprisingly enjoyable even if you don't place any bets. All London stadiums have bars and restaurants.

Catford Stadium Adenmore Road, SE6 (8690 8000) *Races Mon, Thurs, Sat at 7.15pm. Admission £4. Catford/Catford Bridge rail.*

Walthamstow Stadium Chingford Road, W4 (8531 4255) *Races Tues, Thurs, Sat at 7.30pm. Admission £5 or under, or FREE. Walthamstow Central underground.*

Wimbledon Stadium Plough Lane, SW17 (8946 8000) *Races Tues, Fri, Sat at 7.30pm. Admission £5 or under. Wimbledon underground/rail.*

Gymnasium Equipment and Athletics Facilities

Barnet Copthall Stadium Great North Way, NW4 (8457 9915) *Use of facilities costs £2 per day. Mill Hill East underground.*

Crystal Palace National Sports Centre Ledrington Road, SE19 (8778 0131) *Admission: £2.25 per day. Crystal Palace rail.* This complex has an extensive range of facilities.

Primrose Hill Primrose Hill Road, NW3 *FREE to use. Chalk Farm/Camden Town underground.* There has been an open-air gymnasium here since Victorian times, and nowadays there is a choice of around 20 different types of exercise equipment.

Parliament Hill Track Highgate Road, Hampstead Heath, NW5 (7435 8998) *Costs £1.70 per day. Gospel Oak Rail.*

Victoria Park Victoria Park Road, E9 (8985 1957) *FREE. Mile End underground.* A fitness trail with some gym equipment.

Winn's Common Plumstead, SE18 *FREE. Plumstead rail.* A small selection of outdoor gym equipment.

West Ham Park Upton Lane, E7 *FREE. Plaistow underground.* A keep fit trail with a few items of gym equipment.

Haircuts

London College of Fashion 20 John Prince's Street, W1 (7514 7400) *Open Mon–Fri 10am–5pm during term time. Oxford*

Circus underground. Men and women are both welcome. Call to make an appointment for a FREE haircut.

Toni and Guy Hairdressing Academy 75 New Oxford Street, WC1 (7836 0606) *Tottenham Court Road/Holborn underground*. Look out for vouchers for FREE haircuts by competent students, advertised in free magazines like *Girl About Town* and *Midweek*. Otherwise cuts are £5 each.

Kite Flying

Primrose Hill, Richmond Park and Blackheath Common are all popular kite-flying spots. The London Tourist Board (0870 5887711) can tell you about FREE kite festivals being held throughout the year in the capital, which includes Blackheath, SE3 (8808 1280) on Easter Sunday and Monday.

Lectures, Talks and Discussions
Admission is *free*.

The Albany Centre Douglas Way, SE8 (8692 0231) *Open Mon–Sat 10am–6pm. New Cross underground/rail*. There are poetry readings, and occasional tours of the theatre explaining the workings backstage, from lighting to sound.

Architectural Association 34–36 Bedford Square, WC1 (7636 0974) *Open Mon–Fri 10am–7pm; Sat 10am–3pm. Tottenham Court Road underground*. Weekly afternoon and evening lectures.

Architecture Foundation The Economist Building, 30 Bury Street, SW1 (7839 9389) *Open Tues, Wed, Fri noon–6pm; Thurs, Sat, Sun 2–6pm. Green Park underground.* This campagning charity has urban planning debates.

British Museum Great Russell Street, WC1 (7636 1555) *Open Mon–Sat 10am–5pm; Sun 2.30–6pm. Russell Square underground.* Weekday lectures at 1.15pm; gallery talks Tues–Sat 11.30am and talks at other times from Sat–Tues.

Camden Arts Centre Arkwright Road, NW3 (7435 2643) *Open Tues–Thurs noon–8pm; Fri–Sun noon–6pm.* Artists give informal talks about their works on display. Ring for details.

Explore Worldwide *venues in central London (01252 344161).* This travel company offers informative two-hour slide lectures every two weeks or so. Although the shows obviously mention the holidays they sell, there's an opportunity to learn about other lands, different cultures and ancient sites around the world, hiking in mountain regions, wildlife and natural history etc. Ring for a ticket.

Geffrye Museum Kingsland Road, E2 (7739 9893) *Open Tues– Sat 10am–5pm; Sun 2–5pm. Old Street underground.* Talks on Saturdays at 2pm and 3.30pm and other talks related to special exhibitions.

Greenwich Borough Museum 232 Plumstead High Street, SE18 (8855 3240) *Plumstead rail.* Afternoon talks given once a month on a wide range of subjects.

Gresham College Barnard's Inn Hall, EC1 (7831 0575) *Open Mon–Fri 9.30am–5pm. Chancery Lane underground.* Request a free programme detailing the year's lectures, which tend to run from September to November and February to May, when there could be anything from two or three a month to nearly 20. The lectures are on astronomy, divinity, geometry, law, music, physics and rhetoric, as founder, City merchant Sir Thomas Gresham, insisted they should be when establishing the college in 1597. Nowadays the College also delivers lectures on commerce and occasionally other subjects such as literary London.

Guildhall School of Music and Drama Silk Street, Barbican, EC2 (7628 2571) *Barbican/Moorgate underground*. Occasional talks on aspects of music and drama.

Holland Park Illchester Place, Kensington, W8. (7602 9483) *Holland Park underground*. Summer talks about the wildlife and history of the park are given at the Ecology Centre.

Instituto Cervantes 22 Manchester Square, W1 (7935 1518) *Open Mon–Thurs 9.30am–6.30pm; Fri 9.30am–5pm. Marble Arch/ Bond Street underground*. Ring for details of lectures and talks with a Spanish theme.

Italian Cultural Institute 39 Belgrave Square, SW1 (7235 1461) *Open Mon–Fri 9.30am–5pm. Knightsbridge underground*. Regular lectures on Italian themes.

Museum of London 150 London Wall, EC2 (7600 3699) *St Paul's underground*. Regular lunchtime lectures and gallery talks.

National Gallery Trafalgar Square, WC2 (7747 2885) *Charing Cross underground/rail*. Lunchtime lectures every day, except Sun.

National Portrait Gallery 2 St Martin's Place, WC2 (7306 0055)

Open Mon–Sat 10am–6pm; Sun 2–6pm. Charing Cross underground/rail. Daily lectures.

Polish Cultural Institute 34 Portland Place, W1 (7636 6032) *Open Mon–Wed, Fri 10am–4pm; Thurs 10am–8pm. Regent's Park underground.* Regular lectures with a Polish theme.

Riverside Studios Crisp Road, Hammersmith, W6 (8741 2255) *Open Mon–Sat 10.30am–11.30pm; Sun noon–11.30pm. Hammersmith underground.* Occasional talks and discussions.

Royal Institution 21 Albemarle Street, W1 (7409 2992) *Green Park underground.* Generally once a term, or three times a year, the Institution organises a free lunchtime talk on a general scientific subject. Ring to join the free mailing list. There are also lectures where an admission charge is levied.

Royal Society of Arts 8 John Adam Street, WC2 (7930 5115) *Lectures are usually at 6pm on weekdays. Seat reservations and a lecture programme for the year available from the Lecture Booking Office by letter or phone. Charing Cross underground/rail.* Early booking is advisable for these popular lectures by members on a broad range of topical themes such as art, architecture, commerce, industry, science and the media. There are also occasional lectures for children.

St Mary-Le-Bow Cheapside, EC2 (7248 5139) *Bank underground.* During the academic year on Tuesdays at 1.05pm the rector talks to a prominent figure (such as an actor or politician) about current affairs, their personal outlook, where the universe ends etc. Admission is on a first-come-first-served basis.

Tate Gallery, Millbank SW1 (7887 8000) *Open Mon–Sat 10am–5.50pm; Sun 2–5.50pm. Pimlico underground.* Daily lectures.

Valence House Museum Becontree Avenue, Dagenham (8595 8404) *Open Tues–Fri 9.30am–1pm; 2–4.30pm; Sat 10am–4pm. Chadwell Heath rail.* Lectures concerning aspects of the collection from time to time.

Wallace Collection Hertford House, Manchester Square, W1 (7935 0687) *Open Mon–Sat 10am–5pm; Sun 2–5pm. Bond Street underground.* General tours daily and occasional specialist lecture tours.

Watermans Arts Centre 40 High Street, Brentford, TW8 (8847 5651) *Open Tues–Sat 10.30am–11pm; Sun 10.30am–10.30pm. Gunnersbury underground/rail.* Occasional talks.

Whitechapel Art Gallery Whitechapel High Street, E1 (7522 7878) *Open Tues–Sun 11am–5pm; Wed until 8pm. Aldgate East underground.* Occasional talks.

William Morris Gallery Lloyd Park, Forest Road, Walthamstow, E17 (8527 3782) *Open Tue–Sat 10am–1pm; 2–5pm and first Sun in each month, 10am–noon, 2–5pm. Walthamstow Central underground/rail.* Occasional lectures relating to William Morris and the Arts and Crafts movement.

Libraries

Details of a selection of various libraries follow, where you are free to browse or study. There are some big libraries with comprehensive collections included and also some of London's libraries with specialist collections.

To find out where your standard local borough libraries

are, consult the *Yellow Pages*. If you haven't got a copy, you'll find one at your local library. Yes, what a conundrum.

Many people use their library just to read the newspapers and magazines provided. Libraries are often also a good source of information concerning events, services, organisations and courses in the area.

Many local libraries hold FREE children's activities in the school holidays, which could be anything from pottery or dance workshops to puppet shows and storytelling.

The Barbican Library The Barbican Centre, Silk, Street, EC2 (General library: 7638 0569, children's library: 7628 9447) *Open Mon–Fri 9.30am–5.30pm (Tues until 7.30pm), Sat 9.30am–12.30pm. Barbican underground.* The City's leading lending library. Membership (if you wish to borrow) is open to those living, working or studying in the City of London and regular visitors to the centre.

Battersea Reference Library Altenburg Gardens, SW11 (8871 7467) *Open Mon–Fri 9am–9pm; Sat 9am–5pm. Clapham Junction rail.* Contains special collections on William Blake, Edward Thomas, building and architecture and the occult.

British Library 96 Euston Road, Somers Town, NW1 (7412 7000) *Open Mon–Thurs 10am–8pm; Fri, Sat 9.30am–5pm. King's Cross/Euston underground/rail.* The mother of all libraries.

British Music Information Centre 10 Stratford Place, W1 (7499 8567) *Open Mon–Fri noon–5pm. Bond Street underground.* The Centre offers an information service on contemporary classical British music using their extensive collection of recordings, scores, videos and other materials.

Finsbury Reference Library 245 St John Street, EC1 (7689 7960) *Open Mon, Thurs 9.30am–8pm; Tues, Sat 9.30am–5pm; Fri 9.30am–1pm. Angel/Farringdon underground.* Specialises in art, design photography and the Sadlers Wells collection.

Geffrye Museum Kingsland Road, E2 (7739 9893) *Open Tues– Sat 10am–5pm; Sun 2–5pm. Old Street underground.* Reference library and furniture trade archive.

Goethe-Institut Library 50 Princes Gate, Exhibition Road, SW7 (7411 3400) *Open Mon–Thurs 10am–8pm; Sat 10.30am–1pm. South Kensington underground.* A collection concerning Germany.

Guildhall Library Aldermanbury, off Gresham Street, EC2 (7606 3030) *Open Mon–Sat 10am–5pm; Bank/Moorgate underground.* An unrivalled collection of books, illustrations, maps, prints and manuscripts about London. There's an exhibition room containing famous books and manuscripts.

Homerton Library Homerton High Street, E9 (8985 8262) *Open Mon 10am–5pm; Tues 10am–7pm; Thurs 1–7pm; Fri 10am– 6pm; Sat 9am–12.30pm; 1.30pm–5pm. Homerton rail.* Special collections on Australasia and the Americas.

Horniman Museum London Road, Forest Hill, SE23 (8766 7663) *Open Tues–Sat 10.30am–6pm; Sun 2–6pm. Telephone for appointment. Forest Hill rail.* Reference library concerned with the museum's exhibits.

Instituto Cervantes 22 Manchester Square, W1 (7935 1518) *Open Mon–Thurs 9.30am–6.30pm; Fri 9.30am–5pm. Marble Arch/ Bond Street underground.* An extensive Spanish library.

Italian Cultural Institute Library 39 Belgrave Square, SW1 (7235 1461) *Open Mon–Fri 9.30am–5pm. Knightsbridge underground.* An extensive library concerning Italy and Italian culture, including videos and CDs.

Keats House Keats Grove, Hampstead, NW3 (7435 2062) *Library open by appointment. Hampstead underground.* A library concerned with the life and work of the Romantic poet.

Kensington Central Library Phillimore Walk, W8 (7937 2542) *Open Mon, Tues, Thurs, Fri 10am–8pm; Wed 9.30am–1pm; Sat 9.30am–5pm. High Street Kensington underground.* Specialises in genealogy, heraldry and folklore.

Limehouse Library 638 Commercial Road, E14 (7987 3183) *Open Mon, Tues, Thurs 9am–8pm; Wed, Fri 9am–5pm; Sat 9am–12.30pm; 1.30–5pm. Limehouse DLR.* Has special sections on French, Portuguese and German literature.

Maida Vale Library Sutherland Avenue, W9 (7641 3659) *Open Mon–Fri 9.30am–7pm; Sat 9.30am–5pm. Maida Vale underground.* Special sections on social justice and criminology, and military history.

Map Library Department of Geography, University College London, 26 Bedford Way, WC1 (7679 2000 ext 5537) *Open Mon–Fri 9am–1pm; 2–5pm but telephone in advance. Euston Square/Warren Street underground.* If it's maps you want, this is the place to see them. Also over 600 atlases to complete the collection.

Marylebone Library Marylebone Road, NW1 (7641 1037) *Mon–Fri 10am–7pm; Sat 9.30am–5pm. Baker Street underground.* The location of the library ensures there is a special section on Sherlock Holmes, in addition to ones on medicine and dentistry.

Mayfair Library 25 South Audley Street, W1 (7641 4903) *Open Mon–Fri 9.30am–7pm; Sat 9.30am–1pm. Bond Street underground.* Special collections of literature in European and other languages.

Museum of London 150 London Wall, EC2 (7600 3699) *Open Tues–Sat 10am–5.50pm. Telephone for appointment. St Paul's underground.* A wide range of books concerning London.

Natural History Museum Cromwell Road, SW7 (7942 5000) *Open Mon–Fri 10am–5pm. Proof of identity required. South Kensington underground.* Large reference library.

National Maritime Museum Romney Road, SE10 (8858 4422) *Open Mon–Fri 10am–5pm. Proof of identity required. Greenwich/Maze Hill rail.* Has one of the biggest reference libraries relating to anything maritime.

National Sound Archive British Library, 96 Euston Road, Somers Town, NW1 (7412 7440) *Open Mon–Thurs 10am–8pm; Fri, Sat 9.30am–5pm. South Kensington underground.* Library of catalogues, periodicals, etc., and listening service.

Newspaper Library Colindale Avenue, NW9 (7412 7353) *Open to over-18s Mon–Sat 10am–5pm. Proof of identity with signature required. Colindale underground.* If you want to see the Battle of Waterloo edition of *The Times*, or other editions of newspapers and periodicals, this branch of the British Library is the place to come.

Photographer's Gallery 5 and 8 Great Newport Street, WC2 (7831 1772) *Open Tues–Sat 11am–7pm. Leicester Square underground.* Reference library.

Polish Cultural Institute Library 34 Portland Place, W1 (7636 6032) *Open Mon–Wed, Fri noon–3pm. Regent's Park underground.* A relatively small library with around 4,000 books concerned with aspects of Poland.

Royal Geographical Society Lowther Lane, 1 Kensington Gore, SW7 (7591 3040) *Open Mon–Fri 10am–1pm; 2–5pm. South Kensington underground.* The excellent library of this society dedicated to exploration is open to non-members by appointment.

Rudolph Steiner House 35 Park Road, NW1 (7723 4400) *Open Mon–Fri 11am–1pm; 2–5pm. Baker Street underground.* Works of and about Steiner, which visitors are welcome to browse and study. Steiner (1861–1925) was an Austrian philosopher who developed his own spiritual and mystic teaching designed to develop the whole human being.

St Bride Printing Library St Bride Institute, Bride Lane, EC4 (7353 4660) *Open Mon–Fri 9.30am–5.30pm by appointment. St Paul's underground.* This reference library covering the history of printing has original wooden printing presses from the 1800s on display, and the librarian may even have time to explain how they worked.

Science Reference and Information Service 25 Southampton Buildings, Chancery Lane, WC2 (7323 7494) *Open Mon–Fri 9.30am–9pm; Sat 10am–1pm. Chancery Lane underground.* Special collections include patents, inventions, markets and products, industry and technology.

Shoreditch Library Pitfield Street, N1 (7739 6981) *Open Mon, Tues, Fri 10am–5pm; Thurs 1–7pm; Sat 9am–5pm. Old Street* *underground.* Special collections on small manufacturing industries.

Swiss Cottage Library 88 Avenue Road, NW3 (7413 6533) *Open Mon, Thurs 10am–7pm; Tues, Fri 10am–6pm. Swiss Cottage underground.* Has an Ordnance Survey map collection as well as *The Times* newspaper from 1785 on microfilm.

Wellcome Institute History of Medicine Library The Wellcome Building, 183 Euston Road, NW1 (7611 8888) *Open Mon, Wed, Fri 9.45am–5.15pm; Tues, Thurs 9.45am–7.15pm; Sat 9.45am–1pm. Euston underground/rail.* A large collection on the history of medicine.

Wellcome Trust Information Service Library The Wellcome Building, 183 Euston Road, NW1 (7611 8888) *Open Mon–Fri 9.45am–5.pm; Euston underground/rail.* Wholly concerned with medicine, it keeps up to date with medical research and advances.

Westminster Central Reference Library 35 St Martin's Street, WC2 (7641 4636) *Open Mon–Fri 10am–8pm; Sat 10am–5pm. Charing Cross underground/rail.* A comprehensive library that includes international telephone directories, maps, special collections on theatre, cinema, ballet, art, antiques and architecture, and a register of British companies.

William Morris Gallery Lloyd Park, Forest Road, Walthamstow, E17 (8527 3782) *Open Tues–Sat 10am–1pm; 2–5pm and first Sun in each month, 10am–noon, 2–5pm. Walthamstow Central underground/rail.* The archive and reference library are open by appointment.

The Life of a Ligger: There Is Such a Thing as a Free Lunch

If you have the ruthlessness, ingenuity, confidence, cheeky personality and possibly, sometimes, the stupidity required, you can turn the art of obtaining something for nothing, or getting in where you're not invited, into something approaching a full-time occupation.

This behaviour, known as 'ligging', 'blagging', or 'freeloading', is an especially popular pastime with many members of the media industry, who are almost required to master the art as part of their basic training.

And there's no end to it. With persistence, if you're able to pass yourself off as a half-competent hack travel writer, there are enough newspapers, magazines, airlines, ferry companies, car hire firms, tour operators and tourist offices out there to sponsor your international trips whether your piece actually appears in a publication or not.

But you need to be impudent enough to do it. If you possess this quality, one opportunity leads to another. You could, say, drop in on a freebie function such as the preview of a Cork Street art exhibition (which usually take place on Tuesdays) by entering at the same time as a group of others that you had seen who were about to walk in, or when the signing-in book was unattended.

Over the food and wine most generously provided by your host, you could get talking to a friend of a celebrity having a party later in the evening. What a coincidence it is, you exclaim, that you know the celebrity too (not letting on that the time you met him was when you obtained his autograph in the year Mrs Thatcher became prime minister). Obviously, your new acquaintance concludes that it would be ludicrous for you not to attend the party. You realise that this means you won't be able to slip anonymously into a press screening of that big film you've been anxiously awaiting, that's showing in an hour in a preview theatre in Wardour Street.

At the shindig you meet a commissioning editor of a national broadsheet who is so merry by way of intoxication that he'd commission a pot of paint let alone you, the London-based theatre/food/sports reporter (delete according to freebies not required) for the *Philadelphia Examiner/ Arctic Airways In Flight Magazine/Prague Gazette*. And so on . . .

The best way to deal with the PR people at the door of a promotional party, who are there to weed out hangers-on like you, is to make one of them think they've met you before. Public relations is all about meeting people all of the time, and they probably wouldn't know you from Adam even if they had once met you. So it's best to start the conversation by asking 'How are you? You've lost some weight/changed your hair. I suppose it's been a while.' Unless the PR person is absolutely *sure* you're an impostor, she's hardly going to risk causing a scene by ejecting you at such an important occasion.

If you want to avoid buying a round of drinks in a bar, drop down to tie a shoelace as the group approaches the bar, catching up with everyone when the round is bought.

If you know or know of someone who's a member of a London club, needless to say it would be very wrong to sign yourself in there under their name. If you did, of course, they would be approached for payment of the bill you ran up while on the premises (If you were to do this, it's as well to bear in mind that you may later be approached by the fraud squad.)

A couple of waiters working in hotels recently confided to me that they never bother to check whether names of hotel guests and their room numbers tally – indeed often they just request the room number from guests. The less moral would think it a pity not to use the opportunity such lack of diligence presents. To use bar and restaurant areas of larger hotels – small establishments may know patrons by sight – have a glimpse at the front desk as you enter to note how rooms are numbered: two digits or three for example. Such knowledge should suffice for provision of various hotel services, although it would be prudent to do some regular training of the 100-metre sprint prior to doing this.

When playing golf, try starting at the sixth hole and finishing at the fifth and you'll have no need to bother the management for the payment of green fees.

Each time you see a printing shop, call in and say you want to get some invitations printed, and ask whether they have any samples. Help yourself to any that are for future parties, weddings, conferences and other functions that appeal, explaining that you need them to facilitate the design of your own invitation.

It's best to visit restaurants in groups of at least 11 if the service charge is 10 per cent and groups of 13 if the service charge is 12.5 per cent. Get the group to agree beforehand to split the bill equally, saying that dissecting it with a calculator after the meal is so very tacky. When the bill comes, stress to the other members of the party how important it is to add 10–12.5 per cent to the total. This takes care of your share of the costs. It's a bit rotten to deprive the waiter or waitress of a tip, but at least you get a good meal for nothing.

If you are in employment, by loosely defining your job title you can again get something for nothing. Suppose, for example, you work as teaboy at a rock magazine. Even if only one of the ten record companies you approach for a review copy of the latest release by a favoured band doesn't make enquiries to find that coffee-making and rubbish-bin-emptying take up the bulk of your workload, at least you've been sent one free CD, and with any luck they'll be keen to send you more.

Ligging opportunities are all around. If a crowd is walking into a house to join a party, a good ligger will always join them. There are endless excuses were he or she to be caught out. I mean, can you read half the house numbers clearly in a darkened street? It's best to go in brandishing a bottle of wine, which you can instantly return to the car on the pretext of having left your lights on by mistake. When you return to the celebrations, if someone asks who you're with, you can simply say John, Jane or David – there's usually someone of that name present.

Ligging is only at the expense of your conscience and

perception of morality. And at least if you go too far, accommodation will be free too – a spell in prison.

Magazines and Newspapers

There's a wealth of FREE literature available in London without you having to search out the local library – which anyway has probably been closed down, or has had half the books thrown out to make way for racks of videos (invariably decrepit 70s TV serials such as *Colditz* and *Poldark*), condensed talking books (not so often for those with failing sight as for the bone idle) and CDs (usually *The Best of Chicago* plus *Rumours* and *Hotel California* and a couple of Bob Dylan recordings from his boring phase because all the best stuff is always out on loan).

You'll be awash with that upmarket type of magazine that really only exists to help flog expensive appartments thrust through your letterbox if you have a swanky enough address. If you don't, you'll have to make do with the more downmarket titles stuffed in your face first thing in the morning at central train stations and also available from street dispensers.

Yet some of these publications can be surprisingly good. *Midweek* is probably the best written of the capital's free publications. Many of the contributors also write for or go on to write for the national media. It is distributed from around 8am to 10am at major rail and underground stations on Mondays and is also available from dispensers.

Girl About Town and *Ms London* are also distributed from

8am to 10am at major rail and underground stations and from dispensers. They are aimed at young working women, and if you disregard the dubious adverts for bargain basement hen night venues and cocktail bars, there's often good articles about relationships, careers and fashion and film interviews and reviews.

There are also several free weekly newspapers available from central London street dispensers (in The Strand, WC2, and Earl's Court Road, SW5, for example) such as *New Zealand News UK*, *TNT Southern Cross* and *SA Times*, which apart from the occasional vaguely interesting travel article are chiefly only of interest to their targeted audiences, namely New Zealanders, Australians and South Africans respectively.

Trailfinder Magazine is another publication available from central street dispensers and is published three times a year. Although it promotes a travel agency, in each issue it includes six or seven travel articles accompanied by excellent colour photography.

Galleries is an impressive monthly magazine on the current art scene, available from many commercial art galleries. Galleries and artists are indexed and there is further information included.

Makeovers and Beauty Care

See also *Cosmetics and Perfumes* p. 69.

The Body Shop *Over 40 branches around London, for details call head office, 01903 73150.* Branches offer FREE makeovers (or if you wish, just selected items such as eyes or lips), application tips and advice, and some also give skincare, handcare and footcare demonstrations. Full makeovers take around 20–30 minutes, but if you are in a hurry they can provide express makeovers in 10 minutes. Unlike some stores, the staff will not apply a whole bucket's worth of make-up to your face. An appointment is often neccessary, and it's usually best to avoid lunchtimes and Saturdays.

Markets

Some of London's street markets, such as Brixton and Brick Lane, are dominated by particular ethnic groups and therefore serve as an excellent introduction to the diversity of peoples living in the capital. The oldest markets, such as Brick Lane, Petticoat Lane and Portobello Road, preserve some of London's history while reflecting the changing times and fashions.

Many markets can be a great experience even if you have no intention of buying anything. Some sell unusual or interesting wares, while others, though selling the ordinary and drab, reflect the economic fortunes of the area or simply add real colour and personality to their neighbour-hoods in their own rights.

Bermondsey (New Caledonian) Market Bermondsey Square, SE1 *Open Fri 5am–1pm. Bermondsey underground.* Brisk business occurs at this antique dealers' market which consists of hundreds of stalls with an overwhelming variety of goods. It is best seen before dawn when scores of torches flicker as buyers examine the goods.

Berwick Street Market Berwick Street, W1 *Open Mon–Sat 9am–5pm. Tottenham Court Road underground.* Dating back to the 1840s, this busy, boisterous fruit, veg and general food market retains much of its character despite the huge volume of pedestrian and vehicular traffic. Prices plunge after about 4pm.

Borough Market Stoney Street, SE1 *Open Fri noon–5pm; Sat 9am–5pm. London Bridge underground/rail.* A wonderful enclosed market with a great atmosphere selling a great diversity of foods including fish, game, fruit and veg, breads and luxury chocolates.

Brick Lane Market E1, E2 *Sun 7.30am–1pm. Aldgate/Shoreditch underground.* This big, ramshackle market offers a real East End experience as Brick Lane and nearby streets come alive with hundreds of stalls selling almost anything.

Brixton Market around Electric Avenue SW9 *Open Mon, Tues, Thurs–Sat 8.30am–6pm; Wed 8.30am–3pm. Brixton underground.* A large, lively, exotic, general market with an Afro-Caribbean flavour. There is reggae music reverberating around the railway arches and the biggest choice of African and Caribbean food in Europe. From goat meat, calfheads and exotic fish to mango, yam and okra. The presence of Rastafarian priests and the smell of incense complete the exotic atmosphere, which is a world away from Harvey Nic's.

Camden Market Camden High Street/Chalk Farm Road, NW1 *Open Thurs–Sun 9am–5pm. Camden Town/Chalk Farm underground.* Busiest and best at the weekend, there are several markets in the area offering great variety, such as Inverness Street, a local food market, and the weekend

Stables and Camden Canal Markets with collectables, as well as the indoor Electric Ballroom Market. Camden Lock, where it all began, occupies renovated warehouses. In the summer months the markets are enhanced by street theatre, music and art shows.

Camden Passage Upper Street, N1 *Open Tues, Wed, Sat 8am—4pm; Thurs, Fri 9am—5pm. Angel underground.* This Islington market is transformed from a civilised antiques market on Wednesday (with books on Thursday) to a lively flea market on Saturday.

Church Street Market Church Street, NW8, W2 *Open Tues—Sat 9am—5pm. Edgware Road underground.* Church Street has had a market since the 1840s. Nowadays this lively local facility sells anything from bric-a-brac, groceries and clothes to antiques. Nearby Bell Street Market, also in Lisson Grove (open Sat 9.30am—5pm) is smaller yet chaotic.

Columbia Road Flower Market Columbia Road, E2 *Open Sun 8am—2pm. Shoreditch/Liverpool Street underground.* The prettiest street market in the capital, with loads of plants and flowers on display, and if you wait until after 1pm, stall-holders start almost giving stuff away.

Covent Garden Market The Piazza, WC2 *Daily 9am—4pm. Covent Garden underground.* Stalls with crafts, overpriced junk and antiques.

Gabriel's Wharf 56 Upper Ground, SE1 *Open Tues—Sun 11am—6pm. Waterloo underground/rail.* There are colourful craft workshops with a small crafts market on Fridays 11am—3pm. You can also start good riverside walks from here.

Greenwich Markets College Approach, Stockwell Street and

Greenwich High Road, SE10. *Open Sat, Sun 9am–5pm. Greenwich/Maze Hill rail/Cutty Sark/Greenwich DLR.* Greenwich has had a market for nearly 1,000 years. The impressive array of antiques, clothes, books, music and crafts stalls has done much to exacerbate the parking and pollution problems in Greenwich centre in recent years.

Kensington Market Kensington High Street, W8 *Mon–Sat 9.30am–6pm. High Street Kensington underground.* Either packed with great fashion, or full of seedy trash, according to your view and age.

Leadenhall Market Gracechurch Street, EC3 *Open Mon–Fri 8am–4pm. Bank underground.* Built in 1881 this small but picturesque Victorian covered market in the City, with its impressive ironwork facade with stalls for various foods, is especially lively at lunchtime.

Leather Lane Leather Lane, EC1 *Open Mon–Fri 11am–2pm. Chancery Lane/Farringdon underground.* An old Cockney market.

Merton Abbey Mills Merton Abbey Mills, SW19 *Open Sat/Sun 10am–5pm. Colliers Wood underground.* Up to 200 stalls selling arts, crafts, food and bric-a-brac by the River Wandle.

Northcote Road Markets Northcote Road, SW11 *Antiques market open Mon–Sat 10am–6pm; Sun noon–5pm. General market Mon, Tues, Thurs, Sat 9am–5pm; Wed 9am–1pm. Clapham Junction rail.* A mix of goods on sale, from a covered antiques market, juggling equipment and unicycles to Halal butchers and West Indian greengrocers.

Petticoat Lane Middlesex and Wentworth Streets, E1 *Open Sun*

9am–2pm; partially open Mon–Fri 10am–2.30pm. Liverpool Street/Aldgate underground. Over 200 years old, and with over a thousand stalls on Sundays, it's a real experience, packed with people and goods from the humdrum to the bizarre.

Portobello Road W11 *Open daily around 9am–5pm. Notting Hill Gate/Ladbrooke Grove underground.* Crammed with junk, books, clothing, jewellery and antiques. There are some interesting shops around it all, especially around the Westway flyover. There's a cosmopolitan atmosphere, best on Saturdays when it's busiest and when there are often street performers and buskers.

St Martins-in-the-Fields Trafalgar Square, WC2 *Open Mon–Sat 11am–5pm. Charing Cross underground/rail.* A small crafts market with homemade jewellery, knitwear and ethnic crafts, toys, hats etc (although garish souvenirs have increasingly been emerging).

St James's Piccadilly, W1 *Fri, Sat 10am–5pm. Piccadilly Circus underground* A small outdoor craft market in the pretty paved garden.

Shepherd's Bush Market Uxbridge and Goldhawk Roads W12 *Shepherd's Bush underground.* Lock-ups, stalls and shops, some with Asian and African clothes and foods.

Spitalfields Market Commercial Street, between Lamb Street and Brushfield Street, E1. *Open Mon–Fri noon–2.30pm; Sun 10am–5pm. Liverpool Street underground.* Occupying Victorian buildings of the original fruit and veg market, this has grown greatly in recent years. Crafts and antiques, and organic produce. If you're looking for breakfast or lunch, there's a row of stalls offering a range of snacks.

Walthamstow Market Walthamstow High Street, E17 *Tues, Thurs, Fri, Sat 9am–5pm; Morris Gallery: Tues–Sat 10am–1pm, 2–5pm. Walthamstow Central underground.* The UK's longest street market with a mile of around 500 stalls selling food, leather, clothing and fabrics. Look out for the impressive town hall, a classical building in a Swedish-influenced interwar style. Nearby is the William Morris Gallery (Forest Road, E17, 8527 3782) on Forest Road, an attractive Georgian mansion with grounds and a museum covering William Morris's life and work. It also houses a collection of Pre-Raphaelite paintings.

Museums and Collections
Admission is *free* unless otherwise stated.

Alexander Fleming Laboratory Museum St Mary's Hospital, Praed Street, W2 (7725 6528) *Open Mon–Thurs 10am–1pm; also Mon–Thurs 2–5pm by appointment. Adults £2, concessions £1. Paddington underground/rail.* A recreation of the lab in which Fleming discovered penicillin.

Alfred Dunhill Museum 48 Jermyn Street, SW1 (7290 8615) *Open Mon–Fri 9.30am–5pm by appointment. Piccadilly Circus underground.* The history of the firm with examples of motoring accessories, watches, pipes, lighters and pens made by Dunhill.

Baden-Powell Museum Queen's Gate, SW7 (7584 7030) *Open by appointment. South Kensington/Gloucester Road underground.*

Memorabilia, mementoes and pictures tell the story of scouting, which Lord Baden-Powell began in 1907.

Bank of England Museum Threadneedle Street, EC2 (entrance in Bartholomew Lane) (7601 4444) *Open Mon–Fri 10am–5pm. Bank underground/DLR.* Housed within the Bank of England itself in the heart of the City of London, the museum covers the history of the Bank from 1694 to the high-tech period of today. There are interactive videos and displays including a modern dealing desk, ancient gold bars, banknotes and coins and Roman pottery and mosaics uncovered when the bank was rebuilt.

Bethnal Green Museum of Childhood Cambridge Heath Road, E2 (8980 2415) *Open daily except Fri, 10am–5.50pm. Bethnal Green underground.* This branch of the Victoria and Albert Museum has nostalgia by the pram-load, including toys, dolls, teddy bears, nursery furniture, children's clothes, puppets, games and costumes. There are over 40 dolls' houses alone and there would be more if they could get the planning permission. Also temporary exhibitions. There are children's activities in the school holidays and at half term including workshops and theatre performances ($£1–£2$) and soft-play sessions for the under-7s ($£1$).

Bexley Museum, Hall Place Bourne Road, Bexley (01322 526574) *Open Mon–Sat 10am–5pm; Sun (summer only) 11am–5pm. Bexley rail.* Among the displays are ones on natural history, archaeology and geology in the locality. There's some Roman pottery and a collection of butterflies, and also temporary exhibitions, usually concerning the Bexley area.

Black Cultural Archives Museum 378 Coldharbour Lane, SW9 (7738 4591) *Open Mon–Sat 10.30am–6pm; archives by appoint-*

ment. Brixton underground/rail. Explores the history of black people in Britain from Roman times onwards, augmented with regular temporary exhibitions.

BOC Museum Association of Anaesthetists, 9 Bedford Square, WC1 (7631 1650) *Telephone for an appointment to view. Tottenham Court Road underground.* A themed exhibition based on the use of anaesthetics generally runs each year from February to November.

Bramah Tea and Coffee Museum 1 Maguire Street, SE1 (7378 0222) *Open daily 10am–6pm. Adults £4, concessions, children £3. London Bridge underground/rail.* Learn all about the history of these beverages at this small museum.

British Dental Association Museum 64 Wimpole Street, W1 (7935 0875 ext 209) *Open Mon–Fri 10am–4pm by appointment. Oxford Circus/Bond Street underground.* If you're brave enough, come and see equipment and re-created surgeries presenting the history of dentistry in Britain.

British Library 96 Euston Road, NW1 (7412 7000) *Open Mon, Wed, Thurs, Fri 9.30am–6pm; Tues 9.30am–8pm; Sat 9.30am–5pm; Sun 11am–5pm. King's Cross underground/rail.* Beautiful collections of manuscripts and books, famous autographs, maps, heraldry, music and bibles, including King John's Magna Carta (1215) and Handel's *Messiah*. There's 7th- to 17th-century illuminated manuscripts and displays of oriental illuminated manuscripts and printed books. There are also temporary exhibitions and various events.

British Museum Great Russell Street, WC1 (7636 1555) *Open Mon–Wed, Sat, Sun 10am–5.30pm; Thurs, Fri 10am–8.30pm. Tottenham Court Road/Russell Square underground.* Founded in 1753, this, the capital's most popular attraction (it attracts over 6 million visitors annually) and one of the world's great museums, shows the works of man from prehistoric times onwards. There are permanent displays of antiquities from Egypt, Greece and Rome, and there are prehistoric, Romano-British, Medieval, Renaissance, modern and oriental collections. There are temporary exhibitions of coins, medals, prints and drawings. You should also see the Rosetta stone, the Elgin Marbles, Egyptian mummies and children's trails. The museum has regular lectures, gallery talks and films. If you need a break from the endless exhibits (over 6 million of them), grassy Russell Square, WC1, is nearby.

British Optical Association Museum The College of Optometrists, 10 Knaresbrough Place, SW5 (7839 6000) *Open by appointment, although closed for redevelopment until early 2003. Earl's Court underground.* Spectacles, opera glasses, opthalmoscopes and other memorabilia going back three centuries.

Bromley Museum The Priory, Church Hill. Bromley BR6 (01689 873826) *Open Sun–Fri 1–5pm; Sat 10am–5pm; closed Sun Nov–Mar. Orpington rail.* Uncovering how people lived in the Bromley area from prehistoric times to the present, it includes such items as Saxon jewellery and a typical 1930s dining room.

Brooking Architectural Museum University of Greenwich, Dartford Campus, Oakfield Lane, Dartford, Kent (01380 816565) *Open by appointment, Mon–Fri 9am–5pm. Dartford rail.* A large collection of architectural items going back 500 years which includes doors, sections of staircase, latches and windows, some from the likes of Windsor Castle and 10

Downing Street. If you're restoring an old house, examples from the relevant period can be found beforehand.

Bruce Castle Museum Lordship Lane, Tottenham, N17 (8808 8772) *Open Tues–Sun 1–5pm; guided tours by arrangement with curator. Wood Green underground.* Standing in Bruce Castle Park, this Elizabethan/Jacobean/Georgian building with its 16th-century tower has a museum concerning local and postal history.

Burgh House The Hampstead Museum, New End Square, NW3 (7431 0144) *Open Wed–Sun noon–5pm. Hampstead underground.* This Queen Anne house has displays on the history of Hampstead including local residents such as DH Lawrence, as well as prints by Constable.

Canal Museum 12–13 New Wharf Road, N1 (7713 0836) *Open Tues–Sun 10am–4.30pm. Adults/children over 8 £2.50, concessions £1.25. King's Cross underground/rail.* A small museum housed in a 150-year-old warehouse telling the story of those who made a living on canals.

Capel Collection Third Floor, London Chest Hospital, Bonner Road, Victoria Park, E2 (7377 7608) *Open by written appointment. Bethnal Green underground.* A small collection of instruments and books relating to chest medicine.

Carlyle's House 24 Cheyne Row, SW3 (7352 7087) *Open Apr–Oct Wed–Sun 11am–5pm. Adults £3.50, children 5–16 £1.75. Sloane Square underground.* Historian Carlyle lived at this Queen Anne house from 1834 until his death in 1881 and entertained guests including Dickens and George Eliot.

Chartered Insurance Institute Museum 20 Aldermanbury, EC2 (8989 8464) *Opening times vary. Moorgate/St Paul's under-*

ground. A small museum with display cases illustrating the history of insurance. There's such things as antique fireman's gear, a Victorian fire engine and a large collection of fire-marks, signs used in the past to indicate that a building was insured.

Church Farmhouse Museum Greyhound Hill, NW4 (8203 0130) *Open Mon, Wed–Sat 10am–1pm; 2–5.30pm; Tues 10am–1pm; Sun 2–5.30pm. Hendon Central underground.* A fascinating museum of domestic and local history and the decorative arts within an old gabled farmhouse, which was built in 1659. There is a period scullery, kitchen and dining room and changing exhibitions. Sunny Hill Park is behind the museum.

Clink Prison Museum 1 Clink Street, SE1 (7403 6515) *Open daily May–Oct 10am–10pm; Nov–Apr 10am–6pm. Adults £4, children, concessions £3. London Bridge underground/rail.* Housed in a warehouse that was a prison from the 12th to 17th centuries, this attraction is a small, less scary alternative to the London Dungeon, with information on murderers, rats, torture and other gruesome things.

Clockmakers' Company Museum The Clockroom, Guildhall Library, Aldermanbury, EC2 (7332 1868) *Open Mon–Fri 9.45am–4.45pm. Bank/Moorgate underground.* 700 exhibits, which go back as far back as the 14th century and include the first electric clock, a gas-powered clock, royal timepieces and marvellous grandfather clocks, illustrate 500 years of timekeeping. Try and visit on the hour, at noon if possible.

Clowns Museum 1 Hillman Street, E8 (7608 0312) *Open first Friday of month noon–5pm and first Tuesday of the month*

6.30–11pm and by arrangement. Hackney Central rail. Artefacts relating to clowns, with a joke and clown shop attached.

Crossness Engines Industrial Museum Belvedere Road, SE2 (8311 3711) *Tours by arrangement one Sunday and one Tuesday each month at 1.45pm and occasional open days. Adults £3, under-16s FREE. Abbey Wood rail.* The tour is of the old works dating from 1865, which contains four of the largest rotative beam engines in the world. An impressive relic of the industrial age.

Crystal Palace Museum Cottage Yard, Anerley Hill, Sydenham, SE19 (8676 0700) *Open Sun 11am–5pm. Crystal Palace rail.* Set in the 200-acre Crystal Palace park, this small museum explores the history of Sir Joseph Paxton's Victorian Crystal Palace.

Cuming Museum 155–157 Walworth Road, SE17 (7701 1342) *Open Tues–Sat 10am–5pm. Elephant and Castle BR/underground.* Southwark's history from Roman times is unravelled. There are special displays on Dickens and Shakespeare, superstition through the ages, a dynamo built by Faraday, ships in bottles, and temporary exhibitions.

Dr Johnson's House 17 Gough Square, EC4 (7353 3745) *Open Mon–Sat 11am–5pm. Adults £4, concessions £3, under-14s £1.* Dr Samuel Johnson lived here for 10 years compiling the first comprehensive English dictionary. There is a video about Johnson's life and works as well as paintings and curios.

Dickens' House Museum , 48 Doughty Street, WC1 (7405 2127) *Open Mon–Sat 10am–5pm. Adults £4, concessions £3, children £2. Chancery Lane underground.* A literary honeypot, with a drawing room furnished in keeping with the year 1839 and plenty of evocative Dickensia.

Erith Museum Erith Library Walnut Tree Road, Erith, Kent (01322 336582) *Open Mon, Wed, Sat 2.15–5pm. Erith rail*. A small museum concerned with the history of Erith.

Fan Museum 12 Crooms Hill, Greenwich, SE10 (8305 1441) *Open Tues–Sat 11am–5pm; Sun noon–5pm. Adults £3.50, children, concessions £2.50; Tues 2–5pm FREE to OAPs and disabled. Cutty Sark DLR/Greenwich DLR/rail*. An early-18th-century building with around 3,000 antique fans from around the world. The museum traces the history of the fan, fan manufacture and changing fashions.

Farady Museum Royal Institution, 21 Albemarle Street, W1 (7409 2992) *Open Mon–Fri 9am–5pm. Admission £1. Green Park underground*. A small museum celebrating the achievements of Michael Faraday, the 'father of electricity'. There is a recreation of his lab.

Fenton House Hampstead Grove, NW3 (7435 3471) *Open March Sat, Sun 2–5pm; Apr–Oct Wed–Fri 2–5pm; Sat, Sun 11am–5pm. Adults £4.30, children 5–15 £2.15; entrance to garden FREE. Hampstead underground*. Built in 1693, this is one of Hampstead's earliest houses and contains a collection of early keyboard instruments as well as other exhibits.

Firepower Royal Arsenal, Woolwich SE18 (8855 7755) *Open daily 10am–5pm. Admission prices vary. Woolwich Arsenal rail*. A new £15m museum replacing the previous Museum of Artillery and covering the history of the Royal Regiment of Artillery. There are various displays of artillery as well as a multimedia presentation re-creating using artillery in the 20th century.

Florence Nightingale Museum St Thomas' Hospital, 2 Lambeth Palace Road, SE1 (7620 0374) *Open Mon–Fri 10am–5pm; Sat, Sun 11.30am–4.30pm. Adults £4.80, children, concessions £3.60. Waterloo underground/rail.* Displays celebrating the famous nurse.

Forty Hall Museum Forty Hill, Enfield, Middlesex (8363 8196) *Open Sat, Sun 1–4pm. Enfield Chase rail.* An imposing Caroline mansion with elaborate Jacobean ceilings, which as a museum struggles for a unified theme. Among other things it houses 17th- and 18th-century furniture, local history and ecology displays, childhood mementoes and an exhibition of the history of advertising and packaging.

Freemasons' Hall Museum Freemasons' Hall, WC2 (7831 9811) *Open Mon–Fri 10am–5pm; most Sats 10.30am–1pm. Tours (including the Grand Temple) 11am, noon, hourly from 2pm–6pm. Holborn/Covent Garden underground.* Although Freemasons have a reputation for secrecy, they have no qualms about opening their headquarters, the Grand Lodge, to the public. There are collections including jewellery, medals and regalia associated with Masonic ritual. The huge marble and jade temple is majestic.

Freud Museum 20 Maresfield Gardens, NW3 (7435 2002) *Open Wed–Sun noon–5pm. Adults £4, concessions £2, under-12s FREE. Finchley Road underground.* Exhibits at famous psychoanalyst Sigmund Freud's home until his death in 1939 include the famous couch on which his patients lay for analysis.

Fulham Palace Museum Bishop's Avenue, SW6 (7736 3233) *Open Mar–Oct Wed–Sun 2–5pm; Nov–Feb Thurs–Sun 1–4pm. Adults £1, concessions 50p, FREE to under-16s. Putney Bridge underground.* A small museum covering the history of this building, which was home to the bishops of London until 1973.

Geffrye Museum Kingsland Road, E2 (7739 9893) *Open Tues–Sat 10am–5pm; Sun noon–5pm. Old Street underground.* Recently enlarged, the museum was named after the Lord Mayor of London in 1685, Sir Robert Geffrye, who bequeathed the row of almshouses here and a chapel for the poor. The museum is primarily concerned with interior design and, with tremendous attention to detail, presents fascinating room displays showing homes from before 1600 to the present. There's also attractive gardens with mature trees and a restful walled herb garden (open Apr–Oct) providing further botanical interest. In the summer there are activities for children such as treasure hunts, juggling and face painting, and music in the museum or garden. There are also regular free family events, summer outdoor evening concerts and children's workshops at weekends and during school holidays exploring such things as painting techniques, printing, mirror making and dyeing.

Gilbert Collection Somerset House, The Strand, WC2 (7240 5782) *Open Mon–Sat 10am–6pm; Sun & bank holidays noon–6pm. Temple underground. £4.* Impressive collections of gold, silver and mosaics. The palatial building possesses one of London's finest views of the Thames.

Grange Museum of Community History Neasden Lane, NW10 (8452 8311/8908 7432) *Open Mon–Fri 11am–5pm; Sat 10am–*

5pm. Neasden underground. Dating from around 1700 the building was originally part of a farm and now has exhibitions about the local area, the London Borough of Brent. There are temporary displays, a local history library and period rooms including a reconstructed draper's shop. Visitors may picnic in the enclosed garden and conservatory and there's a children's play area.

Grant Museum of Zoology and Comparative Anatomy Biology Department, Darwin Building, University College, Gower Street, WC1 (7679 2000) *Open Wed, Fri 1–5pm. Euston Square/Goodge Street underground.* Opened in 1928, the collections in this teaching hospital cover the whole of the animal kingdom with many rare and extinct specimens including one of only five known Quaqqa skeletons, a type of zebra extinct since the 1850s.

Greenwich Borough Museum 232 Plumstead High Street, SE18 (8855 3240) *Open Mon 2–7pm; Tues, Thurs–Sat 10am–1pm; 2–5pm. Plumstead rail.* Displays include a history of the borough, local geology and archaeology and a wildlife gallery plus temporary exhibitions. Children's workshops are held in the school holidays as well as an activities club each Saturday.

Guards' Museum Wellington Barracks, Birdcage Walk, SW1 (7414 3271) *Open daily 10am–4pm. Adults £2, concessions £1, FREE to under-16s. St James's Park underground.* The museum covers the British Army's five Guards regiments founded in the 17th century.

Gunnersbury Park Museum Gunnersbury Park, Popes Lane, W3 (8992 1612) *Open Mar–Oct Mon–Fri 1–5pm; Sat, Sun 1–6pm; Nov–Feb daily 1–4pm. Acton Town underground.* This early-

19th-century mansion within the park has a collection of topographical items, transport displays with coaches of the Rothschild family, costume, toys and archaeology relating to the locality, the boroughs of Ealing and Hounslow. There are temporary exhibitions too. As well as the surrounding park, which houses other historic buildings, Kensington Cemetery is adjacent.

Hackney Museum Central Hall, Mare Street, E8 (8986 6914) *Open Tues–Fri 10am–12.30pm; 1.30–5pm; Sat 1.30–5pm. Bethnal Green underground/Hackney Central rail.* Explores the rich and surprising local history of the area's cosmopolitan population from Viking times. Everyday items evoke the past, and objects from around the world give an insight into Hackney's diverse populations. There's a multimedia computer program, temporary exhibitions and children's activities too.

Handel House Museum 25 Brook Street, W1 (7495 1685) *Open Tues, Wed, Fri, Sat 10am–6pm; Thurs 10am–8pm; Sun noon– 6pm. Adults £4.50, children, concessions £3.50. Bond Street underground.* A new museum in the house that was the famous composer's home for 36 years.

Harrow Museum and Heritage Centre Headstone Manor, Pinner View, Middlesex, HA2 (8861 2626) *Open Wed–Fri 12.30pm– 5pm; Sat, Sun 10.30am–5pm. Harrow and Wealdstone underground/rail.* This medieval site has, as well as the museum with regular temporary exhibitions, a moat and grounds with plenty of wildlife.

Hogarth's House Hogarth Lane, Great West Road, W4 (8994 6757) *Open Apr–Oct Tues–Fri 1–5pm, Sat, Sun 1–6pm; Nov, Dec, Feb, Mar Tues–Fri 1–4pm, Sat, Sun 1–5pm. Turnham Green* *underground*. English engraver and painter William Hogarth (1697–1764) lived in this 17th-century house for his last 15 years to get some peace and quiet. Nowadays even an estate agent couldn't convince you that this patch of London is tranquil, being the place to be if you like traffic congestion and being conveniently situated for the start of the M4 and the Hammersmith flyover. Engravings, drawings and other mementoes are on display, and there's a pretty garden.

House of Detention Clerkenwell Close, EC1 (7253 9494) *Open daily 10am–6pm. Adults £4, children £2.50, concessions £3.* Not an S&M parlour, but a macabre collection of memorabilia from prisons that existed here from 1616 to 1890. Exhibits in the restored cells tell the story of the prison system from its sadistic 17th-century beginnings to the more enlightened Victorian era.

Horniman Museum 100 London Road, Forest Hill, SE23 (8699 1872) *Open Mon–Sat 10.30am–5.30pm; Sun 2–5.30pm. Forest Hill rail.* A great museum of a standard you'd expect in central London, rather than tucked away on the outskirts. It houses a varied and ever-interesting collection including an aquarium and over 6,000 musical instruments from around the world, many of which can be heard, touched and played, with occasional demonstrations and interactive videos. There's a big collection of ethnographical and natural history displays, a library, lectures, workshops, concerts, children's activities and special exhibitions. The latest addition is the solar-powered Centre for Understanding the Environment, concentrating on ecological issues. Horniman Gardens, with its small collection of animals, is on the same site and worth a visit.

Hunterian Museum Royal College of Surgeons of England, 35–43 Lincoln's Inn Fields, WC2 (7869 6560) *Open Mon–Fri 10am– 5pm. Holborn/Temple underground.* A medical museum that began with eminent 18th-century research surgeon John Hunter's huge collection of anatomical, pathological and zoological specimens and that has since been enlarged. It examines how the body adapts to change, those caused by accident or disease and reproduction and birth. There are fossils and the results of experiments, as well as skeletons of a giant, a dwarf and some infamous 19th-century murderers. The Odontological Museum is also at the College (see p. 125).

Imperial War Museum Lambeth Road, SE1 (7416 5000) *Open daily 10am–6pm. Lambeth North underground/Waterloo underground/rail.* The nation's museum of 20th-century war is imaginative and lively and includes lots of rockets, planes, tanks and suchlike but also effective reconstructions including a walk-through experience of trench warfare. Adjacent to the museum is the Tibetan Peace Garden at the Geraldine Mary Harmsworth Park, which is intended to symbolise understanding between cultures. There are contemporary western sculptures and ancient eastern images, Himalayan flowers, shrubs and Buddhist symbols.

Islington Museum Gallery Town Hall, Upper Street, N1 (7354 9442) *Open Wed–Sat 11am–5pm; Sun 2–4pm. Highbury and Islington underground.* Temporary exhibitions, lasting around six weeks, relating to the area.

The Iveagh Bequest Kenwood, Hampstead Lane, NW3 (8348 1286) *Open daily Nov–Mar 10am–4pm; Apr–Sept 10am–6pm; Oct*

10am−5pm. Archway/Golders Green underground. English Heritage's splendid neoclassical mansion has an impressive collections of paintings, an 18th-century jewellery collection and the highest quality antique furniture.

Jewish Museum 129–131 Albert Street, NW1 (7284 1997) *Open Mon−Thurs 10am−4pm; Sun 10am−5pm. Adults/children over 5 £3.50, concessions £1.50. Camden Town underground.* Covering the history of Jews in Britain, objects used in religious ceremonies are displayed.

Keats House Keats Grove, Hampstead, NW3 (7435 2062) *Open Tues−Sat noon−5pm; also 10am−noon by appointment and for tours. Adults £3, concessions £1.50, under-16s FREE, entry to garden FREE. Hampstead underground.* This pretty Regency house, where tragic Romantic poet John Keats lived and wrote 'Ode to a Nightingale' as well as many other works, has letters, manuscripts and relics, and mementoes of his love for his next-door neighbour, Fanny Brawne.

Kew Bridge Steam Museum Green Dragon Lane, Brentford, Middlesex (8568 4757) *Open daily 11am−5pm. Mon−Fri: adults £3, concessions £2, children (5−15) £1; Sat, Sun: adults £4, concessions £3, children 5−15 £2. Gunnersbury underground/ Kew Bridge rail.* A Victorian pumping station that has become a museum tracing water supply. On Saturday and Sunday at 3pm the restored steam engine comes to life.

Kew Public Records Office Ruskin Avenue, Richmond (8876 3444) *Open Mon−Fri 9.30am−5pm. Kew Gardens underground/rail.* There are regular exhibitions using items from the huge collection of national archives from the Norman Conquest onwards.

Kingston Museum and Art Gallery Wheatfield Way, Kingston, Surrey (8546 5386) *Open Mon, Tues, Thurs–Sat 10am–5pm. Kingston rail.* An Edwardian museum depicting the area's past, with a special exhibition featuring clothes and mementoes of important Kingston residents.

Leighton House 12 Holland Park Road, W14 (7602 3316) *Open Mon–Sat 11am–5.30pm. Garden open Apr–Sept 11am–5.30pm. High Street Kensington underground.* An extraordinary, opulent and exotic Victorian house built in 1866 for the then President of the Royal Academy, Frederic, Lord Leighton, by George Aitchison. The stunning domed Arab Hall, with its unusual, Middle-Eastern tiles, mosaic floor and fountain and pool, was added in 1879. There are a variety of works on display and a tranquil garden.

Lifetimes Croydon Clocktower, Katharine Street, Croydon, CR9 (8253 1030) *Free admission Wed 4.45–6pm. East/West Croydon rail.* Part of the new Croydon Clocktower cultural complex, Lifetimes is based upon the experiences of Croydon people from 1830 to the present day and there are reconstructions, models, many belongings lent by local people, changing displays, a 'hands-on' room and touch-screen computers. The organisers claim that there's so much information it would take over two days to see and hear it all.

Livesey Museum 682 Old Kent Road, SE15 (7639 5604) *Open Mon–Sat 10am–5pm. Elephant and Castle underground.* A small and friendly children's museum with temporary, lively hands-on exhibitions exploring a single theme. For example, an exhibition on air covered pollution, aerodynamics, asthma, alternative energy, rainforests and the weather. Visitors could launch a hot-air balloon, explore computer programs, an electric car and air cannon, and create a mini tornado. There's a toddlers play area, and older children appreciate the push-button exhibits. There are further exhibits in the courtyard. Parking in the local side streets is free, which is a rarity these days.

London Fire Brigade Museum 94a Southwark Bridge Road, SE1 (7587 2894) *Tours Mon–Fri 10.30am, 12.30am, 2.30pm; by appointment. Adults £3, children 7–14, concessions £2. Borough underground.* Tours of this small museum last two hours and cover the history of firefighting in the capital since the Great Fire of 1666. Exhibits include fightfighting equipment from the past.

London Museum of Jewish Life 80 East End Road, N3 (8349 1143) *Open Mon–Thurs 10.30am–5pm; Sun 10.30am–4.30pm. Adults £2, concessions, children over 12 £1. Finchley Central underground.* A Holocaust exhibition and displays on sweatshop and East End life.

London Scottish Regimental Museum 95 Horseferry Road, SW1 (7630 1639) *Open by appointment. St James's Park underground.* Medals, photos and other memorabilia relating to this distinguished regiment formed in 1859.

Martinware Pottery Collection Southall Library, Osterly Park Road, Southall, Middlesex (8574 3412) *Open Tues, Thurs, Fri 9am–7.45pm; Wed, Sat 9am–5pm. Southall rail.* This collection of slightly eccentric pottery made by the Martin family from 1873 to 1923 is housed in an annexe of the reference library and includes a variety of tiles, jugs, pots and other items. Bigger examples of their work are displayed at the Pitshanger Manor Museum.

Museum in Docklands Warehouse 1, West India Quay, Docklands, E14 *Open Mon—Sat 10am—6pm; Sun noon—6pm. Admission prices vary.* Charting the history of Docklands and the Port of London, the exhibits, reconstructions and multimedia displays cover Roman trading, medieval and colonial expansion and last century's decline and regeneration.

Museum of Domestic Architecture and Design Middlesex University, Bounds Green Road, N11 (8362 5244) *Open Tues—Sat 10am—5pm; Sun 2—5pm. Bounds Green underground.* The collection includes wallpaper and textile designs.

Museum of Garden History St Mary-at-Lambeth, Lambeth Palace Road, SE1 (7401 8865) *Open Feb Mon—Fri 11am—2pm; Mar—Dec Mon—Fri 10.30am—4pm; Sun 10.30am—5pm. Waterloo underground/rail.* As well as exhibits relating to garden history there is a recreated 17th-century garden.

Museum of the Honorable Artillery Company Armoury House, City Road, EC1 (7382 1537) *Open by appointment. Moorgate underground.* The company was founded in 1537 and exhibits include uniforms, porcelain and swords.

Museum of London 150 London Wall, EC2 (7600 3699) *Open Mon—Sat 10am—5.50pm; Sun noon—5.50pm. Barbican/St Paul's underground.* Claiming to be the largest and most comprehensive city museum in the world, it tells the story of London and its people beginning with the first hunter-gatherers of 400,000 years ago, to the city that was founded by the Romans in around 50AD, and on to the 1500-square-kilometre metropolis of today. There are displays of the homes and workplaces of Londoners, fine and applied arts and the products of science and industry. The museum also has interactive exhibitions, sculptures, a Victorian shop, a barber's shop, a 1930s car, the Lord Mayor's state coach, Selfridge's lift and a display on the Great Fire. Regular drop-in workshops and events.

Museum of Richmond Old Town Hall, Whittaker Avenue, Richmond, Surrey (8332 1141) *Open Tues–Sat 11am–5pm. Adults £2, concessions £1, FREE to under-16s. Richmond underground/rail.* Covering Richmond's history from prehistoric times onwards.

Museum of St Bartholomew's Hospital West Smithfield, EC1 (7601 8152) *Open Tues–Fri 10am–4pm. Barbican/St Paul's underground.* The story of the hospital from 1123 to today told with the use of video, audio recordings, medical instruments and other memorabilia.

Museum of the Order of St John St John's Gate, St John's Lane, EC1 (7253 6644) *Open Mon–Fri 10am–5pm; Sat 10am–4pm with half-hour guided tours Tues, Fri and Sat 11am and 2.30pm. Farringdon/Barbican undergound/rail.* The museum is housed in a gatehouse built in 1504 that was the entrance to the medieval priory of the Order of St John of Jerusalem, which, among other charitable deeds, founded St John Ambulance. There is a collection of books dating from 1425, armour, paintings, ceramics, furniture, silver and medical instruments, insignia and other treasures of the Knights of St John. There are also displays looking at the people and personal memorabilia of St John Ambulance including its role in the Boer and World Wars. The 17th-century elaborate model of Jerusalem's Holy Sepulchre is well worth a look despite being very politically incorrect:

it's carved from ebony, ivory and mother of pearl. There is also a 12th-century crypt. Opposite St John's Gate at Priory House is a new museum, the St John Ambulance Exhibition, with training equipment, photographs and other displays.

Museum of the Royal Pharmaceutical Society of Great Britain 1 Lambeth High Street, SE1 (7735 9141) *Open by appointment Mon–Fri 9am–5pm. Vauxhall/Lambeth North underground.* Covering five centuries of medicinal drugs, focusing on those who invented, sold and took them.

Musical Museum 368 High Street, Brentford, Middlesex (8560 8108) *Open Apr–Oct Sat, Sun 2–5pm; also July, Aug 2–4pm. Adults £3.20, concessions £2.50. Gunnersbury underground/ Kew Bridge rail.* A collection of automatic musical instruments.

National Army Museum Royal Hospital Road, SW3 (7730 0717) *Open daily 10am–5.30pm. Sloane Square underground.* The history of the British, Indian and Colonial forces from 1485, with reconstructions of the life of a soldier through the years and from the jungles of Burma to the deserts of Sudan. There's a model of the Battle of Waterloo using over 70,000 model soldiers, Florence Nightingale's jewellery, items removed from the Gulf War battleground just after it ended, and even the skeleton of Napoleon's horse. The audio-visual displays, relics, personal mementoes, uniforms and weapons, portraits and prints are augmented with temporary exhibitions and events. A visit combines well with a look at the Great Hall and Chapel of the Royal Hospital and its grounds, Ranelagh Gardens.

Natural History Museum Cromwell Road, SW7 (7942 5000) *Open*

Mon—Sat 10am—5.50pm; Sun 11am—5.50pm. Charge for some exhibitions. South Kensington underground. Now incorporating the former Geology Museum (the earthquake simulator is the main attraction there), this huge museum is impressive both inside and out. A magnificent Victorian cathedral-like building, but with absorbing up-to-date displays and an unrivalled collection of animals, plants, minerals and fossils. Galleries concentrate upon one subject, such as ecology, the environment or one of the most popular, dinosaurs. It's so big it's best to amble round, making discoveries as you go, otherwise plan your assault with ruthless efficiency to cram in as much as possible.

National Maritime Museum, Romney Road, SE10 (8858 4422) *Open daily 10am—5pm. Cutty Sark DLR/Greenwich DLR/ rail.* A wide range of traditional and interactive exhibits concerning pioneering sea travel, maritime London, naval uniforms, Nelson and many other maritime subjects.

National Postal Museum King Edward Building, King Edward Street, EC1 (7239 5420) *Open Mon—Fri 9.30am—4.30pm St Paul's underground.* Probably the world's best collection of British postage stamps, including the world's first, the Penny Black. As well as more than 250,000 stamps, there are artefacts such as scales, model mailcoaches, paintings, letter boxes, etc.

National Sound Archive 29 Exhibition Road, SW7 (7412 7430) *Open Mon—Thurs 10am—5pm; Fri, Sat 10am—8pm. South Kensington underground.* The audio section of the British Museum, this collection reflects the development of recorded sound from early wax cylinders onwards. Ring to make an appointment to listen from a choice of thousands and thousands of recordings including folk, classical, popular and ethnic music from around the world as well as speech and drama.

North Woolwich Old Station Museum Pier Road, E16 (7474 7244) *Open Jan–Nov Sat, Sun 1–5pm; extra times in school holidays. North Woolwich rail/Beckton DLR.* A restored Victorian station building centring on the London and North Eastern Railway with trains, timetables, a 1920s ticket office, models, photographs, station signs and a turntable pit. Occasional films. Working locomotive first Sunday each month from April to October.

Nelson Collection Lloyds of London, 1 Lime Street, EC3 (7327 6260) *Open by appointment, at least seven days' written notice required. Monument underground.* Exhibits include silver, letters, ceremonial swords and other memorabilia.

Odontological Museum Royal College of Surgeons of England, 35–43 Lincoln's Inn Fields, WC2 (7869 6560) *Open Mon–Fri 10am–5pm. Holborn/Temple underground.* Examines the history of odontology and dentistry. There is an excellent collection of comparative pathology, 19th-century preparations of skulls and teeth by the father of British dentistry, Sir John Tomes, and early extraction instruments and dentures. There are examples of 'phossy jaw' caused by the phosphorous used in manufacturing matches in the last century, and which led to the 'Match Girl Strike' in the 1880s. The Hunterian Museum (see p. 116) is also at the College.

The Old Operating Theatre Museum and Herb Garret 9a St Thomas Street, SE1 (7955 4791) *Open daily 10am–4pm. Adults*

£3.25, concessions £2.25, children £1.60. *London Bridge underground/rail.* Florence Nightingale trained at this restored operating theatre built in 1821 which is a grim reminder of surgery before both antiseptic and anaesthetic. The museum, housed in the attic of a disused church, is reached via a small spiral staircase.

Pavlova Memorial Museum Ivy House, North End Road, NW11 *Open Sat 2–5pm. Golders Green underground.* Ivy House was home to great Russian ballerina Anna Pavlova from 1912 to 1931 and now has a small collection of memorabilia.

Percival David Foundation of Chinese Art 53 Gordon Square, WC1 (7387 3909) *Open Mon–Fri 10.30am–5pm. Euston Square/Goodge Street underground.* Hundreds of examples of Chinese ceramics from the 9th to the 18th centuries, covering the Song, Yuan, Ming and Qing dynasties, all housed in a converted Georgian townhouse in Bloomsbury.

Petrie Museum of Egyptian Archaeology Egyptology Department, by Bloomsbury Science Library, University College London, Malet Place, Gower Street, WC1 (7679 2884) *Open Tues–Fri 1–5pm; Sat 10am–1pm. Goodge Street/Warren Street underground.* A collection begun by Victorian archaeologist Sir Flinders Petrie, the father of Egyptian archaeology, in 1884 with additions by his colleagues and successors, exhibited to show the development of Egyptian culture, technology and day-to-day life. There is pottery, jewellery, toys and the world's oldest dress. The museum reckons to have the biggest and finest collection of ancient Egyptian antiquities in any university in the world.

Pitshanger Manor Museum and Gallery Walpole Park, Mattock Lane, Ealing, W5 (8567 1227) *Open Tues–Sat 10am–5pm. Ealing Broadway underground.* Although there is a display of Martinware pottery, it could be argued that this isn't strictly a museum in the usual sense unless you count the Grade I listed house as the exhibit. Set in a park, there's plasterwork from the mid-18th century to be seen and it is interesting from an architectural point of view to see what neoclassical architect Sir John Soane did to the building at the start of the 19th century, when he turned it into a Regency villa. There's also an art gallery holding contemporary exhibitions.

Police Traffic Museum South East Traffic Unit, Catford Garage, 34 Aitken Road, SE6 *Open by appointment requested in writing: staff are on police duty and therefore visits can be cancelled at short notice. Bellingham rail.* A small museum connected with traffic patrol, which includes vehicles from the 1960s onwards.

Polish Institute Museum 20 Princes Gate, SW7 (7589 9249) *Open Mon–Fri 2–4pm; first Sat in month 10am–4pm. South Kensington/Knightsbridge underground.* A large collection covering Polish history and culture with emphasis on World War II.

Pollocks Toy Museum and Shop 1 Scala Street, W1 (7636 3452) *Open Mon–Sat 10am–5pm. Adults £3, children 3–18 £1.50. Goodge Street underground.* Based around the contents of the East London toy shop of Benjamin Pollock (1856–1937), which specialised in toy theatres, there's a wealth of old-fashioned toys.

Public Record Office Museum Ruskin Avenue, Kew, Richmond, Surrey (8876 3444) *Open Mon—Fri 10am—5pm.* Of the millions of documents from government departments from the 11th century onwards housed here, records displayed include the first national census, the Domesday Book (1086), medieval charters, Shakespeare's will, the Gunpowder Plot papers and details of the funeral of the 'Grand Old' Duke of York.

Pumphouse Educational Museum Lavender Pond Nature Park, Lavender Road, off Rotherhithe Street, SE16 (7231 2976) *Open Mon—Fri 9.30am—3pm. Rotherhithe underground.* Surrounded by a nature park and pond, this traces the story of Rotherhithe with objects found on the Thames foreshore.

Puppet Centre, Battersea Arts Centre Lavender Hill, SW11 (7228 5335) *Open Mon—Fri 2—6pm. Clapham Junction rail.* Around 50 of the Centre's collection of 500 puppets are on display at any one time as well as related memorabilia.

Ragged School Museum 46–50 Copperfield Road, E3 (8980 6405) *Open Wed, Thurs 10am—5pm and first Sun of month 2—5pm. Mile End underground.* Ragged schools were for the poorest families in Victorian society, providing basic education for children, free meals and help with finding work. The museum is based on a ragged school founded by Dr Barnardo. By 1870 it was the biggest in London. The captivating exhibitions on East End life include a typical Victorian classroom. There are children's activities and workshops including classroom re-enactments.

Royal College of Physicians Collection 11 St Andrew's Place, NW1 (7935 1174) *Open by appointment with the librarian. Regent's Park/Great Portland Street underground.* A collection that includes portraits, landscapes, photographs, medals, sculptures and engravings, some dating back to the 16th century.

Royal Hospital Chelsea Museum Royal Hospital Road, SW3 (7730 5282) *Open Mon–Fri 10am–noon, 2–4pm; Sat 2–4pm. Sloane Square underground.* Charles II founded this hospital for veteran soldiers and it remains the home of over 400 Chelsea Pensioners who wear distinctive scarlet coats and tricorne hats. The small museum has pictures (including Van Dyck's famous picture of Charles I and family), medals and uniforms connected with the Royal Hospital. There's a chapel and Great Hall and neat, pretty grounds – Ranelagh Gardens.

Royal London Hospital Museum and Archive St Augustine with St Philip's Church, Newark Street, E1 (7377 7608) *Open Mon–Fri 10am–4.30pm. Whitechapel underground.* Located in the basement of a fine 19th-century church that is now a medical library, the development and role of the hospital is illustrated. Joseph Merrick, the 'Elephant Man' was a patient in the 1880s and this is documented.

Royal Military School of Music Museum Kneller Hall, Kneller Road, Twickenham, Middlesex (8898 5533) *Open by appointment only. Whitton rail.* Housed in a huge Jacobean-style mansion which is also home to the Army's music academy, this small museum has historic musical instruments including a double bass made in 1650, uniforms of bandsmen of the British Army, and other associated items.

Royal Mint Sovereign Galleries 7 Grosvenor Gardens, SW1 (7931 7977) *Open Mon–Fri 10am–4pm. Victoria underground/rail.*

An exhibition in a Victorian townhouse that unravels the 500-year history of gold sovereigns.

Rugby Football Union Museum Gate 7, Rugby Football Union Stadium, Rugby Road, Twickenham, Middlesex (8892 8877) *Open Mon–Fri 9.30am–1pm; 2.15–5pm. Twickenham rail.* The history of the game is alas displayed rather unimaginatively.

St Bride's Church Crypt Museum St Bride's Church, Bride Lane, off Fleet Street, EC4 (7353 1301) *Open daily 9am–5pm; guided tours by appointment. Cannon Street underground.* The 'parish church of the press' or the 'cathedral of Fleet Street', this is the eighth church on the site since the 6th century. The museum holds many relics including Roman remains, medieval walls and historic printing presses and a library concerned with print techniques. The 73-metre church spire inspired the modern-day wedding cake when a local baker modelled his wedding cakes on it and was then copied by others. That the church is called St Bride's is a coincidence.

Salvation Army International Heritage Centre 101 Queen Victoria Street, EC4 (7367 6570) *Open Mon–Fri 9.30am–3.30pm; Sat 9.30am–noon. King's Cross underground/rail.* Recounting the story of this religious movement set up by William Booth in 1865 to help the poor. There is an hour-long recorded commentary available.

Science Museum Exhibition Road, SW7 (7942 4454) *Open daily 10am–6pm. South Kensington underground.* An enormous museum (seven floors plus the relatively new Wellcome Wing) devoted to science and technology. Exhibitions include the exploration of space, firefighting, nuclear physics, computing, chemistry and medicine. There's a real lunar command module, locomotives and aircraft. Children especially love the endless push-button exhibits and can also solve scientific problems first hand that are posed by the equipment in the Launch Pad area.

Sir John Soane's Museum 13 Lincoln's Inn Fields, WC2 (7405 2107) *Open Tues–Sat 10am–5pm. Lecture tours Sat 2.30pm; £3. Also open first Tues of each month 6–9pm for candlelit viewing. Holborn underground.* Each year 50,000 people visit this 1812 beautiful, unusual, eccentric and unpredictable museum which lies behind the facades of three Georgian town houses. It displays Soane's eccentric collection of plasterwork, paintings, models of buildings – and chillingly, of tombs complete with skeletons – as well as drawings, antiquities, sculptures and books from around the world that took nearly half a century to assemble. The items displayed are staggering in volume and variety and even hold the attention of very young children, especially since a surprise is around every corner, false walls swing back to reveal second walls of pictures, or a new alcove crammed with more treasures invariably appears. Soane, a bricklayer's son who became one of Britain's most influential architects, bequeathed his collection to the nation on the understanding that nothing was removed or changed.

Thames Police Museum Thames Divisional HQ, 98 Wapping High Street, E1 *Open by written appointment. Wapping underground.* The history of the marine police, with artefacts from 1798 including weapons, uniforms and model boats.

Theatre Museum Russell Street, WC2 (7943 4700) *Open Tues– Sun 10am–6pm. £4.50 adults, £2.50 concessions, FREE for* *under-16s and over-60s.* An absorbing, thorough look at the history of the theatre, with fun interactive exhibits for kids, occasional stage make-up demonstrations and family events during school holidays.

Valence House Museum Becontree Avenue, Dagenham, Essex (8595 8404) *Open Tues—Fri 9.30am—1pm, 2—4.30pm; Sat 10am—4pm. Chadwell Heath rail.* A largely 17th-century moated manor house with local artefacts including Stone and Iron Age implements and Anglo-Saxon weapons and jewellery, as well as displays of 17th- and 20th-century interiors.

Vestry House Museum Vestry Road, Walthamstow, E17 (8509 1917) *Open Mon—Sat 10am—1pm, 2—5pm. Walthamstow Central underground/rail.* Housed within an 18th-century work-house, there are many original features such as a Victorian police cell and displays on local domestic life 100 years ago. Exhibits displaying lifestyles from the Stone Age onwards.

Victoria and Albert Museum Cromwell Road, SW7 (7938 8500) *Open daily 10am—5.45pm; Wed 10am—10pm. Some exhibitions and special events may carry a charge. South Kensington underground.* An exciting museum, possibly the world's greatest of fine and applied arts, with around four million exhibits from all periods and areas of the world. Ten acres of gallery space display sculpture, jewellery, enamels, weapons, silver, miniatures, watercolours, musical instruments, furniture, pottery, glass, a dress collection and changing exhibitions and displays. Highlights include the glass staircase, the Charles Rennie Mackintosh displays and costume gallery. There's a good panoramic view of London from the Constable Gallery in the Henry Cole Wing

---

and family workshops and various activities. Regular talks and tours.

Vintage Wireless Museum 23 Rosendale Road, SE21 (8670 3667) *Open by appointment only Mon–Sat 11am-7.30pm. West Dulwich rail.* There are not only radios here, there's also the first ever TV set, telephones and thousands of other items.

Wandsworth Museum The Courthouse, Garratt Lane, SW18 (8871 7074). Wandsworth rail. *Open Tues–Sat 10am–5pm; Sun 2–5pm.* Local history.

Wellington Museum Apsley House, 149 Picadilly, W1 (7499 5676) *Open Tues–Sun 11am–5pm. Adults £4.50, concessions £3, under-18s FREE. Hyde Park Corner underground.* Family home of the First Duke of Wellington, the rooms in this sumptuous building are adorned with pictures and gifts from foreign monarchs.

Whitewebbs Museum of Transport Whitewebbs Road, Enfield, Middlesex (8367 1898) *Open Mon–Fri 10am–5pm; but check first. Crews Hill rail.* Vintage vehicles including cars, bikes and a fire engine dating from 1912.

William Morris Gallery Lloyd Park, Forest Road, Walthamstow, E17 (8527 3782) *Open Tues–Sat 10am–1pm, 2–5pm and first Sun in each month, 10am–noon, 2–5pm. Walthamstow Central underground/rail.* Socialist designer William Morris lived in this delightful 18th-century house with its own grounds from 1848 to 1856 and his furniture, wallpapers and fabrics are on display as well as ceramics, furniture and other works by associates including Rossetti and Burne-Jones. There are al so pictures and sculptures by Rodin.

William Morris Society Kelmscott House, 26 Upper Mall, W6 (8741 3735) *Open Thurs, Sat 2–5pm. Hammersmith underground.* Designer and author Morris lived here at the end of his life and there's memorabilia, examples of his work and a printing press used to publish his work.

Wimbledon Lawn Tennis Museum Centre Court, All England Tennis Club, Church Road, SW19 (8946 6131) *Open daily 10.30am–5pm; during championships spectators only. Adults £5, concessions £4. Southfields underground.* Racquets, balls and memorabilia of the stars, a reconstruction of an Edwardian match and videos of past championships take visitors through over 150 years of the game.

Wimbledon Society's Museum The Village Club, Ridgeway, 26 Lingfield Road, SW19 (8296 9914) *Open Sat, Sun 2.30–5pm. Wimbledon underground.* A little museum about the history of the area, run by volunteers.

Music
All are *free* unless otherwise stated.

Acoustic Cafe 17 Manette Street, WC1 (7439 0831) *Tickets from £3. Tottenham Court Road underground.* Country, folk and rock.

Alexandra Palace and Park Wood Green, N22 (8365 2121) *Wood Green underground/Alexandra Palace rail.* FREE live music in the form of Grove Shows every third Sunday.

The Barbican Centre Silk Street, EC2 (7638 4141) *Admission £5 upwards. Barbican/Moorgate underground.* Jazz, classical, contemporary, blues, medieval, even Russian gypsy music . . . It's all here. Generally on weekday evenings 5.30–7pm and Sundays 12.30–2.30pm there are FREE performances at the Performance Platform on the ground floor.

Blackheath Concert Halls 23 Lee Road, SE3 (8463 0100) *Blackheath rail*. Usually once a month from 7.30–10.30pm on a Thursday, there's a FREE jazz play-in, a jam session hosted by a professional trio. Otherwise, musical events, from punk to classical, begin at £2.50 a ticket.

Borderline Orange Yard, Manette Street, W1 (7734 2095) *Admission from £5. Tottenham Court Road underground*. Rock and country.

Bread and Roses 68 Clapham Manor Street, SW4 (7498 1779) *Clapham Common underground*. FREE admission to this pub specialising in world music.

Brixton Artists' Collective 35 Brixton Station Road, SW9 (7733 6957) *Open Mon–Sat 10am–6pm. Brixton underground*. Occasional cultural events (FREE) featuring music and also possibly visual arts, poetry and acting.

Bull and Gate 389 Kentish Town Road, NW5 (7485 5358) *Admission almost always under £5. Kentish Town underground/rail*. A nightly trio of rock bands.

Bull's Head 373 Lonsdale Road, SW13 (8876 5241) *Admission from £4. Barnes Bridge rail*. Jazz.

Cecil Sharp House 2 Regent's Park Road, NW1 (7485 2206) *Admission from £3. Camden Town underground*. Folk music evenings.

Crystal Palace Tavern 108 Tanner's Hill, SE8 (8692 1536) *New Cross underground/rail.* FREE evening performances ranging from blues to pop, R&B to punk.

Dingwalls Middle Yard, Camden Lock, Chalk Farm Road, NW1 (7267 1577) *Tickets from £5 midweek. Chalk Farm underground.* Ever-popular rock venue.

Dublin Castle 94 Parkway, NW1 (7485 1773) *Admission £5 or under. Camden Town underground.* Pub with live rock.

Earl's Court Exhibition Centre Warwick Road, SW5 (7385 1200) *Some tickets from £5 for rock concerts put on here. Earl's Court underground.*

Fiddler and Firkin 14 South End, Croydon (8680 9728) *Admission FREE. East Croydon rail.* A pub with anything from rock and pop to funk and soul on a couple of weekend evenings.

Forum 9–17 Highgate Road, Kentish Town, NW5 (7284 1001) *Tickets starting at £5. Kentish Town underground/rail.* A good medium-sized rock venue.

Garage 20–22 Highbury Corner, N5 (8963 0940) *Admission £4 upwards. Highbury and Islington underground/rail.* Mainly indie bands play at this venue.

Geffrye Museum Kingsland Road, E2 (7739 9893/8368) *Old Street underground.* In the summer there is occasional FREE music in the museum or garden.

The George Inn 77 Borough High Street, SE1 (7407 2056) *London Bridge underground.* This National Trust-owned pub built in 1676, the only remaining galleried coaching inn in London, has FREE live traditional English music performed on the first Monday of most months from 8pm.

Greenwich Park SE10 (8858 2608) *Greenwich/Maze Hill rail, Cutty Sark DLR.* From around late June to late August there are band performances usually Sun 3–4.30pm; 6–7.30pm at the bandstand. Also from Tues–Sun from 12.30pm mid-June to early Sept typically, there's light music played by duos at the cafeteria.

Grosvenor Chapel South Audley Street, W1 (7499 1684) *Hyde Park Corner underground.* Regular FREE lunchtime classical recitals.

Guildhall School of Music and Drama Silk Street, Barbican, EC2 (7628 2571) *Barbican/Moorgate underground.* There is a rich selection of FREE regular classical concerts and recitals – often two or three a day – during term time, as well as other events such as modern music concerts, jazz concerts and open rehearsals at the school or other venues. Telephone for a programme of events.

Hammersmith and Fulham Irish Centre Blacks Road, W6 (8563 8232) *Hammersmith underground.* Various Irish music events, often either FREE or under £5.

Hampstead Heath NW3. (8348 9930) *Hampstead underground.* Sunday afternoon FREE band performances on the bandstands at Parliament Hill and Golders Hill in the summer vary from brass, steel and jazz bands to light orchestras.

Harrow Arts Centre Uxbridge Road, Hatch End, HA5 (8428 0124) *FREE jazz at lunchtime on the last Sunday in the month. Pinner underground.*

Harrow Museum and Heritage Centre Headstone Manor, Pinner View, HA2 (8861 2626) *12.30–2pm; Sunday lunchtimes. FREE.*

Harrow and Wealdstone underground/rail. Jazz, blues and music from the '30s to '50s in the 16th-century timber-framed tithe barn.

Hope and Anchor 207 Upper Street, N1 (7354 1312) *Admission under £5. Highbury and Islington underground/rail.* Pub rock.

Horniman Gardens 100 London Road, Forest Hill, SE23 (8699 2339/1872) *Forest Hill rail.* FREE summer Sunday band concerts in the bandstand.

Hyde Park W1, W2, SW7 (7298 2100) *Hyde Park Corner/Marble Arch underground.* From mid-June to early September there is live cafeteria music, bandstand concerts on Sunday afternoons from late June to late August and occasional further musical recitals and concerts.

Instituto Cervantes 22 Manchester Square, W1 (7935 1518) *Open Mon–Thurs 9.30am–6.30pm; Fri 9.30am–5pm. Marble Arch/Bond Street underground.* Occasional FREE concerts put on by this Spanish Institute – telephone for details.

Italian Cultural Institute 39 Belgrave Square, SW1 (7235 1461) *Open Mon–Fri 9.30am–5pm. Knightsbridge underground.* Telephone for details about FREE concerts organised by this body that promotes Italian culture.

Kensington Gardens W2, W8 (7298 2100) *Lancaster Gate/High Street Kensington underground.* FREE early evening classical recitals June–August at the bandstand.

Lauderdale House Community Arts Centre Highgate Hill, Waterlow Park, Highgate Hill, N6 (8348 8716) *Archway underground.* Occasional FREE concerts and many for under £5 adult admission, usually classical music, with regular jazz evenings too.

London Arena Limeharbour, Isle of Dogs, E14 (7538 1212) *Some tickets from £5. Crossharbour DLR.* Major rock and pop venue.

The Maple Tree 52 Maple Road, SE20 (8778 8701) *Anerley rail.* This public house presents occasional FREE music concerts on Saturday evenings.

Morley College 61 Westminster Bridge Road, SE1 (7928 8501) *Lambeth North underground.* Regular FREE Tuesday lunchtime concerts at 1pm; including piano recitals, duets and trios.

National Portrait Gallery 2 St Martin's Place, WC2 (7306 0055) *Charing Cross underground/rail.* Occasional FREE music recitals.

Ocean 270 Mare Street, E8 (8533 0111) *Tickets from £1. Hackney Central rail.* A new venue with three different performance spaces.

100 Club 100 Oxford Street, W1 (7636 0933) *Admission starting at £5. Oxford Circus/Tottenham Court Road underground.* Jazz and indie.

Paradise Bar 460 New Cross Road, SE14 (8692 1530) *Admission is either free or under £5. New Cross underground/rail.* A wide range of bands in the evenings including jazz, folk, rock and soul.

Polish Cultural Institute 34 Portland Place, W1 (7636 6032) *Open Mon–Wed, Fri 10am–4pm; Thurs 10am–8pm. Regent's Park underground.* Telephone for details of occasional FREE Polish music concerts organised by the institute.

Queen's Park Kingswood Avenue, NW6 (8969 5661) *Queen's Park underground*. FREE Sunday bandstand concerts Aug–Sept typically ranging from jazz and swing to Caribbean and brass.

Regent's Park NW1 (7486 7905) *Regent's Park / Camden Town underground*. From May to late August there is FREE live cafeteria music, weekend bandstand concerts and occasional musical recitals.

Richmond Park Holly Lodge, Richmond, Surrey (8948 3209) *Richmond underground / rail*. From late June to the early September there is light music performed most days at Pembroke Lodge at lunchtimes and in the early afternoons.

Rock Garden The Piazza, Covent Garden, WC2 (7240 3961) *Covent Garden underground*. Small central rock venue with admission from £4.

Ronnie Scott's Club 47 Frith Street, W1 (7439 0747) *Tickets occasionally under the £5 mark. Tottenham Court Road underground*. Top-quality jazz.

Royal Academy of Music Marylebone Road, NW1 (7873 7300) *Baker Street underground*. There are around 10 orchestral concerts, chamber music performances and recitals each week during term time, but tickets are required in advance for larger, particularly popular performances.

Royal Albert Hall Kensington Gore, SW7 (7589 3203) *Adult admission £3 upwards. South Kensington underground*. As well as the Proms, which runs from mid-July to mid-September, the Hall hosts a wide range of pop and classical concerts.

Royal College of Music Prince Consort Road, SW7 (7589 3643) *South Kensington underground*. Around 5 FREE chamber performances each week during each term at the college at 1.05pm. Also occasional FREE masterclasses and regular larger evening events.

Royal National Theatre South Bank, SE1 (7452 3400) *Waterloo rail/underground*. Early through to contemporary music from around the world including jazz, classical and folk performed in the foyer usually at 6pm Mon–Fri and 1pm Sat.

St Alfege Church Nelson Road, SE10. (8853 2703) *Greenwich rail/Cutty Sark DLR*. Regular FREE lunchtime concerts.

St James's Church Clerkenwell Close, EC1 (7251 1190) *Farringdon underground/rail*. Regular FREE classical lunchtime concerts.

St James's Park The Mall, SW1 (7298 2000) *St James's Park underground*. Bandstand concerts daily at lunchtime and in the early evening from the end of June to the end of August.

St John's Church Smith Square, SW1 (7222 1061) *Admission generally £5. Westminster underground*. Classical Thursday lunchtime concerts at 1pm.

Shepherd's Bush Empire Shepherd's Bush Green, W12 (7771 2000) *Tickets often start at £5. Shepherd's Bush underground*. Mainly rock at this ex-BBC theatre.

South Bank Centre Belvedere Road, South Bank, SE1 (7960 4242) *Tickets are regularly FREE or under £5. Waterloo underground/rail*. The Royal Festival Hall, Queen Elizabeth Hall and Purcell Room have a wide variety of music concerts. Also, in the Royal Festival Hall foyer, there is a wide range of FREE live music Wed–Sun 12.30–2pm; including blues, country, jazz, classical, folk and music from other lands. On Friday evenings, 5.15–6.45pm there's 'commuter jazz', also in the foyer.

Southwark Cathedral Montague Close, SE1 (7407 2939) *London Bridge underground/rail*. Usually an organ recital on Mondays and a music recital on Tuesdays 1.10–2pm.

Spitz Old Spitalfields Market, 109 Commercial Street, E1 (7392 9032) *Tickets from £4. Liverpool Street underground/rail*. Rock, jazz, and various other styles.

Station Tavern 41 Bramley Road, W10 (7727 4053) *Latimer Road underground*. FREE folk, R&B and acoustic blues every evening at 9pm and Sunday lunchtimes.

The Swan 215 Clapham Road, SW9 (7978 9778) *Admisison either FREE or under £5. Stockwell underground*. Irish live music in this popular pub.

Trinity College of Music 11 Mandeville Place, W1 (7935 5773) *Bond Street underground*. In each 12-week term there are generally three or four FREE performances of chamber music and recitals each week at the Barbirolli Lecture Hall or the Hinde Street Methodist church nearby.

Tufnell Park Tavern 162 Tufnell Park Road, N7 (7272 2078) *Tufnell Park underground*. FREE. Modern jazz, vintage jazz, world jazz, jazz/funk and just plain old ordinary jazz plus blues and R&B on a couple of evenings a week, usually Saturday and Sunday.

Underworld 174 Camden High Street, NW1 (7482 1932) *Tickets from £4. Camden Town underground.* Indie rock below the World's End pub.

Union Chapel Compton Terrace, N1 (7226 1686) *Tickets from £3. Highbury and Islington underground/rail.* Live rock and folk echo from this church.

University of London Union Manning Hall, Malet Street, WC1 (7664 2030) *Tickets from £5. Goodge Street underground.* Student venue with rock acts.

The Venue 2a Clifton Rise, SE14 (8692 4077) *Admission price varies. New Cross underground/rail.* Alternative and indie rock and a popular line in cover bands at the weekend.

Vortex 139 Stoke Newington Church Street, N16 (7254 6516) *FREE or under £5. Stoke Newington rail.* Jazz.

Waterlow Park Highgate High Street, N6 (7911 1648) *Archway underground.* Jazz and light music in the summer. FREE.

Watermans Arts Centre 40 High Street, Brentford, TW8 (8847 5651) *Gunnersbury underground/rail.* FREE Sunday lunchtime music from 12.30pm including jazz, funk, blues and rock.

Water Rats 328 Gray's Inn Road, WC1 (7837 7269) *Admission from £4. King's Cross underground/rail.* Indie rock music pub.

West Ham Park Upton Lane, E7 (8472 3584) *Plaistow underground.* Bandstand music in the summer on Sundays.

Westminster Abbey Dean's Yard, Parliament Square, SW1 (7222 5152) *Westminster underground.* The choir can be appreciated at regular services (around 30 a week), and there's an organ recital at 5.45pm on Sundays.

WKD 18 Kentish Town Road, NW1 (7267 1869) *Many concerts cost under £5 or are FREE. Camden town underground.* Popular venue for rock, reggae, world music and other styles.

Wigmore Hall 36 Wigmore Street, W1 (7935 2141) *Tickets start at £5. Bond Street underground.* Regular classical concerts and recitals.

MUSIC IN CITY CHURCHES

A number of the City's many churches organise FREE lunchtime concerts, usually beginning around 1–1.15pm on weekdays and lasting under an hour. The City of London Information Centre, St Paul's Churchyard, EC4 (7332 1456/7606 3030) can give details of the day's concerts and their publication, *City Events*, gives monthly details. Some other churches around London also put on lunchtime concerts. The standards are almost always high for these performances, which range from solos to chamber orchestras.

All Souls Langham Place, W1 (7580 3522) *Oxford Circus underground.* Occasional free concerts, especially organ recitals.

St Anne and St Agnes Gresham Street, EC2 (7606 4986) *Mon and Fri at 1.10pm. St Paul's underground.* Also other events such as Bach, jazz and Lutheran choral vespers.

St Bride Fleet Street, EC4 (7427 0133) *Frequent concerts at 1.15pm; Tues, Wed, Fri. Blackfriars underground/rail.*

St Georges Hanover Square, 2a Mill Street, W1 (7629 0874) *Oxford Circus underground*. Recitals usually Thurs.

St Giles Cripplegate Barbican, EC2 (7588 3013) *Barbican/Moorgate underground*. Small-scale classical works.

St James's Church Piccadilly Piccadilly, W1 (7734 4511) *Thurs, Fri and also many Weds and some Sats at 1.10pm. Also some evening concerts (not free). Piccadilly underground*. Big on Baroque.

St Lawrence Jewry Gresham Street, EC2 (7600 9478) *Piano recitals on Mondays at 1pm and organ recitals on Tuesdays at the same time. Bank underground*.

St Margaret's Broad Sanctuary, SW1 (7222 6382) *Occasional choirs weekdays 1–2pm. Westminster underground*.

St Margaret Lothbury Lothbury, EC2 (7606 8330) *Thursdays at 1.10pm. Bank underground*.

St Mary-le-Bow Cheapside, EC2 (7248 5139) *Medieval and Renaissance works on Thursdays at 1.05pm. St Paul's underground*.

St Mary-le-Strand Strand, WC2 (7836 3126) *Aldwych underground*.

St Michael's Cornhill, EC3 (7626 8841) *Organ recitals on Mondays at 1pm. Bank underground*.

St Olave's Hart Street, EC3 (7488 4318) *Wednesdays and Thursdays at 1.05pm. Tower Hill underground*.

St Sepulchre-without-Newgate Holborn Viaduct, EC1 (7248 1660) *Chancery Lane underground*.

Opera

Broadgate Centre Eldon Street, EC2 (7588 6565) *May–Sept Mon–Fri 12.30–2pm. Liverpool Street underground/rail.* Opera often features in the Broadgate Arena summer entertainments.

Covent Garden Piazza Covent Garden, WC1 (7304 4000) *Covent Garden underground.* The Royal Opera House approximately three times a year relays a free live performance of opera or ballet to up to 6,000 people standing outside in the Piazza. There are 260 seats for the elderly and disabled. Just as well it's free – the price for a box consisting of four seats in the Opera House can top £1,000 for some performances.

London Coliseum St Martin's Lane, WC2 (7632 8300) *Tickets from £3. Charing Cross underground/rail.* Home of the English National Opera, the Coliseum is often associated with high ticket prices but sometimes these are available very cheaply.

Organised Walks and Tours

The Countryside Hotline Gives advice about places of interest and where to walk. Phone 7222 8000 for details.

Epping Forest Countrycare Produces a leaflet detailing the year's guided walks programme around the Epping Forest area. Call 01992 788203.

Greenwich Guided Walks *Organised by the Greenwich Tour Guides Association (8858 6169). Leave at 12.15pm and 2.15pm* *daily from Greenwich Tourist Information Centre, Pepys Building, Cutty Sark Gardens, Greenwich SE10. Cost: £4 (concessions £3).* The walks through historic Greenwich last 90 minutes.

Houses of Parliament tours Parliament Square, SW1 (Commons: 7219 4272, Lords: 7219 3107) *Book a £3.50 guided tour of both Houses in advance through Ticketmaster (7344 9966). Westminster underground.* 'Line of route' tour: during the recess, parties can take a tour at any time on weekdays. When the Houses are sitting, hourly official tours are available weekdays before noon and on Friday afternoons. Groups must be sponsored by a Member of Parliament or peer. If you are not a UK citizen, apply to your Embassy or High Commission or write to The Public Information Office of the House of Commons. Groups should be no larger than 16 people. Tickets are not required but guides expect a gratuity of around £25 per party. 'Big Ben' tour: contact your MP, Embassy or High Commission to book the FREE 45-minute tours Mon–Fri at 10.30am, 11.30am and 2.30pm. 'Lord Chancellor's apartments' tour: FREE tours on Tues/Thurs mornings but long waiting list. Phone 7219 2184 for cancellations.

Inland Waterways Association For guided walks along canals and other inland waterways, contact this organisation (7586 2510) who have details of two to four walks each month on Wednesdays at 6.30pm and Sundays at 2.30pm.

Jack the Ripper Mystery Walk *Wed, Sun 8pm; Fri 7pm. Adults £5, concessions £3.50. (8558 9446). Aldgate underground station.* A two-hour walk.

Kensington Gardens, Hyde Park and St James's Park These

organise occasional guided walks featuring various aspects of their history, wildlife, gardens, plant life and personalities. For details telephone 7298 2100.

The London Wildlife Trust Organises guided walks with a wildlife theme. Telephone 7261 0447.

Original London Walks *Cost £5 adult, £4 senior citizens and students, FREE for children under 14. Most start at central underground stations. (7624 3978).* Offers around 100 walks from a repertoire of 200 consistently good two-hour walks each week. They include Dickens' London, Shakespeare's London, Diana, Princess of Wales, Hidden Pubs of Old London Town, Beatles Magical Mystery Tour, the Oscar Wilde Walk, Jack the Ripper Haunts, Spies and Spycatchers and Legal London.

The Blood and Tears Walk *Cost £5. (8348 9022).Starts from outside Barbican underground station.* Examines the more gruesome elements of London's history. There's also a Shakespeare City Walk from Blackfriars underground.

The Ramblers' Association *Hotline (7370 6180) gives information on their FREE guided walks for the week.* The Association also organises a Festival of Summer Walks in mid–late August.

Tourist Information Centres Provide details of guided and self-guided walks and tours. (See the Tourist Information Centres, p. 213.) They also provide FREE or inexpensive booklets and leaflets.

Westminster School Tour Westminster School, Little Dean's Yard, London SW1 (7963 1010) *First three weeks of April. Admission £2. Guided tours of up to 20 by arrangement. Westminster under-*

ground. Westminster has occupied the Abbey's medieval monastery buildings since 1540 and this tour reveals the pre-Reformation world of the Abbey as well as a glimpse of the past and present life of an English public school.

Parks and Open Spaces

See also *Wildlife Activities* section, page 233.

Abney Park Cemetery Stoke Newington High Street, N16 *Open daily Apr–Sept 9am–5.30pm; Oct–Mar 9am–3.30pm. Stoke Newington rail.* A mature wildlife-rich mixed woodland.

Alexandra Palace and Park Wood Green, N22 *Wood Green underground/Alexandra Palace rail.* Wander around the Victorian 'Ally Pally' and 200-acre grounds, and see the panoramic views, a small animal enclosure, children's playground, conservation area and boating lake. There are children's shows and workshops during the summer at the Grove Community Centre.

Avery Hill Park Avery Hill Road, SE9 *Falconwood rail.* Though not particularly beautiful, this has a covered Victorian Winter Gardens with many species of tropical and temperate plants, one of the finest collections outside the Royal Botanical Gardens at Kew.

Battersea Park Queenstown Road, SW8 *Battersea Park rail.* Bordered on one side by the river – with views across the water to Chelsea – there's a lot packed into the 200 acres here including the Japanese Peace Pagoda, a herb garden, the tranquil Old English Garden, an art gallery, a big adventure playground for 5 to 16-year-olds, a deer enclosure, lakes, tree trails and nature trails. Maps, brochures and other information is available from the Park Office to the left of the Albert Bridge entrance, and also from the Pump House, which has a video on the park's history.

Beckenham Place Park Beckenham Hill Road, Beckenham, Kent *Beckenham Hill rail*. Tennis courts nestle among the parkland.

Bishop's Park and Fulham Palace Grounds Bishop's Avenue, Fulham Palace Road, SW6 *Putney Bridge underground*. This was once the biggest moated sight in England, but unfortunately the moat has been filled in. Still, you can stroll around the charming herb garden and its Tudor gateway.

Blackheath Blackheath SE3 *Blackheath rail*. The 170 acres are rich in history: the Danes camped here in 1011, and James I introduced golf to England here. Greenwich Park is on one side, unspoilt Blackheath Village on the other. There are three ponds, one used for boating at the weekend. An architectural gem, The Paragon, is off South Row, SE3.

Brockwell Park Dulwich Road, SE23 *Herne Hill rail*. A hilly expanse of green.

Bushy Park Hampton Court Road, Middlesex, TW12 *Hampton Wick rail*. North of Hampton Court Palace, this royal park of 1,099 acres has deer and a children's playground but is best known for the large Waterhouse Woodland Gardens and grand Chestnut Avenue. A children's play programme is organised in the summer.

Calthorpe Project Community Garden 258–274 Gray's Inn Road, WC1 *King's Cross underground/rail*. A relaxing retreat.

Charlton Park Charlton Park Road, SE7 *Charlton rail*. A big expanse of open parkland by the impressive Jacobean Charlton House. There's a small playground. Cross Charlton Park Road and walk in leafy, wooded Maryon Wilson Park, which has a small collection of animals on display.

Chelsea Physic Garden 66 Royal Hospital Road, SW3 (7352 5646) *Open Apr–Oct Wed noon–5pm; Sun 2–6pm. Adults £4, children 5–16, concessions £2. Sloane Square underground.* Founded in 1673 by the Society of Apothecaries, this is a peaceful 4-acre botanical garden in the heart of London. Guided and self-guided tours available.

Chislehurst Common Chislehurst, Kent *Chislehurst/Petts Wood rail*. There are dozens of footpaths including the Petts Wood Circular Walk, where you'll walk past working farms and woods that house bats, weasels, rabbits and foxes.

Chiswick House Gardens Burlington Lane, W4 *Turnham Green underground*. Although there is a charge to enter the neo-classical villa, the wooded, 60-acre gardens are free to all. There are statues, temples, a lake, and an information centre with details of park trails and a display about the garden's history.

Clapham Common Clapham, SW4 *Clapham Common underground*. A welcome expanse of green with ponds and a playground within a large concentration of residential streets.

Claybury Woods entrance via Claybury Hospital, off Manor Road, Woodford Green *Woodford underground*. Lots of ancient woodland with an old orchard.

Coldfall Wood Crichton Avenue, N10 *East Finchley underground*. Thirty-five acres of ancient woodland.

Coram's Fields 93 Guildford Street, WC1 *Russell Square underground*. Although only a few acres, there's a paddling pool, an animal enclosure and playground equipment. Adults are only admitted if accompanied by a child.

Crobham Hurst Upper Selsdon Road, South Croydon *South Croydon rail*. Unspoilt woodland.

Crystal Palace Park Sydenham, SE19 *Crystal Palace rail*. There's a maze, a children's play area, a tiny museum about the huge Victorian glasshouse, Crystal Palace, which was installed here but later destroyed by fire, and even a collection of full-scale Victorian models of 29 dinosaurs.

Dulwich Park College Road, SE21 *North/West Dulwich rail*. A Victorian park of 75 acres with a good collection of trees and regular events organised by the Park Rangers. Neighbouring, smaller Belair Park was laid out in the late-18th century in the classic English landscape fashion.

Eltham Common Well Hall Road, SE9 *Eltham rail*. A grassy expanse merging into glorious Oxleas Woods.

Epping Forest Epping, Essex *Epping/Loughton underground*. This gigantic, ancient forest (over 6,000 acres plus an extra 2,000 acres acquired over the years to protect the forest from development) is never more than a mile from a road yet it is simple to get lost here. Genuine countryside, much of the area is designated as a Site of Special Scientific Interest. There are regular organised two-hour walks every four to six weeks. About 500 deer roam in the forest and deer sanctuary and there are over 360 rare animal and plant species present.

Finsbury Park N4. *Finsbury Park underground*. A Victorian park with a boating lake, playgrounds and an adventure playground.

Fryent Country Park Fryent Way, Kingsbury, NW9 *Wembley Park underground*. 260 acres of unspoilt countryside with nature walks and a wildlife area.

Gladstone Park Dollis Hill Lane, NW10 *Dollis Hill underground*. This 90-acre park was named after William Gladstone, who regularly visited the park's magnificent Dollis Hill House. There is an arboretum housing hundreds of plants and trees from around the world, an art gallery, a children's playground, a wildlife area and an old walled garden.

Golders Hill Park North End Road, NW11 *Golders Green underground*. A beautiful walled garden and pond and a good selection of animal and bird enclosures. There are children's activities and live music in summer.

Green Park Picadilly, W1/SW1 *Green Park underground*. So-called due to the absence of flowers, it also lacks a lake, yet its mature trees and grassland are a tranquil retreat from the congested centre of town.

Greenwich Park Greenwich, SE10 *Greenwich/Maze Hill rail*. Situated on a hill between Blackheath at the top and the River Thames at the bottom, this park was enclosed in 1433 by order of Henry VI. Successors Henry VIII and Elizabeth I found it a pleasing party venue. Deer were introduced in 1515 and a herd is still in residence in the 13-acre Wilderness. There's a pond with wildfowl, a children's playground, a flower garden and London's longest herbaceous border. There are excellent views, especially at the top of the hill by the Old Royal Observatory (with the meridian line of zero longitude passing through it) where the magnificent panorama takes in the National Maritime Museum, Canary Wharf and Docklands, and on a clear day Tower Bridge and St Paul's Cathedral as well. The Observatory's big red ball drops at 1pm daily. The information centre at the St Mary's Gate entrance has displays about the history of the 183-acre park. In the summer there are various events such as band performances in the bandstand, open air theatre, cafe music, children's entertainment and shows, and a family day with various events.

Ham House Grounds Ham, Richmond, Surrey (8940 1950) *Open Sat–Thurs 10.30am–6pm or dusk if earlier. Richmond rail/underground.* Entry is FREE to the formal Stuart gardens and water meadows of this National Trust-owned residence.

Hampstead Heath and Parliament Hill Hampstead NW3, NW5 *Hampstead underground.* 791 acres of unspoilt heathland four miles from the centre of London, Hamstead Heath is great for walking, with glorious views. There is kite flying on Parliament Hill (with its splendid views of London) at the south end of the heath, a horse riding circuit, organised walks, the art collection at Kenwood, and even some bathing ponds. There are Sunday afternoon band performances on the bandstands at Parliament Hill and Golders Hill and evening Scottish country dancing sessions in the summer. For children there is a playground, an adventure playground, play activities for under-5s (the One O'Clock

Club), dog-free enclosures with play equipment, and in Golders Hill a deer enclosure and an animal enclosure with flamingoes and a variety of birds and animals. In the summer there are shows with clowns, puppets and magicians.

Hampton Court Park and Gardens Hampton Court Road, East Mosely, Middlesex *Hampton Court rail*. Although admission to Wolsey's riverside Hampton Court Palace is not free, its 550 acres of deer–inhabited parkland and the formal gardens are, and are well worth visiting in their own right. The Great Vine, planted in 1768, is supposed to be the oldest in the world.

Highgate Wood Muswell Hill Road, N6 *Highgate underground*. 70 acres of ancient woodland with a good children's playground, nature trails and nature hut. On the other side of Muswell Hill Road is Queen's Wood, a smaller but quieter patch of ancient woodland.

Holland Park Illchester Place, Kensington, W8 *Holland Park underground*. A peacock lawn, rose gardens, a Japanese water garden, woodland, a wildlife pond, an ecology centre and an excellent adventure playground are all crammed into this pretty little park.

Horniman Gardens 100 London Road, Forest Hill, SE23 (8699 1872) *Forest Hill rail*. Has a small children's zoo and a nature trail. If you like working outdoors, volunteers are needed for two hours on Sundays to help with 'ecological management tasks' (ie clearing up and repairing) on the Horniman Railway Trail – phone for details.

Hyde Park Park Lane W1, W2, SW7 *Hyde Park Corner/Marble*

Arch underground. A peaceful place, despite being by some of the world's busiest streets. Although 50,000 people may visit it on a nice summer's day, there's enough space for all in the 350 acres of woods, grassland, river and gardens that originally was a Tudor hunting ground. There is a children's playground and a horse riding track. Speaker's Corner, in the north-east of the park, comes alive on Sunday mornings – it is a venue for free and often barmy speech. There are Sunday afternoon concerts at the bandstand in the summer, and every day at around 10.30am the very colourful Household Cavalry can be seen riding through the park, going from Hyde Park Barracks to Buckingham Palace.

Kensington Gardens Kensington W2, W8 *Lancaster Gate/High Street Kensington underground*. A continuation of Hyde Park, yet this park strikes a different mood, and is particularly suitable for children. There's a flower walk, the huge Round Pond, kite flying, a children's playground, the Albert Memorial, the Serpentine Gallery and the Peter Pan statue. There are puppet shows in the summer.

Kew Gardens (Royal Botanic Gardens) Kew Green, Richmond (8332 5622) *Open 9.30am, closing times vary with dusk. Adults £5, concessions £3.50, children (5–16) £2.50. Kew Gardens underground/rail*. Three hundred acres of magnificent gardens with 30,000 types of plant in fabulous buildings, all set in a beautiful landscape. Seven glasshouses, a museum with interactive exhibition and two art galleries.

Lee Valley Country Park Marsh Lane, N17 *Northumberland Park/Waltham Cross rail*. Stretches 23 miles from Bow in the East End of London to Ware in Hertfordshire. There's a working farm at Hayes Hill, about two miles from Waltham Abbey.

Lesnes Abbey Woods Abbey Road, Belvedere, Kent *Abbey Wood rail*. Named after the 12th-century abbey whose remains are within this 200-acre wood, there's a wealth of wild flowers, birds and a fossil bed. Bostall Heath and woods is adjoining, adding an extra 150 acres of green space.

Maryon Wilson Park Charlton Park Road, SE7 *Charlton rail*. Tranquil, leafy, wooded Maryon Wilson Park has a small collection of animals on display. Also, one side of it is Charlton Park and on the other is picturesque Maryon Park, featured in Antonioni's classic 1966 film, *Blow Up*.

Mile End Park Copperfield Road, E3 *Mile End underground*. The new century has seen a development scheme revitalising this space, which will comprise a sports park complete with stadium and go-karting track, an ecology park, and an arts park with its own outdoor exhibiting space.

Morden Hall Park Morden Hall Road, Morden, Surrey *Morden underground*. This National Trust-owned park has waterways from the River Wandle, a tree-lined avenue, wildlife-rich meadowland, marshland and woodland as well as a riverside walk and an information room with a permanent display on the history of the estate. Old estate workshops house local craftspeople carrying out traditional trades such as furniture restoration, woodturning and stained-glass design and restoration, and their work is on display. A city farm is adjacent.

Mycenae House and Grounds 90 Mycenae Road, Blackheath, SE3 *Westcombe Park rail*. The spacious, mature gardens are often gloriously empty, and there's an art gallery (open Mon, Tues, Thurs–Sat 11am–5pm; Sun 2–5pm) within the house.

Osterley Park Isleworth, Middlesex *Osterley underground*
Although there is a charge to enter the manor house, there is extensive landscaped parkland with beautiful lakes and some 16th-century stables all free to enter.

Oxleas Woods Shooters Hill, SE18 *Falconwood rail.* Oxleas Woods is an 8,000-year-old woodland that is adjacent to Shepherdleas, Jack and Castle Woods, Eltham and Woolwich Commons and Eltham and Avery Hill Parks –1 a massive area of green space. It contains Severndroog Castle, a Gothic tower built in 1784.

Paddington Street Gardens Paddington Road, W1 *Baker Street underground.* A pleasant, restful open space away from the crowds around Baker Street station. Lots of species of trees can be found in this small space. For the young there's a decent-sized playground, and for the very old, in fact dead, there's a finely designed mausoleum, which is all that remains of the 18th-century burial ground these gardens used to be.

Pear Wood Wood Lane, Stanmore *Stanmore underground.* Ancient woodland.

Primrose Hill NW3 *Chalk Farm/Camden Town underground.* Separated from Regent's Park by a busy road and London Zoo, this 61-acre grassy hill has a children's playground, an outdoor gymnasium, and at the top of the hill one of London's six protected viewpoints.

Queen's Park Kingswood Avenue, NW6 *Queen's Park underground.* A small park but welcome in an area somewhat lacking in green space. There is a *pétanque* rink and for children there's a playground, paddling pool and pet's corner. The summer holidays bring children's entertainers such as clowns and jugglers as well as bouncy castles and playschemes with supervised activities. There are also Sunday bandstand concerts in the late summer.

Regent's Park NW1 *Regent's Park/Camden Town underground.* Surrounded on three sides by Nash terraces and Regent's Canal on the fourth, the 300 acres of Regent's Park include three children's playgrounds, the beautiful Queen Mary's Rose Garden (best in June) and a vast lake rich in wildfowl. Walk along the big, flat playing fields and peer in at the animals at London Zoo. There's summer music in the bandstand and cafeteria, even possibly occasional folk dancing, and children's activities during the summer season. If you're meeting someone, be specific about which entrance gate, as there's about 40 of them.

Richmond Park Holly Lodge, Richmond, Surrey *Richmond underground/rail.* The largest Royal park, being over 2,500 acres, Richmond Park has hardly changed over the centuries. It is so well preserved, it remains more natural than many arecountryside in Britain. It is big enough for every one of its 2–3 million annual visitors to find real peace and quiet. There is the Isabella Plantation, a quiet woodland garden as well as hundreds of red and fallow deer, badgers, foxes, lakes and grasslands, and great views. At Adams Pond at Sheen Gate there's a pond for sailing model boats and a flying field for model aircraft. Despite its size, there are only two cafes and two children's playgrounds, but then this is not a 'statues and bandstands' kind of park. Still, in the summer light music is perfomed at Pembroke Lodge and there are children's events such as puppet shows, workshops and storytelling.

Roundwood Park Harlesden Road, NW10 *Willesden Green underground*. An aviary, children's playground, floral displays and a wildlife area.

St James's Park The Mall, SW1 *St James's Park underground*. In the shadows of Buckingham Palace and other interesting and impressive buildings from the Tudor age to modern times, this beautiful but compact park has five acres of lake and a children's playground. There are bandstand concerts in the summer.

Syon Park Brentford, Middlesex *Gunnersbury underground*. Beautiful, classically landscaped gardens with lawns and a lake as well as a big indoor adventure playground, butterfly house, insect house and aquatic exhibition (admission charges for these apply). A great day out for the kids. See also Butterfly House in *Sightseeing and Places of Interest* page 175.

Trinity Square Gardens Tower Hill, EC3 *Tower Hill underground*. Contains a war memorial to merchant seamen lost fighting for their country. A little plaque near the main road marks the site of the execution of 125 people including Thomas Cromwell and Sir Thomas More.

Victoria Embankment Gardens Victoria Embankment, SW1, WC2 *Charing Cross underground/rail*. There are many statues, beautiful flower beds and a lily pond in these gardens by the Thames.

Victoria Park Old Ford Road, E3 *Mile End underground*. A big formal park with lakes, fountains, two playgrounds, a trim trail, a one o'clock club (weekdays 1–4pm) for under-5s and their parents, goats, a herd of deer, and numerous events in the summer.

Victoria Tower Gardens Millbank, SW1 *Westminster underground*. A quiet and scenic riverside garden with statues and a children's play area.

Waterlow Park Highgate High Street, N6 *Archway underground*. Expanses of water, rose gardens and a children's area are in this hilly park of 26 acres next to Highgate Cemetery.

Well Hall Pleasaunce Well Hall Road, SE9. *Eltham rail*. Features a rose garden, wild garden, moat, stream and waterfall.

West Ham Park Upton Lane, E7 *Plaistow underground*. West Ham Park has 77 acres with an adventure playground, children's playground and an impressive botanical collection within the gardens. The summer holidays bring children's entertainers such as clowns and jugglers as well as bouncy castles and playschemes with supervised activities. There are also Sunday bandstand concerts in late summer.

Westminster Abbey Gardens Westminster Abbey, SW1 *Westminster underground*. This beautiful, restful site of over an acre has been the Abbey garden for 900 years, and has lawns, fine trees, a colourful rose garden and a monastic herb garden. All plants are labelled.

Wimbledon Common/Putney Heath SW19, SW15 *Wimbledon underground/rail*. Massive open heath and woodland, stretching for almost two miles. There's a windmill and pond areas that are full of birdlife.

Playgrounds and Adventure Playgrounds

Most London parks contain at least one FREE outdoor playground. The following playgrounds and adventure playgrounds offer FREE admission unless otherwise stated.

Acklam Road 6 Acklam Road, W10 (7969 5058) *Open term times Tues–Sat 3.30–7.30pm; school holidays Mon–Fri 10.30am–5.30pm. Westbourne Park underground/rail.* Lots of activities including swings, a pool table, art, sport and games.

Adventure Kingdom Bromley Civic Centre, Bromley, Kent (8290 1998) *Open daily 10am–7pm. Over-4s £3.35, under-4s £2.80.* Indoor soft play centre.

Angell Town Gordon Grove, SE5 (7737 0956) *Open term times Mon–Fri 3.30–7pm; school holidays (registration fee in summer) Mon–Fri 11am–6pm. Loughborough Junction rail.* Climbing frames, swings and lots of other activities.

Attlee Thrawl Street, E1 (7247 1281) *Open term times Tues, Wed 3.30–7.45pm, Thurs, Fri 3.30–5pm; school holidays Tues, Wed 9.45am–5pm, Thurs, Fri 12.45–7.45pm; Sat 9.45am–4.45pm. Aldgate East underground.* Various play structures, inflatables, etc.

Burgess Community Playground Albany Road, SE5 (7277 1371) *Open term times Tues–Fri 3.30–7.30pm; Sat 11am–5.30pm; school holidays Mon–Fri 10.30am–6.30pm; Sat 11am–5.30pm. Elephant and Castle underground.* An indoor/outdoor adventure playground with sandpits, slides, tennis, tabletennis, football, swings, arts and crafts.

Charlie Chaplin Bolton Crescent, SE5 (7735 1819) *Oval underground*. A playground for disabled children only. To visit, telephone for details.

Crumbles Castle Bingfield Street, N1 (7278 8640) *Open term times Mon−Wed 3.30−7.15pm; Thurs 4−6pm; Sun noon−6pm; school holidays Mon−Fri 10am−1.30pm; 2.30−6pm. King's Cross underground/rail*. Facilities include table tennis, art and craft activities, and outdoor play structures.

Dog Kennel Hill Dog Kennel Hill, East Dulwich SE22 (7274 6197) *Open term times Tues−Thurs 3.30−7.30pm; Sat 10.30am−4.30pm; school holidays Mon−Fri 10.30am−6pm. East Dulwich rail*. Swings, cricket, football, table tennis and other games as well as arts and crafts.

ELHAP 119 Roding Lane North, Woodford Bridge, Essex (8550 2636) *Open Mon−Fri 9am−5pm but telephone first. Woodford underground*. A special needs playground with a fortnightly Saturday club that integrates mainstream children with those with special needs. Also adult day care and holiday playschemes. Play structures, play areas, a giant seesaw, water play, sand play, music, a soft room and play room.

Evergreen Play Association Richmond Road, E8 (7275 9004) *Open term times Tues−Fri 3.30−6.45pm, Sat, Sun 10.30am−5.30pm; school holidays Mon−Fri 10.30am−5.30pm. Dalston Kingsland rail*. Arts and crafts such as pottery, hockey, table tennis, swings, inflatables, a wildlife garden and bees.

Highgate Wood Muswell Hill Road, N6 (8444 6129) *Highgate underground*. Includes an impressive children's playground.

Holland Park Illchester Place, Kensington, W8 (7602 9483) *Hol-*

land Park underground. Contains an excellent adventure playground.

Kid's Corner , 232 Hither Green Lane, SE13 (8852 3322) *Open daily 10am–7pm. Admission prices vary. Hither Green rail.* Indoor adventure play centre.

Kimber BMX/Adventure Playground Kimber Road, SW18 (8870 2168) *Open term times Tues–Fri 3.30–7pm; Sat 11am–6pm; school holidays Mon–Sat 11am–6pm. Southfields underground.* As well as a BMX bike track, and bikes for hire, there is basketball, swings, table tennis and arts and crafts.

Log Cabin 259 Northfield Avenue, W5 (8840 3400) *Open Mon, Wed–Fri 9.30am–6.30pm. Northfields underground.* A playground that offers extensive activities and also has facilities for the disabled. It has a variety of structures including swings and climbing frames, as well as toys, games, a darkroom, inflatables, arts and crafts and a nature area.

Mint Street 56 Southwark Bridge Road, Lant Street, SE1 (7403 3747) *Open term times Mon–Fri 3.30–7pm; school holidays Mon–Fri 10am–5pm. Borough underground.* Has the usual play structures and arts and crafts facilities as well as tennis, table tennis, pool table, hockey and football.

Monkey Business 222 Green Lanes, The Triangle, Palmers Green, N13 (8886 7520) *Open Thurs–Tues 10am–7pm. Cost: £2.75 per hour. Palmers Green underground.* An indoor playground with the now-common assortment of tube slides, ball pools, ropes, mazes and an aerial runway.

The Notting Hill Venture Centre Telford Road, W10 (8969 7919) *Open term times Tues–Sat 3.30–6.45pm; school holidays Mon–Fri 11am–5.45pm. Ladbroke Grove underground.* A football

---

pitch, tennis, basketball, lots of structures, slides and swings as well as crafts such as jewellery making and gardening.

Palace Bishops Avenue, SW6 (7731 2753) *Open Mon—Fri 10am—5pm but by arrangement. Putney Bridge underground.* A special needs playground in the grounds of Fulham Palace that has integration sessions with mainstream children.

Rascals Waterfront Leisure Centre, Woolwich High Street, SE18 (8317 5000) *Open Mon—Fri 9.30am—6pm; Sat, Sun 9.30am—2pm. Admission £3.30 first child, £1.65 extra children. Woolwich Arsenal rail.* An indoor adventure playground with nets, ball ponds, tube slides etc.

Slade Gardens Lorn Road, SW9 (7737 3829) *Open term times Mon—Fri noon—1.30pm, 3.30—7.30pm; school holidays Mon—Fri 10am—7.30pm. Stockwell underground.* Outdoor facilities include football, towers, ropes and swings, and indoors there are various arts and crafts such as model making and painting.

Spike's Madhouse Crystal Palace National Sports Centre, Ledrington Road, SE19 (8778 9876) *Open during school holidays Mon—Fri noon—5pm, Sat, Sun 10.30am—5pm. Cost: £2 per hour. Crystal Palace rail.* An indoor adventure playground with nets, ball ponds, tube slides etc.

Surrey Docks Trident Street, SE16 (7232 0846) *Open term times Tues—Fri 3.30—8pm, Sat 10am—6pm; school holidays Mon—Fri 10am—6pm. Surrey Quays underground.* Activities include netball, basketball, football, climbing. There are also play structures, a pool table, table tennis, arts and crafts, and workshops.

Toffee Park Ironmonger Row, EC1 (7251 0190) *Open term times*

Mon–Fri 3.30–8pm; school holidays Mon–Fri 10.30am–6pm. Old Street underground. 'The children say what they want to do and we organise it,' said one of the staff. There are swings, arts and crafts, a pool table and other games.

Sex

Contraceptives are *free* on the National Health Service to British citizens, EU residents and foreigners working or studying in Britain.

Brook Advisory Centre 233 Tottenham Court Road, W1 (7323 1522) *Goodge Street underground.* Provide FREE contraception to the under-21s. There are centres around London. Call to find your nearest.

Family Planning Association 27 Mortimer Street, W1 (7837 4044) *Goodge Street underground.* Call to find out your nearest branch. Condoms and other contraception, leaflets and advice are available for the asking. Don't be too choosy: requests for a box of fluorescent ribbed passion fruit-flavoured sheaths will probably not be accommodated.

Shops

Although outside London most high streets are identikit, with the same old chainstore shopfronts to be seen at whichever town you're in, the capital certainly has some interesting shops.

Alfie's Antique Market 13–25 Church Street, NW8 (7723 6066)

Marylebone underground. Several floors with antique furniture, jewellery, textiles, pottery etc.

Alfred Dunhill 48 Jermyn Street, SW1 (7290 8615) *Piccadilly Circus / Green Park underground.* This has on display about 200 of the company's collection of around 2,500 pipes from around the world including an Eskimo slate pipe, an emu's foot pipe and a Chinese opium pipe.

Angela Flanders Aromatics 96 Columbia Road, E2 (7739 7555) *Open Sun 9am–2pm only. Shoreditch underground.* Wonderful scents made from fresh herbs and flowers.

Bond Street Shops Bond Street, W1 *Bond Street underground.* The area has plenty of art galleries, especially around Cork St, and lots of antique galleries and an indoor antique market at 124 New Bond Street and Grays antique market off 58 Davies Street. Asprey's (165 New Bond Street) has some incredible luxury goods to admire, as does the likes of Cartier (175 New Bond Street) and Tiffany (25 Old Bond Street). Upmarket auction houses Sotheby's (34 New Bond Street) and Phillips (101 New Bond Street) are both situated in this grand neighbourhood. Hobb's of Mayfair, South Audley Street, is an upmarket delicatessen while Higgins in Duke Street supplies coffee to the Queen.

Borders 203 Oxford Street, W1 (7292 1600) *Oxford Circus underground.* This large bookshop has regular in-store activities including FREE children's activities, readers' and writers' groups, live music, quizzes and author events. There is another branch of Borders at 120 Charing Cross Road, WC2 (7379 8877).

Burlington Arcade off Piccadilly and Old Bond Street, W1 *Picca-*

dilly Circus/Green Park underground. Built in 1819, London's longest and most celebrated shopping arcade of mahogany-fronted shops selling luxury goods is complete with two top-hatted, uniformed beadles to discourage anyone from lowering the tone by running, singing, humming or – horror of horrors – opening an umbrella in the Regency arcade. Piccadilly Arcade, off Piccadilly, is an Edwardian extension of the Burlington Aracade and also has suitably grand traditional shops.

Conran Shop 81 Fulham Road, SW3 (7589 7401) *South Kensington underground.* The sofas may cost the price of a two-up, two-down in the North-East, but you can get some great design ideas here.

Davenport's Magic Shop 7 Charing Cross Underground Shopping Concourse, Strand, WC2 (7836 0408) *Charing Cross underground/rail.* Ask to see a card trick or two and be prepared to be mystified.

Ede and Ravenscroft 93 Chancery Lane, EC1 (7405 3906) *Chancery Lane underground.* A unique, peculiarly British shop, Ede and Ravenscroft are a firm of robe makers supporting the neighbouring law courts and crammed with the paraphernalia of the law. This is where you would go if called to the Bar, or if you had taken silk or were elevated to the Bench. It's full of elegant handmade wigs, crisp jabots and wing collars, gowns and other clothing from another age.

The Emporium 330 Creek Road, Greenwich SE10 (8305 1670) *Greenwich rail/DLR, Cutty Sark DLR.* Fascinating if you like clothing and other stuff from the 1940s to 1970s.

Foyles 113–119 Charing Cross Road, WC2 (7437 5660) *Tottenham*

Court Road underground. A famous, huge, sprawling book-shop.

Gerry's 74 Old Compton Road, W1 (7734 4215) *Leicester Square underground.* Alcohol from all around the world including African peanut liqueur and Peruvian pisco.

Green Park Shops Pall Mall and St James's Street, W1 *Picadilly underground.* Walking around this area takes you past some very upmarket shops. Admire hats at Lock's, antiques at Spinks, handmade shoes at Lobbs, and wines at the early 19th-century Berry Bros & Rudd.

Hamleys 188 Regent Street, W1 (7494 2000) *Piccadilly Circus/ Oxford Circus underground.* The world's biggest toy shop, full of toys sporting some of the world's biggest price tags.

Harrods 87 Brompton Road, SW1 (7730 1234) *Knightsbridge underground.* Visiting London's biggest and most famous store is something of an experience; it is a gigantic golden consumer palace.

Heals 196 Tottenham Court Road, W1 (7636 1666) and 234 King's Road, SW3 (7349 8411) *Goodge Street/Sloane Square underground.* Pricey, but excellent for interior design and furnishing inspiration. A branch of Habitat, with more down-to-earth prices, is adjacent to the Tottenham Court Road Branch.

Liberty 210–220 Regent Street, W1 (7734 1234) *Piccadilly Circus/ Oxford Circus underground.* This shop really stands out, being an eye-catching mock-Tudor department store built in the 1920s from timbers taken from the last Navy sailing ships.

London Architectural Salvage and Supply Company (LASSCO)

St Michael's Church, Mark Street, EC2 (7739 0448) *Old Street underground.* The treasures in this old church are a recycler's dream: garden follies, antique tiles and fireplaces, oak floorboards and hundreds of other curios.

London Doll's House Company 29 The Market, Covent Garden, WC2 (7240 8681) *Covent Garden underground.* It's fascinating to see the level of detail the dolls, houses, furniture and accessories boast here.

Milroy's of Soho 3 Greek Street, W1 (7437 9311) *Tottenham Court Road underground.* More than 400 whiskies are stocked here.

Radio Days 87 Lower Marsh, SE1 (7928 0800) *Open Mon–Sat 11am–5pm. Lambeth North underground.* Packed with memorabilia of every variety including an esoteric collection of 1920s to 1980s vintage magazines. Here you can find anything from hand-sewn 1930s gowns to 1970s flares and 1950s kitsch.

Royal Arcade Connects Albermarle Street with Old Bond Street, W1 *Bond Street underground.* This arcade of select shops was built in 1879 and has high arched bays topped by a grand glass roof.

Smith's Snuff Shop 74 Charing Cross Rd, WC2 (7836 7422) *Open Mon–Fri 9am-6pm; Sat 9.30am–5.30pm. Leicester Square underground.* As well as a big variety of snuff costing under £1, that decadent habit of yesteryear, there are also tobaccos, cigarettes and cigars.

Tobias and the Angel 68 White Hart Lane, SW13 (8296 0058) *Open Mon–Sat 10am–6pm. Barnes Bridge rail.* A shop laid out as a home with a bedroom, sitting room, kitchen and

---

nursery, decorated and furnished with the old and new handmade pieces that the shop sells. These include textiles, furniture, tools and lamps

Twinings 216 Strand, WC2 (7353 3511) *Temple underground.* This small shop selling tea dates from 1710. It claims to be the oldest in the capital to be selling the same goods as the original owners. There's a small museum where the firm's history is illustrated.

Waterstone's 203 Piccadilly, W1 (7851 2400) *Piccadilly Circus underground.* This bookshop, which has FREE events, retains the fine modernist 1930s facade of its predecessor, Simpson's the outfitters.

FOOD SHOPS AND CAFES

Many independent food shops offer free food samples to those who ask, including many of the following. Also included are some cafes.

Algerian Coffee Stores 52 Old Compton Street, W1 (7437 2480) *Leicester Square underground.* A big range of coffees (and teas too) at this store established in 1887.

Barstow and Barr 204 Upper Street, N1 (7359 4222) and Unit 90, Camden Lock, Chalk Farm, NW7 (7428 0488) *The Camden Lock branch is open Sun 11am–5.30pm. Angel/Camden Town underground.* You are welcome to try a small selection from these shops' stock of over 100 cheeses, and also Provence olives.

The Beer Shop 14 Pitfield Street, N1 (7739 3701) *Old Street underground.* A huge selection of beers.

Cafe Brood 1–6 Green Dragon Court, Bridge Arcade, SE1 (7407 0644) *London Bridge rail/underground*. The menu of this popular cafe by Southwark Cathedral has a Belgian slant.

The Cheeseboard 26 Royal Hill, SE10 (8305 0401) *Greenwich rail/ DLR*. Try samples of a huge range of cheeses available for tasting, many obscure. If you buy some, don't complain, as one old gentleman did, that your Red Leicester is orange.

Fortnum and Mason 181 Piccadilly, W1 (7734 8040) *Piccadilly Circus underground*. The grand store continues to cater for the English style of yesteryear.

Fratelli Camisa 53 Charlotte Street, W1 (7255 1240) *Goodge Street underground*. Various cold meats, olives, cheeses etc.

Gambardella 48 Vanbrugh Park, Blackheath SE3 (8858 0327) *Open daily 8am–6pm. Westcombe Park rail*. This down-to-earth cafe has been a fixture of this corner of Blackheath since 1927 and the Formica and mirror-rich decor dates from the 1940s. Most meals are under £5, including fry-ups and pasta.

Garcia and Sons 248–250 Portobello Road, W11 (7221 6119) *Notting Hill underground*. A large, unpretentious Spanish delicatessen now into its 45th year, with a good choice of tapas, chorizo and olives.

Hand Made Food 40 Tranquil Vale, Blackheath SE3 (8297 9966) *Open Mon–Fri 9am–7pm; Sat 9am–5.30pm; Sun 10am–2pm. Blackheath rail*. Like many delicatessens and specialist food shops, Hand Made Food is happy for everything from its fresh food range to be tasted, if this privilege is not abused.

Harrods Knightsbridge, SW1 (7730 1234) *Open Mon–Sat 10am–*

7pm. Knightsbridge underground. A whisk through the huge Food Hall sampling the varied, exotic fare can effortlessly procure you an impressive calorie intake.

Hare Krishna Temple 10 Soho Street, W1 (7437 3662) *Tottenham Court Road underground.* From Monday to Saturday at around 1pm you can enjoy a completely FREE delicious Indian vegetarian meal in the Temple next to the Hare Krishna Restaurant.

The Hive 93 Northcote Road, SW11 (7924 6233) *Open Mon—Sat 10am—6pm. Clapham South underground.* Solely devoted to bees and honey, this fascinating shop has a glass observation hive built into the wall where you can watch over 25,000 bees at work. The owners would appreciate it if you don't break the glass. There are various bee artefacts around the shop including a wasp nest and there's even a 10-minute taped commentary available talking you through these. You can also often watch honey and royal jelly-based cosmetics and beeswax candles being rolled and dipped. There are leaflets and other information available, as well as honey samples to try.

Maison Bertaux 28 Greek Street, W1 (7437 6007) *Tottenham Court Road underground.* This cosy cafe-patisserie is an institution of old Soho with a great selection of gateaux, croissants and eclairs.

Neal's Yard Dairy , Short's Gardens, WC2 (7379 7646) *Open Mon—Sat 9am—7pm; Sun 10am—5pm. Covent Garden underground.* Cheeses from Britain and Ireland principally.

Patisserie Valerie 44 Old Compton Street, W1 (7437 3466) *Leicester Square underground.* Step into this patisserie and you're transported to another era. Established in 1926, it's traditional look is retained with wooden floors and panelling and a window crammed with rich cakes.

Rippon Cheese Stores 26 Upper Taschbrook Street, SW1 (7931 0628) *Open Mon–Fri 9am–6.30pm; Sat 9am–5pm. Pimlico underground.* Quite a choice with over 550 cheeses on offer.

Rococo 321 King's Road, SW3 (7352 5857) *Open Mon–Sat 10am–6.30pm. Sloane Square underground.* This is the place for chocolate, from modest kids' bars to unspeakably delicious truffles made from the world's rarest cocoa bean. Try a sample or two – at your peril.

Rosslyn Delicatessen 56 Rosslyn Hill, NW3 (7794 9210) *Open Mon–Sat 8.30am–8.30pm; Sun 8.30am–5pm. Hampstead underground.* Most weekends there are free tastings of a particular product, but otherwise cheeses, meats, pâtés and olives can usually be tried at most times.

Selfridges 400 Oxford Street, W1 (7629 1234) *Marble Arch/Bond Street underground.* Foods from around the world in the Food Hall of this huge Edwardian department store.

The Spice Shop 1 Blenheim Crescent, W11 (7221 4448) *Ladbroke Grove underground.* Endless herbs, spices, berries, barks and leaves including 20 types of chilli and more than 10 paprikas.

Tea House 15a Neal Street, WC2 (7240 7539) *Covent Garden underground.* More than 50 teas on offer.

Teddington Cheese Station Road, Teddington, Middlesex (8977 6868) *Teddington rail.* Frequent tastings at this specialist shop.

Villandry Delicatessen 170 Great Portland Street, W1 (7631 3131)

Great Portland Street underground. Loads of delicacies from around the globe.

Sightseeing and Places of Interest

A collection of many of London's buildings and monuments of historical and architectural interest and other major – or just plain interesting – sights and attractions. Admission is FREE unless stated.

Abney Park Cemetery Stoke Newington Church Street, N16 (7275 7557) *Open daily Apr–Sept 9am–5.30pm; Oct–Mar 9am–3.30pm. Stoke Newington rail.* An eery, peaceful Victorian Gothic cemetery.

Age Exchange Reminiscence Centre 11 Blackheath Village, SE3 (8318 9105) *Open Mon–Sat 10am–5pm. Blackheath rail.* The past explored via a reconstructed 1930s shop and temporary exhibitions. Members of the centre, aged 60-plus, stage plays examining the past. There's a cafe, classic film club and tea dances.

Africa Centre 38 King Street, WC2 (7836 1973) *Open gallery Mon–Fri 9.30am–5.30pm; Sat 11am–4pm. Covent Garden underground.* This 18th-century building is devoted to African culture and politics. There's a craft shop, an exhibition space and a resource centre with newspapers, magazines, journals and other sources of information about Africa.

Albert Memorial Kensington Gardens by Kensington Gore, SW7 *Gloucester Road/South Kensington underground.* Designed by Sir George Gilbert Scott and completed in 1872, this ostentatious memorial to Queen Victoria's consort is extraordinarily detailed Victoriana in the Gothic tradition. Of the many carvings there are depictions of agriculture, manufacture, commerce and engineering and carvings representing Europe (a bull), Africa (a camel), America (a bison) and Asia (an elephant). If you also spot a can of Fosters it's not representing Australia but is some litter. During the last war the cross at the top of the memorial was blown off – and clumsily replaced the wrong way round. The memorial has had its fair share of critics: even contemporary Victorians called it an 'overgrown reliquary'. Over the road is the Royal Albert Hall, Kensington Gore, SW7, a magnificent red brick and terracotta auditorium topped by a splendid iron and glass dome.

Avery Hill Winter Garden Avery Hill Park, Avery Hill Road, SE9 (8316 8991) *Open daily 10am–noon, 1–4pm. Falconwood rail.* Hundreds of plant species in this domed glasshouse with cold, temperate and tropical greenhouses.

Banqueting House Whitehall, SW1 (7839 7569) *Open Mon–Sat 10am–5pm. Adults £3.80, concessions £3, children 5–15 £2.30. Westminster underground.* Built 1619 and designed by Inigo Jones, the only surviving part of the Palace of Whitehall. A Royal residence until the end of the 17th century – Charles I was executed here. The classical hall has a marvellous ceiling painted by Rubens.

Blue Plaques These have been erected to commemorate the residences of famous people and today there are over 700. They include: **Robert Baden-Powell,** founder of the Scouting movement, 9 Hyde Park Gate, SW7; **John Logie Baird,** who demonstrated television in 1926, 22 Frith Street, W1; **William Bligh,** captain of the *Bounty*, 100 Lambeth Road, SE1; **Thomas**

Carlyle, historian and essayist, 24 Cheyne Row, SW3; **Charles Dickens,** novelist, 48 Doughty Street, WC1; **Benjamin Disraeli,** statesman, 22 Theobalds Road, WC1; **Sir Edward Elgar,** composer, 51 Avonmore Road, W14; **George Eliot,** novelist, 4 Cheyne Walk, SW3; **Benjamin Franklin,** American statesman, 36 Craven Street, WC2; **William Gladstone,** statesman, 11 Carlton House Terrace, SW1; **George Frederic Handel,** musician, 25 Brook Street, W1; **Jimi Hendrix,** guitarist and songwriter, 23 Brook Street, W1; **Dr Samuel Johnson,** writer, 17 Gough Square, EC4; **Rudyard Kipling,** writer, 43 Villiers Street, WC2; **Guglielmo Marconi,** wireless inventor, 71 Hereford Road, W2; **Karl Marx,** philosopher, 28 Dean Street, W1; **Wolfgang Amadeus Mozart,** composer, 180 Ebury Street, SW1; **Sir Isaac Newton,** scientist, 87 Jermyn Street, SW1; **Florence Nightingale,** nurse, 10 South Street, W1; **Samuel Pepys,** diarist, 12–14 Buckingham Street, WC2; **Dante Rosetti,** artist and poet, 110 Hallam Street, W1; **Captain Robert Scott,** Antarctic explorer, 56 Oakley Street, SW3; **Bram Stoker,** novelist, 18 St Leonard's Terrace, SW3; **Mark Twain,** writer, 23 Tedworth Square, SW3; **Ralph Vaughan Williams,** composer, 10 Hanover Terrace, NW1; **James Whistler,** artist, 96 Cheyne Walk, SW3; **William Wilberforce,** abolisher of slavery, 44 Cadogan Place, SW1; **Oscar Wilde,** dramatist, 34 Tite Street, SW3; **Sir Christopher Wren,** architect, 49 Bankside, SE1.

Brompton Cemetery Finborough Road, SW10 (7352 1201) *Open daily 8.30am–dusk. West Brompton underground.* Catacombs by the main entrance welcome visitors to the final resting place of suffragette Emmeline Pankhurst amongst others.

Building Centre 26 Store Street, WC1 (7692 4000) *Open Mon– Fri 9.30am–5.30pm; Sat 10am–1pm. Tottenham Court Road/ Goodge Street underground.* Exhibitions and information concerning all aspects of the building industry including architecture, restoration, interior design and construction. It's a good source of inspiration if you need ideas for improving your home. There are examples of such things as kitchens and bathrooms as well as innovations and materials such as tiles and windows.

Cabaret Mechanical Theatre 33–34 Covent Garden, WC2 (7379 7961) *Open Mon–Sat 10am–6.30pm; Sun 11am–6.30pm. Adults £1.95, children, senior citizens £1.20. Covent Garden underground.* A fascinating collection of over 60 handmade automata which come to life at the touch of a button. Children love it.

Cabinet War Rooms King Charles Street, SW1 (7930 6961) *Open daily 10am–6pm. Adults £5, children FREE. Westminster underground.* A maze of 21 rooms for Churchill's cabinet to meet safely during World War II. The Cabinet, Map and Prime Minister's Rooms were preserved intact when the war ended, and the others have been authentically restored.

Canary Wharf Tower E14 *Canary Wharf DLR.* Love it or hate it, Cesar Pelli's 244-metre-high tower dominates the skyline at the Isle of Dogs and is a striking site when you emerge from the Norman Foster-designed Canary Wharf station.

Centotaph Whitehall, SW1. *Westminster underground.* Lutyens-designed memorial to the two World Wars in the centre of the road.

Charlton House Charlton, SE7 (8856 3951) *Open Mon–Fri 9am–10pm; Sat 9am–5pm. Charlton rail.* Set in spacious grounds, London's best example of a Jacobean house, now a community centre.

Chislehurst Caves Old Hill, Chislehurst (8467 3264) *Open Wed–Sun 11am–4pm. 45-minute tour on the hour, adults £3, children (5–15) £1.50; 90-minute tour, Sun 2.30pm £5, £2.50. Chislehurst rail.* Families with older children love these spooky, man-made labyrinthine caves. Believed to have been started at the time of the Druids, there are signs of Roman and Saxon activity. The caves sheltered thousands from the threat of bombs during World War I and became a town with hospital, school and chapel.

Chiswick House Chertsey Road, W4. (8995 0508) *Open Apr–Sept daily 10am–6pm; Oct daily 10–5pm; Nov–Mar Wed–Sun 10am–4pm. Adults £3.30, concessions £2.50, children (5–16) £1.70. Turnham Green underground.* One of the best examples of 18th-century English architecture and landscaping, it features sumptuous interiors, gilded decoration and fabulous ceiling paintings. There are collections of paintings and furniture, and Italianate gardens with temples, statues and a lake.

Cleopatra's Needle Victoria Embankment, WC2. *Embankment underground.* Presented to the British in 1819 by the Turkish Viceroy in Eygpt, this 3,500-year-old obelisk wasn't installed for another 59 years. A twin is in Central Park, New York.

College of Arms Queen Victoria Street, EC4 (7248 2762) *Open Mon–Fri 10am–4pm. Bank underground.* This impressive 17th-century building is the headquarters of the world of heraldry and has some relevant exhibits.

Covent Garden Piazza WC2 (7836 9136) *Covent Garden underground.* There's always lots happening around the marketplace, with many colourful stalls and shops as well as buskers, street entertainers and street theatre including clowns, acrobats, magicians, musicians and fire eaters. They've been auditioned, so the standard is generally very high.

Cutty Sark King William Walk, SE10 (8858 3445) *Open daily 10am–5pm. Greenwich rail/Cutty Sark DLR. Adults £3.50, children (5–16), concessions £2.50.* Roam the restored decks and crew's quarters of the only surviving three-masted sailing clipper, which used to transport tea from China. In dry dock, the lower hold (that's basement to you, pal) has the largest collection of merchant ship's figureheads.

Daily Express Building 121–128 Fleet Street, EC4 *Blackfriars underground/rail.* An excellent example of art deco architecture, completed in 1932.

Dinosaur Park at Crystal Palace Sydenham, SE19 (8778 7148) *Crystal Palace rail.* Crystal Palace park is home to a collection of full-scale models of 29 dinosaurs, which, although hardly Jurassic Park, are surreal all the same. Scattered over two islands on the park's boating lake, the dinosaurs, all Grade II-listed structures, were made 150 years ago. Fossils found in Wiltshire and Cornwall were among the only clues the Victorian palaeontologists had to work with – the word dinosaur had only recently been invented – but they made few mistakes all the same.

Downing Street SW1 *Westminster underground.* Number 10 has been the Prime Minister's London residence since 1735, and number 11 is the home of the Chancellor of the Exchequer. Yet this sight has probably been of more interest to metalwork enthusiasts than those interested in politics ever since huge protective gates closing off the street were installed by Margaret Thatcher in the 1980s.

East London Mosque 84–98 Whitechapel Road, E1 (7247 1357) *Open by appointment. Whitechapel underground.* A huge red-brick building blending modern design with traditional Middle Eastern themes. At 1.25pm on Fridays the *Jumma* ceremony is attended by around 3,000 local Bangladeshi.

Flaxman Gallery Central Dome, University College, Gower Street, WC1 (7679 2000) *Open Mon–Thurs 8.45–10.30am, Fri 8.45am–7pm; Sat 9.30am–4.30pm. Warren Street/Goodge Street underground.* Plaster casts by neo-classicist John Flaxman (1755–1826) are embedded in the walls of the gallery, which is within the college library. There's also a statue by Flaxman of St Michael.

The George Inn 77 Borough High Street, SE1 (7407 2056) *Open daily during licensing hours. London Bridge underground/rail.* This National Trust-owned pub appeared in Dickens' *Little Dorrit* and is the only remaining galleried coaching inn in London. It was built in 1676. Look out for the tavern clock, dating back to 1745.

Granada Cinema (Gala Bingo Club) Mitcham Road, Tooting, SW17 (8672 5717) *Tooting Broadway tube.* Contact the manager for an appointment to view this Grade I-listed 1931 building, now a bingo hall, with an interior of grand hallways, mirrors and a stunning gothic auditorium that will take you back to the heyday of Hollywood.

Golden Hinde St Mary Overie Dock, Cathedral Street, SE1 (08700 118700) *Opening times vary, check for details. Adults £2.50, concessions £2.10, children (4–13) £1.75. London Bridge under-*

ground/rail. Berthed between London Bridge and South-wark Bridge, this is an excellent full-size reconstruction of Sir Francis Drake's Tudor warship which circumnavigated the globe between 1577 and 1580.

Golders Green Crematorium Hoop Lane, NW11 (8455 2374) *Open daily summer 9am–7pm; winter 9am–5pm. Golders Green underground.* Over a quarter of a million people have been cremated here since 1902, including Peter Cook, Joyce Grenfell, Sigmund Freud, Marc Bolan, Peter Sellers, Alexander Fleming, T.S. Eliot and Kipling – Rudyard, not Mr. Also in Hoop Lane is a Jewish cemetery open Sun–Fri 8.30am–5pm.

Great Ormond Street Hospital for Children Exhibition Peter Pan Gallery, 55 Great Ormond Street, WC1 (7405 9200) *Open by appointment. Russell Square/Holborn underground.* This Georgian townhouse opposite the hospital contains exhibits relating to the history of the renowned hospital.

Greenwich Foot Tunnel Cutty Sark Gardens, Greenwich SE10 and Island Gardens E14. *Open 24 hours. Greenwich rail/Cutty Sark/Island Gardens DLR.* Opened in 1902, the cold, damp, echoey tunnel connects Greenwich with the Isle of Dogs and kids love it. If you don't want to use the steps, the lift service runs Mon–Sat 7am–7pm; Sun 10am–5.30pm; but ring 8854 8888 ext 5493 to confirm. Devotees can also check out nearby Woolwich Foot Tunnel.

Gresham College Barnard's Inn Hall, EC1 (7831 0575) *Open Mon–Fri 9.30am–5pm. Chancery Lane underground.* Telephone to arrange an appointment to see the beautiful centuries-old wood-panelled hall with its illuminated windows in this unusual college that was founded by City merchant Sir Thomas Gresham in 1597. To this day it still puts on interesting lectures for the general public.

Guildhall Gresham Street, EC2 (7606 3030) *Open Apr–Sept daily 9.30am–5pm; Oct–Mar Mon–Fri 9.30am–5pm; Sat 9.30am– 12.30pm. Guided tours by arrangement with the Keeper's Office. Bank underground.* Originally built in 1411 and the centre of the City's local government. Only the walls of the huge Great Hall, crypt and porch survive from the medieval building which was greatly damaged in the Great Fire and the Blitz. The Lord Mayor and Sheriffs are elected here and it is the centre for many traditional ceremonies. Visitors can attend the ceremony-clad meetings of the Lord Mayor's Court of Common Council every third Thursday except in August (ring for more details).

Highgate Cemetery Swain's Lane N6 (8340 1834) *Opening times / tour times vary. Admission, East Cemetery £3, tour of West Cemetery £2. Archway underground.* Beautiful in many places, spooky in others, Karl Marx is one particularly distinguished resident here.

House of St Barnabas-in-Soho 1 Greek Street, W1 (7437 1894) *Open most Mondays and Wednesdays for short guided tours but ring for an appointment. Tottenham Court Road underground.* This charming Georgian mansion built around 1746 has been home to a charity for homeless women since 1862 and provides an insight into a pre-depraved Soho. The tour covers the work of the charity, but visitors also get to see the record rooms and Council Chamber with all their interior decorations preserved including beautiful rococo plasterwork and chandeliers. The courtyard, where Dickens based Dr Alexander Manette's house in *A Tale of Two*

Cities, and a little Byzantine-style chapel are also visited. Longer tours lasting around an hour are also available.

HMS *Belfast* Morgan's Lane, Tooley Street, SE1 (7940 6328) *Open daily Mar–Oct 10am–6pm; Nov–Feb 10am–5pm. Adults £5, concessions £3.90, under-16s FREE. London Bridge underground/rail.* Seven decks and the engine and boiler rooms of this spectacular 1938-built battlecruiser are great fun to explore.

The Inns of Court (Gray's Inn, Lincoln's Inn, Inner Temple and Middle Temple) Holborn, WC2 *Holborn/Temple underground.* London's barristers work from the four Inns – or medieval colleges. All allow public access to parts of their peaceful grounds, the best times usually being mid-morning or mid-afternoon on weekdays. Taking a tranquil walk around the Inns (or Honourable Societies of Barristers) is like taking a big step back in history as wig- and gown-clad lawyers pass by against a backdrop of beautiful buildings going back to medieval times. Despite extensive damage during World War II, **Gray's Inn** has very restful gardens. It's at Gray's Inn Road, WC1 (7458 7800). *Open Mon–Fri 10am–4pm.* **Lincoln's Inn**, Lincoln's Inn Fields, WC2 (7405 1393) *Open Mon–Fri 9am–6pm*, is the most beautiful and least altered of the four. Its well-manicured sweeping lawns were used for executions during the Reformation. Soak up the Oxbridge college type of atmosphere. The best feature of **Middle Temple**, Middle Temple Lane, EC4 (7427 4800) is Middle Temple Hall. This is open most of the year *Mon–Fri 10am–noon, 3–4.30pm – ring and check that the Hall is not in use. Guided tours available.* Completed in 1574, it is a good example of Tudor architecture with an incredible hammerbeam roof looking down on stained-glass windows, a 9-metre table made from a single oak tree and given by Elizabeth I, and various portraits and rich carvings. Nearby is **Temple Church King's Bench Walk, Inner Temple, EC4**. Modelled upon the Church of the Holy Sepulchre in Jerusalem, this is the only circular church in the capital and contains admirable stone effigies and a 13th-century penitent's cell.

Jewel Tower Abingdon Street, SW1 (7222 2219) *Open daily Apr–Sept 10am–6pm; Oct 10am–5pm; Nov–Mar 10am–4pm. Adults £1.50, concessions £1.10, children over 5 80p. Westminster underground.* Opposite the south end of the Houses of Parliament this English Heritage building is one of only two surviving buildings of the original Palace of Westminster. It was built in 1365 by Edward III to house his personal treasure and wardrobe. There is an exhibition and a video.

Kensal Green Cemetery Harrow Road, W10 (8969 0152) *Open Mon–Sat 8.30am–5pm; Sun 10am–5pm. Kensal Green underground.* Opened in 1833, this was the first commercial Victorian graveyard. It boasts inhabitants including Trollope, Thackeray and Isambard Kingdom Brunel.

Kenwood House and the Iveagh Bequest Hampstead Lane, NW3 (8348 1286) *Open daily Nov–Mar 10am–4pm; Apr–Sept 10am–6pm; Oct 10am–5pm. Hampstead/Golders Green underground.* Kenwood, English Heritage's splendid neoclassical mansion remodelled c.1765 by Robert Adam, sits on the edge of Hampstead Heath and contains one of England's most impressive collections of paintings including pictures by artists such as Rembrandt, Vermeer, Hals, Reynolds, Turner and Gainsborough as well as an 18th-century jewellery collection and the highest quality antique furniture. Just three miles from central London, Kenwood's beautiful landscaped park has sloping lawns and a lake.

King's Road Antiques (including Antiquarius Indoor Antique Market) 135 King's Road, SW3 *Opening times are usually Mon–Sat 10am–6pm. Sloane Square underground*. With Chenil Galleries at 181 King's Road and the Chelsea Antiques Market, 245–253 King's Road, as well as over 30 more antique dealers in sw3 you can browse for hours.

Lambeth Palace Lambeth Palace Road, SE1 (7928 8282) *Waterloo underground/rail*. The imposing Tudor gateway loudly announces what has been the London residence of the Archbishop of Canterbury since 1207. The chapel and sections of the Palace survive that time and there's hammerbeam-roofed Great Hall and a gloomy crypt. Write to the bookings department to arrange a FREE tour, although unfortunately it is booked up for some months.

Leicester Square WC2 *Leicester Square underground*. Living statues, musicians and other street entertainers often perform in this bustling pedestrianised square. Be sure to walk through nearby Chinatown, especially pedestrianised Gerrard Street, with its many authentic Chinese restaurants. Also off Leicester Square is a section of the Charing Cross Road famous for its specialist bookshops.

Linley Sambourne House 18 Stafford Terrace, W8 (8742 3438) *Open Mar–Oct Wed 10am–4pm; Sun 2–5pm. Adults £3, children £1.50. High Street Kensington underground*. This 1870s home of *Punch* cartoonist Edward Linley Sambourne, retains its original fixtures, making it an authentic example of a middle-class home of the period.

Livery Companies' Halls around the City. *A limited number of tickets to view some of their grand, historic halls at various open days are available from the City of London Information Centre, St Paul's Churchyard, EC4 (7606 3030).Bank/St Paul's underground.* Livery companies, forerunners of trade unions set up in medieval times, were guilds of craftsmen and traders (such as goldsmiths, fishmongers, vintners and ironmongers) whose duties now are little more than charitable, social and ceremonial.

London Butterfly House Syon Park, Gunnersbury, Kew Bridge (8560 7272) *Open daily 10am–5.30pm. Admission £3.30. Gunnersbury underground.* Situated in Syon Park, landscaped by Capability Brown, this covered garden of tropical plants, water cascades and flowers houses over 1,000 butterflies from all over the world. You can see the butterflies feeding, courting and laying eggs. A display of foreign insects and spiders is next door.

London Wall Near Tower Hill underground station, EC3. *Tower Hill underground.* Adjacent to the station is the best preserved section of the Roman Wall, which was heightened in the Middle Ages. The wall enclosed 330 acres, stretching from Blackfriars to where the Tower of London now stands.

Mansion House Walbrook Street, EC4 (7626 2500) *Group visits of 14–40 people by application in advance. Bank underground/ DLR.* The official residence of the Lord Mayor during his term in office, this opulent neoclassical building designed by George Dance in 1739 has an impressive Egyptian Hall, State Drawing Rooms and lots of gold plate.

Marble Arch W1 *Marble Arch underground.* Designed in 1828 by John Nash, Marble Arch, based on Rome's Arch of Constantine, was designed to be a gateway to Buckingham Palace. It was moved from the Palace in 1851 to become the gateway to Hyde Park. Across the road on the edge of Hyde Park is Speaker's Corner where on Sunday mornings you can still hear people using their right to free speech to talk about a huge variety of causes.

Marble Hill House Richmond Road, Twickenham, Middlesex (8892 5115) *Adults £3.30, concessions £2.50, children (5–16) £1.70. Open Apr–Sept 10am–6pm; Oct 10am–5pm; Nov–Mar 10am–4pm. Richmond underground/rail.* Wander the extravagant gilded rooms of this riverside retreat of Henrietta Howard, a mistress of King George II, and explore the 66 acres of parkland that surround the impressive Palladian villa.

Merchant Taylors Hall 30 Threadneedle Street, EC2 (7588 7606) *Tours by appointment only: write to the Clerk of Merchant Taylors Hall. Bank/Monument underground.* This livery company has been in existence since 1327 and has remained in this particular street from 1347. The beautiful rooms, painstakenly restored, include the main hall, the great kitchen and a library.

Michelin Building Fulham Road, SW3 *South Kensington underground.* This brash art deco building was decorated in 1911 with tiles, mosaics, stained glass and motoring murals by French artists.

Monument Monument Street, EC2. (7626 2717) *Open daily 10am–5.30pm. Adults £1.50, children (5–15) 50p. Monument underground.* At 62 metres high, this is the world's highest free-standing stone column, a memorial to the Great Fire of 1666. Its height equals its distance from the baker's shop

---

where the fire started. There are lots of steps to climb, but a great view from the top.

Morden College 19 St Germans Place, SE3 (8858 3365) *Open by appointment only. Blackheath/Westcombe Park rail.* Those with a particular interest in architecture or almshouses would appreciate the College, built in its own pleasant grounds in 1695 (possibly to Sir Christopher Wren's design) for 'poor merchants . . . and such as have lost their estates by accidents, dangers and Perills of the Seas.' Nearby is The Paragon, an excellent crescent of Georgian mansions linked by Doric colonades, overlooking Blackheath.

North Greenwich Station Ordnance Crescent, SE10 (7222 1234) *North Greenwich underground.* Norman Foster's striking ultra-modern tube station is the largest in Europe.

Osterley House Osterley Park, off Jersey Road, Isleworth, Middlesex (8232 5050) *Open House: Apr–Oct Wed–Sun 1–4.30pm; Park: daily 9am–dusk. House: Adults £4.30, children (5–15) £2.15. Osterley underground.* Built in 1576, it has grand state rooms, Tudor stables and lots of parkland walks.

Pet Cemetery Near Victoria Gate entrance, Hyde Park, W2 (7298 2112) *Open by appointment. Queensway/Lancaster Gate underground.* Has graves for pets buried before 1903.

Piccadilly Circus SW1 *Piccadilly Circus underground.* Alfred Gilbert's fountain statue, Eros, the first to be made from aluminium, is dwarfed by the array of gigantic neon advertisements.

Prince Henry's Room 17 Fleet Street, EC4 (7936 4004) *Open Mon–Sat 11am–2pm. Temple underground.* Built in 1611 and named after James I's eldest son, the oak-panelled, plaster-ceilinged building contains Samuel Pepys memorabilia.

Ranger's House Chesterfield Walk, Blackheath, SE3 (8853 0035) *Open Apr–Sept daily 10am–6pm; Oct daily 10am–5pm; Nov–Mar Wed–Sun 10am–4pm. Adults £2.80, concessions £2.10, children over 5 £1.40. Blackheath/Greenwich rail.* A handsome 18th-century red-brick villa overlooking Greenwich Park with full-length Jacobean and Stuart portraits and other paintings.

The Roman Bath 5 Strand Lane, WC2 *Temple/Embankment underground.* The remains of this National Trust-owned bath, restored in the 17th century, and which may be Roman, is visible through a window from the pathway.

Rose Theatre 56 Park Street, SE1 (7593 0026) *Open daily 10am–5pm. Adults £3, concessions £2.50, children £2. London Bridge underground/rail.* A sound and light show about the history of the theatre, whose remains were discovered a decade ago.

Royal Academy of Arts Burlington House, Piccadilly, W1 (7300 5959) *Open daily 10am–6pm. Piccadilly Circus/Green Park underground.* Although admission prices to exhibitions here exceed the scope of this book, the building itself, including the 1990-built new Sackler Galleries, and some sculptures, including Michelangelo's Tondo, can be admired for FREE.

Royal Geographical Society Lowther Lane, Kensington Gore, SW7 (7589 5466) *Open Mon–Fri 10am–1pm, 2–5pm. South Kensington underground.* Only the main hall and map room of this Society, which is wholly concerned with exploration, are open to the public (and the library is too by appointment), but there are over 750,000 maps as well as paintings, expedition reports and mementoes including those belonging to Livingstone and Stanley.

Royal Hospital Royal Hospital Road, SW3 (7730 5282) *Open Mon–Sat 10am–noon, 2–4pm; also May–Sept Sun 2–4pm. Sloane Square underground.* This elegant building with grassy courtyards was built for Charles II by Sir Christopher Wren (who has made more of a mark on London's construction industry than Wimpey and Barratt Homes put together) to house veteran soldiers, and it remains the home of the Chelsea Pensioners who wear distinctive scarlet or navy-blue uniforms. See the hospital chapel off the central courtyard and the grand Great Hall. There's also a small museum and the well-kept, pretty grounds, Ranelagh Gardens.

Royal Mews Buckingham Palace Road, SW1 (7839 1377) *Open Aug–Sept Mon–Thurs 10am–4.30pm; Oct–July Tues–Thurs noon–4pm. Adults £4.30, under-17s £2. Green Park underground.* A chance to see a working department of the Royal Household. You see one of the finest working stables, a sight that is especially popular with horse-loving children. The horses are stabled in tiled stalls, there's a gleaming tack room, state coaches including the Gold State Coach used for the Queen's Coronation in 1953, private driving carriages, paintings and other such stuff.

Royal Naval College King William Walk, Greenwich SE10 (8269 4747) *Open daily 10am–5pm. Adults £3, concessions £2, FREE for accompanied under-16s and for all after 3.30pm. Greenwich/Maze Hill rail, Cutty Sark DLR.* This group of buildings, originally a naval hospital which became a college in 1873, were designed by Webb (17th century), Wren (18th century) as well as by Hawksmoor, Ripley and Vanbrugh. Now partly occupied by the University of Greenwich, the Chapel and spectacular Painted Hall are open to the public.

Royal Observatory Planetarium Greenwich SE10 (8312 6575) *Open daily Apr–Sept 10am–5pm, Oct–Mar 10am–5pm. Adults £2, children 6–16 1.50, children under 6 not admitted. Greenwich/Maze Hill rail, Cutty Sark DLR.* The Royal Observatory is £6 adult admission, but its sister building, London's only live planetarium, is a cheap alternative presenting one or two shows daily about the mysteries of the skies.

St Katherine's Dock E1 (7488 2400) *Tower Hill underground.* Stroll around the yachts, barges and a lighthouse ship at this marina and admire the restored 19th-century buildings by the Tower of London. There's live music regularly during summer lunchtimes.

St Pancras Station Euston Road, NW1 *King's Cross underground.* Particularly striking on first sight, this is classic Victorian architecture in a Gothic style. The arch, spanning 74 metres, was an astonishing feat in the 1860s.

Shri Nathji Sanatan Hindu Temple 159 Whipps Cross Road, E11 (8989 7539) *Open daily 9am–8pm. No shorts, miniskirts, sleeveless tops etc. Leytonstone underground.* A large temple with shrines to Krishna, Durga, Rama and Shiva.

Shri Swaminarayan Mandir Brentfield Road, Neasden, NW10 (8961 5031) *Open 9am–6pm. No shorts, miniskirts, sleeveless* *tops etc. Neasden underground.* Described as the 'Eighth Wonder of the World' by the *Reader's Digest*, this is the only traditional Hindu *mandir* (temple) outside India. Constructed from 3,000 tons of limestone and 2,000 tons of marble, the elaborate carving involved more than 15,000 Indian craftspeople. Children as well as adults from all cultures enjoy the spectacle of going to one of the short (25-minute) services, which are at 11.45am and 7pm daily.

Somerset House The Strand, WC2 (7845 4600) *Open Mon–Sat 10am–6pm; Sun noon–6pm. FREE except the Courtauld Gallery, Gilbert Collection. Covent Garden/Temple underground.* In the magnificent recently restored sweeping classical courtyard you can sit by the fountains, picnic and at weekends and during school holidays enjoy free entertainment. There's also a terrace and the recently restored Seaman's Hall. Activities include walks, talks, workshops and live music. There is skating on the ice rink (admission charge) around mid-December to early January. The Courtauld Gallery (adults £4, concessions £3, FREE to under-18s) has an impressive collection of Impressionist/post-Impressionist masterpieces, while the Gilbert Collection (adults £4, FREE to under-18s and students; FREE to all Mon 10am–2pm) displays gold, silver and mosaic decorative arts.

Spanish and Portuguese Synagogue Heneage Lane, off Bevis Marks, EC3 (7626 1274) *Open Sun–Wed 11.30am–2pm; Fri 11.30am–12.30pm. Telephone to arrange a short tour (donation requested) which are usually Sun 11.45am, Mon, Wed noon, Tues 11.30am. Aldgate/Liverpool Street underground.* Almost everything in this Wren-influenced building is original, including the furniture. Built by Jewish refugees in 1701, this beautifully decorated synagogue is the oldest in Britain.

Speaker's Corner North-east corner of Hyde Park, W2 *Marble Arch underground*. Soapbox orators have ranted their eccentric or sometimes sensible views at this forum of free speech since 1872 and have included Winston Churchill, Karl Marx and George Bernard Shaw. Popular subjects nowadays are religion, political philosophies, vegetarianism, pacifism and the end of the world. It must be noted that there has been an increase in bigoted speakers or disruptive religious militants of late. It's busiest on Sunday afternoons.

Staple Inn Holborn, WC1 *Courtyard open Mon–Fri 8am–8pm. Chancery Lane underground.* An especially fine half-timbered building with overhanging gables built in 1586 that provides a rare glimpse of London before the Great Fire.

Strawberry Hill St Mary's College Campus, Strawberry Hill, Twickenham (8240 4114) *Open most Sundays from Easter to Oct, 2–4.30pm; otherwise by appointment. Adults £4.75. Strawberry Hill rail.* A striking neo-Gothic folly with opulent interiors rich in details such as fan-vaulting copied from Westminster Abbey.

Sutton House 2 Homerton High Street, E9 (8986 2264) *Open Feb–Nov Wed, Sun 11.30am–5.30pm. Adults £2.10, children (5–16) 60p. Bethnal Green underground.* A National Trust-owned Tudor mansion with Tudor, Jacobean and Georgian interiors as well as medieval foundations.

Thames Barrier Unity Way, Woolwich, SE18 (8305 4188) *Visitor centre: open Mon–Fri 10am–5pm; Sat, Sun 10.30am–5.30pm.*

Adults £3.40, children (5–16), concessions £2, otherwise FREE. Charlton rail/North Greenwich underground. Even without entering the visitor centre you can easily appreciate this impressive feat of engineering, with its 10 huge movable steel gates, from the riverside. Completed in 1984 and built to protect London from tidal flooding, it is the largest barrier of its type in the world and is especially impressive when fully raised during the annual test (usually in early October, ring for the date and times). There's a pleasant riverside walk and a children's play area.

Tower Bridge EC3 (7407 0922) *Tower Hill underground.* Made of steel but clad in stone so as not look out of place next to the Tower of London (one of London's most historic sites though not cheap to enter). The bridge is occasionally raised to allow big vessels through – ring to find out when.

Tower Bridge Piazza at Butlers Wharf Shad Thames, SE1 (7403 6604) *London Bridge underground/rail.* There are some interesting shops including 'Oils and Spices' which sells . . . well, oils and spices. There are art galleries around the fountain sculpture, 'Waterfall 1991', and around this exhibit are scattered a walkman, harmonica, books and other items which on closer inspection turn out to be sculptures too. There's a good view of Tower Bridge off the piazza at the junction with Shad Thames and Horsleydown Lane, next to the Anchor Brewhouse (where John Courage purchased a small brewhouse in 1787) in this area of cobbled streets and wonderful river views. Nearby is Hay's Galleria, Tooley Street, SE1 (7403 4758), an elegant arcade of shops. It has an enormous glass atrium in a Victorian style, and an interesting fountain sculpture, 'The Navigators'.

Trafalgar Square WC2 *Charing Cross underground/rail.* The famous square designed by Nash to celebrate the great naval victory of 1805 has at its centre possibly London's most well-known landmark, Nelson's Column. The 52 metres of 1840s Corinthian column and statue dominates the Square, which plays host to political demonstrations and New Year celebrations. There are lots of sights on or near Trafalgar Square including Admiralty Arch and The Mall, the National Gallery, St Martin-in-the-Fields and Whitehall, which leads to the Palace of Westminster and Westminster Abbey.

2 Willow Road 2 Willow Road, NW3 (7435 6166) *Open Nov, Mar Sat noon–5pm; Apr–Oct Thurs–Sat noon–5pm. Adults £4.30, children (5–15) £2.15. Hampstead underground.* A striking house built in 1939 from a pioneering design by Erno Goldfinger, containing a collection of 20th-century art.

Tyburn Convent 8 Hyde Park Place, W2 (7723 7262) *Guided tours of the shrine daily at 10am, 3.30pm, 5.30pm. Marble Arch underground.* The Benedictine nuns here, who may never leave the covent, have a shrine to the Tyburn martyrs, 105 Catholics executed during the Protestant Reformation. The building is near Marble Arch, which was London's principal public execution site from the 12th to the 18th centuries when it had a three-legged gibbet known as the Tyburn tree. There are various relics and pictures of the martyrs and a model of the tree in the shrine. There are occasional 'Monastic afternoons' with a talk, slide show, tea, tour and vespers.

University College London Gower Street, WC1 (7387 7050) *Open*

Mon–Fri 9am–5pm. Euston Square/Russell Square/Goodge Street underground. The Friends' Room can provide a map and leaflet making up a self-guided tour of this impressive neoclassical building. Known as the 'godless college' as it was founded for students who couldn't enter Oxford or Cambridge because they were not Anglicans. The College Exhibition in the North Cloisters tells the story of the founding of the college and features famous staff and students of the past including Sir Stafford Cripps and Marie Stopes. In the South Cloisters of the main building is the skeleton of the philosopher Jeremy Bentham, whose ideas inspired the founders of the college. He is displayed in a hermetically sealed mahogany case in his original clothing complete with a wax death mask. The University College London also houses the Percival David Foundation of Chinese Art, the Petrie Museum of Egyptian Archaeology, the Flaxman Gallery, the Strang Print Room (mentioned under Art Galleries as 'University College Art Collection'), the Grant Museum of Zoology (listed under Museums) and a Map Library (listed under Libraries).

John Wesley's House and Chapel 47 City Road, EC1 (7253 2262) *Open Mon–Sat 10am–4pm; Sun 10am–2pm. Adults £4, concessions, children £2; FREE entry after 11am service. Old Street/Moorgate underground.* The house of John Wesley (1703–91), father of Methodism, stands next to his chapel and tomb in 'this acre of Christian heritage'. It includes seven historic buildings, mainly Georgian, two chapels, two courtyards, two museums, two pulpits and organs, and a statue of Wesley. His house contains personal items and furniture including his preaching gown, bureau, three-cornered hat and an experimental electric-shock machine.

Directly opposite is Bunhill Fields (also City Road, EC1), once a plague pit and then a burial ground for over 120,000 bodies. You can view moss-covered headstones of Daniel Defoe, John Bunyan and William Blake. The northern section is a peaceful garden.

Westminster Hall Parliament Square SW1 (7219 4273) *Contact your MP to arrange a tour, which take place each morning Parliament sits.* Built in 1099, this is the oldest remaining part of Westminster and has been the scene of many important historical events including the abdication of Edward II and the sentencing to death of Anne Boleyn. The hall has a 14th-century cantilever roof, the earliest and largest in the world.

Whitechapel Bell Foundry 32–34 Whitechapel Road, E2 (7247 2599) *Open Mon–Fri 9am–5pm. Aldgate East underground.* There is a £7 charge to tour the foundry itself – which cast America's Liberty Bell and 'Big Ben' – but the small museum is FREE.

Whitefriar's Crypt Freshfields, 65 Fleet Street, EC4 (7936 4000) *Open by appointment with the premises manager. Blackfriars underground.* Discovered by building developers in 1987, this is part of a medieval Carmelite monastery. Although you can visit the crypt by arrangement with the law firm resident in the building, it can clearly be seen from the street by looking over the railings into the basement, or walking down the steps on the left.

Whittington Stone Highgate Hill, N19 *Archway underground.* This monument, installed in 1821 to mark the spot famous 15th-century mayor Dick Whittington was supposed to have heard the bells summoning him to 'turn again', is worth a look if you are in the area.

Winchester Palace Southwark, Clink Street, SE1 (7222 1234) *London Bridge underground/rail.* An unusual circular window features in the remains of this 13th-century town house later damaged by fire.

Woolwich Foot Tunnel North Woolwich Pier, Pier Road, E16/Ferry Approach, SE18. *Open 24 hours with lift service Mon–Sat 7.30am–6pm; Sun 9am–4pm; but ring 8854 8888 ext 5493 to confirm. North Woolwich/Woolwich Dockyard/Woolwich Arsenal rail.* Kids love this walk under the Thames. See also neighbouring Greenwich Foot Tunnel.

Woolwich Ferry North Woolwich Pier, Pier Road, E16/Ferry Approach, SE18. *Open Mon–Fri 6am–8.30pm; Sat 6am–10pm; Sun 11.30am–7.30pm. North Woolwich/Woolwich Dockyard/Woolwich Arsenal rail.* Although the paddlesteamers dating from 1889 are no more, kids love the short journey across the Thames.

BANKS

London's grand and traditional private banks, conveniently located near each other, provide an interesting insight into London's past.

Child and Co. 1 Fleet Street, EC4 (7353 4080) *Temple underground.* Established in 1559, it has a small museum with banking memorabilia.

Coutts 440 Strand, WC2 (753 1000) *Charing Cross underground/rail.* Although you can hardly fail to miss Coutts' brash, modern facade each time you leave Charing Cross station, it too has a rich history going back to 1692, and is most well known for being the purveyor of the Queen's cash-point card and other banking requirements. Telephone the archivist to arrange a tour of Coutts, which covers over 300 years of the bank's history. Although he deprecatingly described the historical displays as being 'a poor man's Bank of England Museum,' you get to see the boardroom with its splendid 18th-century hand-painted Chinese wall-paper and a replica 17th-century goldsmith's shop.

Drummonds 49 Charing Cross Road, WC2 (7839 1200) *Charing Cross underground/rail* Tucked away in a corner of Trafalgar Square, Drummonds, which is a branch of the Royal Bank of Scotland, boasts a grand banking hall with antique clocks and chandeliers. Customers can still sign their cheques with goose quills dipped in pewter inkwells. There are eight muskets housed in a cabinet by the entrance, which the bank bought to protect employees from the mob after the Gordon Riots of 1780.

Goslings 19 Fleet Street, EC4 (0845 7550088) *Temple underground*. Also has memorabilia.

Hoare's 37 Fleet Street, (7353 4522) *Temple underground*. A particularly good example of a bank of long ago.

CLOCKS

London has some interesting timepieces.

Big Ben Palace of Westminster (the Houses of Parliament) at Parliament Square, SW1 *Westminster underground*. The elabor-ate clock tower is particularly impressive at night when the clockface is lit up. A close-up visit, including a walk behind the huge clockface, is by application to your MP, although there may be a long wait to get on a tour. Strictly speaking, 'Big Ben' is not the name of the clock but of the huge bell that produces that famous ring.

Selfridges Clock 400 Oxford Street, W1 *Bond Street/Marble Arch underground*. There is a fine art deco clock at the main entrance.

But there's also clocks that do more than just tell the time. These put on a show.

Neal's Yard Wholefood Warehouse Shorts Gardens, WC2 *Covent Garden underground*. Here there is an inventive clock where the minute hand is a tube gradually filling with water until, on the hour, bells ring and the water tips out from watering cans onto flowers. Until a redesign, it soaked passers by too.

The Fortnum & Mason Clock 181 Piccadilly, W1 *Piccadilly Circus underground*. It springs into life on the hour when models of Mr Fortnum and Mr Mason meet and bow to each other. The Eton school anthem follows, and then the shopkeepers disappear.

Swiss Centre Clock Leicester Square, W1 *Piccadilly Circus/Leicester Square underground*. The clock plays tunes on a glockenspiel to a procession of alpine animals at noon, 6pm, 7pm and 8pm and at additional times at weekends.

Clockmakers' Company Museum The Clockroom, Guildhall Library, Aldermanbury, EC2 (7606 3030) *Open May–Sept daily 10am–5pm; Oct–Apr Mon–Sat 10am–5pm. Bank/Moorgate underground*. Hundreds of exhibits here illustrate 500 years of timekeeping. Try and visit on the hour, at noon if possible.

Sightseeing After Dark

Many of London's buildings and monuments look even more striking lit up at night than in the day. Areas not to be missed at night include boisterous Covent Garden, WC2, the Las Vegas-style nocturnal version of Harrods (hope they're on economy-seven), Knightsbridge, SW7, the space-station Lloyds Building, Leadenhall Street, EC3, wild Soho, W1, the Tower of London, Tower Hill, EC3 and of course, Piccadilly Circus, W1.

St James's to Parliament Square *St James's/Westminster under-ground*. A good place to start is the bridge over the lake in **St James's Park,** which is open until dusk. From here you can see **Buckingham Palace** floodlit over the lake. **The Mall,** bordering the park, is one of London's finest thoroughfares at night having the Palace at one end and **Admiralty Arch** at the other and fine Regency Nash terraces in between. Admiralty Arch is a huge Edwardian trio of arches domi-nating the south-west corner of **Trafalgar Square.** Passing through the huge arches you come to the illuminated fountains, statues and impressive buildings of Trafalgar Square, including an impressively floodlit **St Martin-in-the-Fields,** one of London's grandest churches. **Whitehall** on the right, is lined by well-lit, generally 18th-century buildings and at the end of this wide, elegant road is **Parliament Square** with **The Houses of Parliament** and **Westminster Abbey,** the oldest and most eminent of London's great churches. A floodlit **Big Ben** towers over the 1862-built **Westminster Bridge,** which is over 25 metres wide.

Victoria Embankment *Westminster underground*. A walk along **Victoria Embankment, SW1, WC2 and EC4** takes you from **Westminster Bridge** to **Blackfriars Bridge** and passes permanently moored ships and various prominent buildings. On the way **Hungerford Foot Bridge** provides an unforgettable panorama of the river from **Cleopatra's Needle** to the **Festival Hall** at the South Bank Centre and slightly further on, **Waterloo Bridge** has particularly good views of the illuminated river, taking in Westminster and the City.

Bankside, SE1 *Waterloo rail/underground*. The riverside walk at Bankside, SE1, by Southwark Bridge, has good views of the City and St Paul's. Pepys watched the City burn in 1666 from an alehouse here, and the flames must have looked rather pretty, especially when reflected upon the water. Opened in 1894, majestic Tower Bridge, was built incorporating Gothic towers so that it harmonises with the Tower of London nearby, and this has led many people to assume it was built in the Middle Ages.

Battersea Bridges *Battersea rail*. Two bridges worthy of a visit include the triple-arched Albert Bridge, sw3/sw11, whose elaborate Victorian ironwork is enhanced by hundreds of white lights and the nearby Chelsea Bridge, sw1/sw8.

Canary Wharf Tower West India Docks, Isle of Dogs, E14. Even at night you can't escape Canary Wharf Tower. **The Telecom Tower** Cleveland Street, W1, is a bit more modest.

Marble Arch W1 *Marble Arch underground*. This and the huge

Wellington Arch, Hyde Park Corner, SW1, are particularly impressive at night. The latter houses a police station.

St Paul's Cathedral Ludgate Hill, EC4 *St Paul's underground.* Considered to be Christopher Wren's masterpiece despite being widely disliked when it opened for business in 1710, warrants a nighttime glimpse.

Westminster Cathedral Ashley Place, SW1. *Victoria underground/ rail.* The imposing Byzantine-style principal Catholic Church is worth seeing lit up at night.

Skating

Serpentine in Hyde Park to Embankment *Most Wednesday evenings at 7pm. Hyde Park Corner/Marble Arch underground.* If you own skates or rollerblades, as well as travelling the capital for FREE, you can join hundreds of other enthusiasts for a mass skate from the Serpentine in Hyde Park to the Embankment.

Somerset House The Strand, WC2 (7845 4600) *Check for times and admission charges. Charing Cross/Covent Garden/Temple underground.* From mid-December to early January you can ice-skate in the open air at Somerset House.

Swimming

London contains many swimming pools and most of these are unexceptional. Therefore those detailed below are either FREE, cheaper or better value than the norm or offer more than the average. Sportsline (7222 8000) can advise of your nearest pool.

Brockwell Lido Dulwich Road, Herne Hill, SE24 (7274 3088) *Open May—Sept Mon—Fri 7—10am, noon—7pm; Sat, Sun 11am—7pm. Adults, morning £2, afternoon £4; children under 16 morning £1.50, afternoon £2.50. Children under 5 FREE. Herne Hill rail. A 1930s pool on the edge of leafy Brockwell Park.*

Chelsea Sports Centre Chelsea Manor Street, SW3 (7352 6985) *Open Mon—Fri 7am—10pm; Sat 8am—6pm; Sun 8am—10pm. Adults £2.70, under-16s £1.40. Sloane Square underground. Teaching pool and 25-metre pool.*

Finchley Lido Great North Leisure Park, High Road, Finchley, N12 (8343 9830) *Open Mon 6.45—8.30am, 9am—6.30pm; Tues, Thurs, Fri 6.45am—9.30pm; Wed 6.30am—8pm; Sat, Sun 9am—4.30pm. Adults £2.70, concessions £1.35—£1.95. Finchley Central underground.*

Highbury Pool Highbury Crescent, N5 (7704 2312) *Open Mon—Fri 6.30am—9pm; Sat 7.30am—7pm; Sun 7.30am—9pm. Adults £2.80, under-16s £1.20. Highbury and Islington underground/rail.*

Oasis Sports Centre 32 Endell Street, WC2 (7831 1804) *Indoor pool open Mon—Fri 6.30am—6.30pm; Sat, Sun 9.30am—5pm; outdoor pool open Mon—Fri 7.30am—9pm; Sat, Sun 9.30am—5pm. Adults £2.90, under-16s £1.19. Holborn underground.*

Parliament Hill Lido Hampstead Heath, off Gordon House Road, Kentish Town NW5 (7485 3873) *Open daily May—Sept 7—9.30am, 10am—6pm; Oct—Mar daily 7—9.30am. Adults £3.70, children £1.50; FREE 7—9.30am. Mixed bathing. Hampstead underground.*

Ponds on Hampstead Heath It's FREE to swim in the following open-air ponds hidden by trees on Hampstead Heath. Being chlorine-free it is inadvisable to touch the slimy ground. Look out for anglers too. These ponds are deep and for competent swimmers only. *Open all year, 7am to sunset. Further details: 7485 4491.*

Hampstead Mixed Bathing Pond *off East Heath Road, Hampstead NW3* **Highgate Men's Pond,** *off Millfield Lane, Highgate N6.* The summer sees men sunbathing naked by this pond, despite it contravening an old health regulation.

Kenwood Ladies' Pond *off Millfield Lane, Highgate, N6.* This pond for women only has a changing hut and shower.

Richmond Pools on the Park Old Deer Park, Twickenham Road, Richmond, Surrey (8940 0561) *Opening times and admission prices vary. Richmond underground/rail.*

Serpentine Lido Hyde Park, W2 (7298 2100) *Open July–Aug Mon–Fri, times and admission prices vary. Knightsbridge underground.*

Seymour Leisure Centre Seymour Place, W1 (7723 8019) *Open Mon–Fri 7am–10pm; Sat, Sun 8am–8pm. Adults £2.15, children 85p. Edgware Road underground.* As well as a relatively inexpensive centrally located pool, there are facilities that include a steam room, sauna and gym.

Tooting Bec Lido Tooting Bec Road, Tooting Bec Common, SW17 (8871 7198) *Open June–Sept daily 10am–8pm. Adults £2.60–£3.10, children £2.10–£2.25. Children under 5 FREE. Tooting Bec underground.*

Waterfront Leisure Centre Woolwich High Street, SE18 (8317 5000) *Open Mon–Fri 7am–11pm; Sat, Sun 9am–9.30pm.*

Admission prices vary. Woolwich Arsenal rail. A large, better-than-average civic swimming pool complex.

Television and Radio Shows

For FREE tickets write (enclosing a stamped, addressed envelope) or ring as far in advance as possible as some shows have huge waiting lists. You may have to wait for some months or even a year or more to see especially popular shows like *Blind Date* and *Top of the Pops* and those with a high celebrity quota. Even so, you may be able to pick up tickets for some popular shows at very short notice.

BBC *Television*: for details of forthcoming shows, write, stating the show you would like to see, to the BBC TV Ticket Unit, Room 301, Television Centre, Wood Lane, London W12 7RJ (8743 8000, recorded information and answerphone: 8576 1227). *Radio*: write to the BBC Radio Ticket Unit, P.O. Box 3000, London W12 7RJ (8576 1227). Most BBC TV shows are recorded at TV Centre in Shepherd's Bush. Most BBC radio shows are recorded at the BBC Radio Theatre at Broadcasting House, W1; the Hippodrome, North End Road, NW11; and the Maida Vale Studios, Delaware Road, W9. Ask to join the BBC's mailing list to get up-to-date news.

ITV *For LWT, Carlton and other ITV shows write to The Ticket Unit, London Television Centre, Upper Ground, London SE1 (7620 1620).* The Duty Office at Carlton Television (7615 1515/7240 4000) or Channel 4 (7306 8333) can give you details of shows coming up.

Channel 5 *Contact the Channel 5 Duty Office, P.O. Box 55, Nottingham NG1 5HE (08457 050505).*

Independent TV Production Companies Companies such as Hat Trick (*Have I Got News For You* etc.) and Smith and Jones' Talkback place classified advertisements in publications such as *Time Out* and *Private Eye* when tickets are available. Or you could contact individual independent production companies themselves.

Powerhouse (7240 2828) can fix up free tickets for programmes on all channels.

Theatre, Live Comedy and Shows

The Albany Douglas Way, SE8 (8692 4446) *Ticket prices vary. New Cross rail.* As well as a very varied theatre programme, there's comedy, dance and music.

Barbican Centre Silk Street, EC2 (7638 8891) *Tickets from £5. Barbican underground.* London home of the Royal Shakespeare Company, there's an excellent variety of modern and classical plays, and musicals.

Battersea Arts Centre (BAC) Lavender Hill, SW11 (7223 2223) *Tickets from £4 and 'pay what you can' on Tuesdays. Clapham Junction rail.* BAC continually presents an exciting and diverse range of theatre productions and other events. You can see them for FREE if you can spare some time in the evenings, joining the friendly Front of House team as a volunteer. Call 7223 6557 for details.

Bird's Nest Theatre, 32 Deptford Church Street, SE8 (8694 2255)

Tickets from £4. Deptford rail. A pub theatre with a varied programme including work by new writers as well as the classics.

Blackheath Halls 23 Lee Road, Blackheath SE3 (8463 0100) *Tickets from around £5 for adults, £3 for children. Blackheath rail.* Children's puppet and theatre productions are often performed on Saturday afternoons at around 3pm.

Bridewell Theatre Bride Lane, EC1 (7936 3456) *Tickets from £5. Chancery Lane underground.* A small theatre specialising in racy musicals.

Brockley Jack Theatre 410 Brockley Road, SE4 (8291 6354) *Ticket prices vary. Crofton Park rail.* A small theatre with a variety of productions.

Bushy Park Hampton Court Road, Middlesex, TW12 (8979 1586) *Hampton Wick rail.* The summer entertainment season often includes FREE open air theatre performances, usually Shakespeare in July. Other open spaces in the Richmond Borough occasionally have FREE summer theatre performances – ring the arts section on 8332 0534 for details.

Chelsea Centre World's End Place, King's Road, SW10 (7352 1967) *Tickets from £5. Sloane Square underground.* Often premieres new works.

Cosmic Comedy Club 177 Fulham Palace Road, W6 (7381 2006) *Hammersmith underground.* Admission is FREE on Tuesday evenings, with untried stand-up comedy acts facing the audience, while on Thursdays you pay on leaving, however much you think is worth paying.

Downstairs at The Kings Head 2 Crouch End Hill, N8 (8340 1028)

Finsbury Park underground/rail. Admission charges for the Wednesday to Sunday comedy shows at 8.30pm vary from FREE upwards.

East Dulwich Cabaret East Dulwich Tavern, 1 Lordship Lane, SE22 (8299 4138) *Monday and Thursday comedy nights here are £3 adult admission, £2 concessions. East Dulwich rail.*

The Gate Theatre The Prince Albert, 11 Pembridge Road, W11 (7229 0706) *Notting Hill Gate underground*. A good pub theatre with 'pay what you want' on Mondays.

George Inn 77 Borough High Street, SE1 (7407 2056) *Borough underground*. Dating from 1542 and mentioned in *Little Dorrit*, this old pub regularly holds performances of Shakespeare plays in its courtyard in summer.

Greenwich Park SE10 (8858 2608) *Greenwich/Maze Hill rail/ Cutty Sark DLR*. The summer entertainment season often includes FREE open-air theatre performances and theatre and puppet shows for children – ring for details.

Guildhall School of Music and Drama Silk Street, Barbican, EC2 (7628 2571) *Barbican underground*. During term time you can see a whole variety of drama productions for free and the standards are very high indeed. Matinees in the main house and all plays in the studio are FREE. Write to the general office for an events diary.

Kids' Week *Last week of August* A huge entertainment extravaganza in which about 25 West End theatres allow children to see their shows for FREE, although adults have to pay. There are also many free theatre workshops and activities. Ring 0870 0732000 for details.

King's Head Theatre 115 Upper Street, N1 (7226 1916) *Tickets from £4. Angel/Highbury and Islington underground.* An excellent pub theatre staging plays and musicals.

Lauderdale House Community Arts Centre Highgate Hill, Waterlow Park, Highgate Hill, N6 (8348 8716) *Adult admission often under £5. Archway underground.* Saturday afternoon children's shows, cabaret, poetry readings and plays.

Lyric Theatre King Street, W6 (8741 2311) *Tickets from £5. Hammersmith underground.* The first performance of each of the Lyric's own productions (not staged by other theatre companies) is FREE to residents of Hammersmith and Fulham borough.

Orange Tree Theatre 1 Clarence Street, Richmond, Surrey (8940 3633) *Tickets from £5. Richmond underground/rail.* A small space specialising in costume drama.

Oval House 52–54 Kennington Oval, SE11 (7582 7680) *Tickets from £5. Oval underground.* Gay and lesbian works.

Rose Theatre 56 Park Street, SE1 (7593 0026) *Adults £3, concessions £2.50, children 5–15 £2. London Bridge underground/rail.* The 16th-century Rose Theatre is still to be excavated and until then the space is being used for a light and sound presentation about it.

Royal Court Theatre Sloane Square, SW1 (7565 5000) *Tickets occasionally start from an incredible 10p, and all seats are £5 on Mondays and often start from £5 on other days. Sloane Square underground.* Champion theatre of new writing.

Royal George Theatre 85 Tanners Hill, SE8 (8692 2594) *Tickets* *from £5. New Cross rail.* A pub theatre specialising in classic plays.

Shakespeare's Globe New Globe Walk, Bankside SE1 (7401 9919) *Tickets from £5. Blackfriars/Mansion House underground.* From May to September, Shakespeare plays are performed in the open air theatre that is an impressive replica of the original Globe.

Southwark Playhouse 62 Southwark Bridge Road, SE1 (7620 3494) *All tickets cost £5 on Mondays. London Bridge underground/rail.*

Theatre Museum Russell Street, WC2 (7943 4700) *Covent Garden underground.* The museum stages occasional FREE play readings, usually of new works by British writers. If you pay the admission charge (adults £4.50, concessions £2.50, under-16s and over-60s FREE) there are regular theatre make-up demonstrations, activity workshops, costume workshops and other activities.

Theatre Royal Stratford East Gerry Raffles Square, Stratford E15 (8534 0310) *Tickets from £5. Stratford underground/rail.* A wide range of theatre, much of it community-based.

tkts Leicester Square, WC2 *Open Mon–Sat 10am–7pm; Sun noon–3.30pm. Leicester Square underground.* At this booth on the Square, run by the Society of London Theatre, you can get up to four seats for as much as half price on the day of performance only, subject to a £2.50 service fee. It's best to queue from around noon–2pm for matinee tickets and from around 2.30pm for evening tickets.

Unicorn Theatre for Children Unicorn at the Pleasance Theatre,

Carpenters Mews, North Road, N7 (7700 0702) *Tickets for the plays, specifically for 4- to 12-year-olds, start at £5. Caledonian Road underground.*

Tourist Information Centres

Many of these offices can provide a FREE map of central London and public transport plans as well as leaflets and advice. London-wide information is available from London Line, telephone 09068 663344.

Bloomsbury 35–36 Woburn Place, WC1 *Open daily 7.30am– 7.30pm. Russell Square underground.*

British Travel Centre 12 Regent Street, W1 *Open Mon–Fri 9am– 6.30pm; Sat, Sun 10am–4pm. Piccadilly Circus underground.*

Capital Helpline (7484 4000) Will try to answer most tourism queries and also questions about many other subjects too, or refer callers to someone who could help.

Chelsea Information Office Old Town Hall, King's Road, SW3 (7352 1856/7352 6056) *Open Mon–Fri 9am–1pm; 2–5pm. Sloane Square underground.*

City of London Information Centre St Paul's Churchyard, EC4 (7332 1456) *Open Apr–Sept daily 9.30am–5pm; Oct–Mar Mon–Fri 9.30am–5pm; Sat 9.30am–12.30pm. St Paul's underground.*

Croydon Tourist Information Centre Katharine Street, Croydon, Surrey (8253 1009) *Open Mon–Fri 9.30am–6pm; Sat 9am– 5pm. East/West Croydon underground.*

Disabled Access *General enquiries – Tripscope (8994 9294); Access on London Transport – The Unit for Disabled Passengers (7918 3312); Access arrangement for tourist attractions and places of entertainment in London – Artsline (7388 2227).*

Greenwich Tourist Information Centre Pepys House, 2 Cutty Sark Gardens, SE10 (0870 608 2000) *Open daily 10.15am–4.45pm. Greenwich rail/Cutty Sark DLR.*

Hackney Museum Tourist Information Centre Central Hall, Mare Street, E8 (8985 9055) *Open Tues–Fri 10am–12.30pm; 1.30–5pm; Sat 1.30–5pm. Hackney Central rail.*

Harrow Tourist Information Centre Civic Centre, Station Road, Harrow, Middlesex (8424 1103) *Open Mon–Fri 9am–5pm. Harrow and Wealdstone rail.*

Heathrow Airport Terminals 1, 2 and 3, Underground Concourse *Open daily 8am–6pm.*

Hillingdon Tourist Information Centre Central Library, High Street, Uxbridge, Middlesex (01895 250706) *Open Mon, Tues, Thurs 9.30am–8pm; Wed, Fri 9.30am–5.30pm; Sat 9.30am–4pm. Uxbridge underground.*

Hounslow Tourist Information Centre 24 Treaty Centre, Hounslow, Middlesex (8572 8279) *Open Mon–Sat 9.30am–5.30pm. Hounslow Central underground.*

Islington Visitor Centre 44 Duncan Street, N1 (7278 8787) *Open Mon–Sat 10am–5pm. Angel underground.*

Kidsline *(7222 8070) Operational term time Mon–Fri 4–6pm; school holidays Mon–Fri 9am–4pm.* Gives information on shows, activities etc suitable for children.

Lewisham Tourist Information Centre 199–201 Lewisham High Street, SE13 (8297 8317) *Open Mon–Fri 10am–5pm. Lewisham rail/DLR.*

Liverpool Street Station Tourist Information Centre Underground Station, EC2. *Open Mon–Fri 8am–6pm; Sat, Sun 9am–5.30pm.*

London Docklands Visitor Centre 3 Limeharbour, Isle of Dogs, E14 (7512 1111) *Open Mon–Fri 9am–6pm; Sat 10am–4.30pm; Sun 9am–4.30pm. Crossharbour DLR.* Free maps and general information about the area as well as an exhibition and an audio-visual presentation.

London Transport Enquiries Victoria Station, SW1 (7222 1234) *Office open Mon–Sat 8.15am–7.30pm; Sun 8.45am–7.30pm; telephone service open 24 hours. Victoria underground/rail.*

National Trust Tourist Office Blewcoat School, 23 Caxton Street, SW1 (7222 2877) *Open Mon–Fri 10am–5.30pm. St James's Park underground.* The Trust's London centre is housed in this early-18th-century schoolroom.

Redbridge Tourist Information Centre Town Hall, 128–142 High Road, Ilford, IG1 (8478 3020) *Open Mon–Fri 9am–5pm. Ilford rail.*

Richmond Tourist Information Centre Old Town Hall, Whittaker Avenue, Richmond, Surrey (8940 9125) *Open Mon–Fri 10am–6pm; Sat 10am–5pm and in the summer Sun 10.30am–4pm. Richmond underground/rail.*

Selfridges Tourist Information Basement Services Arcade, Oxford Street, W1 (7629 1234) *Open Mon–Wed 9.30am–7pm; Thurs,*

Fri 9.30am–8pm; Sat 9.30am–6.30pm. Bond Street underground.

Southwark Information Centre 6 Tooley Street, SE1 (7403 8299) *Open Easter–Oct Mon–Sat 10am–6pm; Sun 10.30pm–5.30pm; Nov–Easter Mon–Sat 10am–4pm; Sun 11am–4pm. London Bridge underground/rail.*

Tower Hamlets Tourist Information 107a Commercial Street, E1 (7375 2549) *Open Mon–Fri 9.30am–4.30pm. Liverpool Street underground.*

Twickenham Tourist Information Centre Civic Centre, York Street, Twickenham, Middlesex (8891 7272) *Open Mon–Fri 9am–5pm. Twickenham rail.*

Victoria Station Tourist Information Centre Victoria Station forecourt, SW1 (8297 8317) *Open Mon–Sat 8am–7pm; Sun 8am–6pm.*

Waterloo International Terminal Tourist Information Centre Arrivals Hall, South Bank, SE1 (8297 8317) *Open daily 8.30am–10.30pm.*

Voluntary Work

GO London (7643 1341) which is part of Community Service Volunteers, has FREE events every couple of weeks or so at weekends, allowing people to help with various community projects around the capital. There's no payment but you may get a free lunch and refreshments.

Walking in London

Most Londoners walk regularly from work to home, from home to the shops, but walking as a pastime in London is so often overlooked. There is so much to see that it is difficult to take it all in. And when you are crammed into a packed commuter train, you just want to get home: a peaceful, leisurely walk is usually the last thing to be considered. A pity, as one of the best ways to get to know the city is on foot.

Of course, location is the important factor when planning a walk, and for that reason most of us would first consider destinations such as the Lake District, the Highlands of Scotland or the moors of Cornwall if we were going to reserve leisure time for walking.

It would seem ill-advised instead to spend our free hours in this polluted, congested and aggressive capital. Walking the Ridgeway in London means nothing more than going from commuter-hell Hayes railway station in the west to a boring Bromley playing field in the east, a somewhat disappointing experience when compared to its 85-mile counterpart situated on the North Wessex Downs, which flow into the Chilterns. Likewise, one can assume that the Pennine Way, off Cotswold Close in Bexleyheath, leaves much to be desired.

Yet even the most cursory glance at the *London A to Z* map shows that the capital can provide a wealth of walks, and even some peace and quiet for the prospective urban explorer. As Disraeli pointed out, London is a nation, not a city.

The areas around Westminster and the City were what was originally London, but as it grew it swallowed up the villages around it. Until well into the 19th century places like Richmond, Streatham and Islington were able to enjoy a separate existence. Maybe London will eventually become a *notion*, not a city, when it has expanded enough to cover the whole of the south-east.

Britain's capital has the advantage of being suitable for walking. Walking is usually the fastest way to travel around the increasingly gridlocked city. From Leicester Square, for example, you can walk to Soho or Trafalgar Square in just a few minutes. Unlike Paris or Rome, cars actually stop for you. Unlike New York, the chances of being attacked are relatively remote in all but the most dubious of areas.

When on foot you notice the smallest architectural detail, a hidden courtyard, a little alleyway. There is probably more culture crammed into London than anywhere else in the world, and there is no better way to take in a bit of culture than by slowly walking around it. And a walk in London, however long, does not require the use of hiking boots, ropes and distress flares.

Even so, tarmac is somewhat harder on the feet than turf and the impure air can exhaust. The incessant noise and bustle in some locations can add to the stress. It's worth bearing in mind that inner city areas, and especially the City, tend to be quieter at weekends while parks and gardens are emptier on weekdays.

Understanding the intricacies of an Ordnance Survey map is also a skill you will not require. The indexed *London A-Z Street Atlas* (published by Geographers' A-Z Map Co.) is quite easy to comprehend. Less detailed but FREE London maps are available from underground stations and Tourist Information Centres.

Tourist Information Centres (see page 213) can provide details of guided and self-guided walks and tours. They also can provide FREE or inexpensive booklets and leaflets too.

There are even walks that are clearly signposted or walks with waymarks. There are metal discs set in the pavement along the City of London's **Heritage Walk** for example. The 12.7-mile **Silver Jubilee Walk** is marked by a series of silver crowns in the pavement, and Parliament Square is a good place to start from. Free maps for these two are available from the **City of London Information Centre** St Paul's Churchyard, EC4 (7332 1456). *Open April—September daily 9.30am—5pm; October—March Mon—Fri 9.30am—5pm; Sat 9.30am—12.30pm.*

The **London Loop** is a sort of M25 for walkers, a 150-mile circular walk through countryside in outer London, broken up into 24 sections. The **Capital Ring** is a circular walk of 72 miles linking green spaces, rivers and canals a ten-mile radius from Charing Cross. **The London Walking Forum (7793 1116)** can provide leaflets on these.

The London Wall Walk follows the course of the old city wall plaques. **The Museum of London** 150 London Wall, EC2 (7600 3699) can provide a map. *Open Tues—Sat 10am—6pm, Sun 2pm—6pm.*

If your wish is for open space, Greater London has an enormous amount of it. Every Londoner is in walking distance of it, a unique situation. Not endless fields with nothing but a closed pub at the end of them – like you'd find in the Lake District – but hundreds and hundreds of parks, public gardens, commons and meadows making up over 60 square miles of the metropolis. In London there are nearly 400 parks with more than 20 acres.

There's Hyde Park, covering over 350 acres, to little patches of green like Embankment Gardens around Charing Cross, and many, many municipal open spaces that only the locals know about. Indeed, there are substantial pockets of green on almost every page of a London street atlas.

The amount of parkland and open space owned by the 32 London boroughs varies enormously. While Hillingdon has well over 3,000 acres, Islington has about 175. Desperate to imply it is overflowing with lawns and gardens, it has the cheek to call a scrap of land off Upper Street 'Islington Green', despite it being barely bigger than a window box.

Henry James wrote over a hundred years ago: 'It takes London to put you in the way of a purely rustic walk from Notting Hill to Whitehall. You may traverse this immense distance – a most comprehensive diagonal – altogether on soft fine turf amid the song of birds, the bleat of lambs, the ripple of ponds and the rustle of innumerable trees.'

Only the lambs are gone. It is a miracle that one can still begin a walk from Queensway tube station, going through Kensington Gardens, then across Hyde Park and on to

Green Park, ending up in the south-east corner of St James's Park near Parliament Square, with only one or two roads to navigate. Such a stroll must torture property developers, as they dream of the marvellously profitable housing estates the could cram into that huge expanse of greenery.

Of course, when the London parks are empty you can find tranquillity but even – maybe due to the British reserve – in the height of summer you can sunbathe, lying on your back along with 10,000 others, yet still be quite alone.

The 39-mile signposted **Green Chain Walk** in south-east London links the banks of the River Thames with nearly 300 open spaces such as woods, parks and gardens. Along the walk you could see squirrels, voles, foxes, jays and woodpeckers, and if you take a detour at Woodlands Farm at Shooters Hill you will come across a herd of cows and a couple of horses. The route is full of historical buildings, including the moatbridge at Eltham Palace, Severndroog Castle in Jackwood, a 1784 summerhouse, Jacobean Charlton House and the ruins of Lesnes Abbey. **Chislehurst Common** (*Chislehurst/Petts Wood rail*) is on the **Green Chain Walk** and also on the **Petts Wood Circular Walk,** where you'll walk past working farms and woods that house bats, weasels, rabbits and foxes.

For a Green Chain pack of ten weatherproof routecards with maps, directions and features of interest, send a cheque for £3.50 payable to Greenwich Council to their Project Officer, SE London Green Chain, P.O. Box 22119, SE18 6WY. Telephone the Project Office for more details on 8921 5028.

You'd think that few people would rush to a sewage treatment works in search of a worthwhile walk. Yet Thames Water is adamant that its **Creek Trail** at its works in Jenkins Lane, Beckton, Barking, is 'one of the most important ecological locations within the London area.' The wildlife trail has been left in its natural state for 20 years, and has an abundance of reed beds and grassland, and a variety of birds, plants, insects and other wildlife. Because times available for visiting are subject to tides, ring the works on 8507 4721 for further details.

Sewer enthusiasts will also appreciate **The Greenway** at Wick Lane, Bow, E3, a four-mile path running on the top of Thames Water's Northern Outfall Sewer embankment, crossing several rivers but also unfortunately the A11, at which point local roads have to be used.

The four-and-a-half-mile **Parkland Walk** from Alexandra Palace to both Highgate and Queen's Woods at Cranley Gardens, N10 and then Highgate underground station (Holmesdale Road, N6) to Finsbury Park, N4 is a good country-style walk along a disused railway line. At Croydon, the signposted **Downlands Circular Walk** starts at the main car park on Ditches Lane, a mile from Coulsdon South railway station: another easy 'country' walk.

Walking in the countryside proper in Britain often requires generous use of the car beforehand, as one goes in search of signs indicating public footpaths. Even when a footpath is discovered, it may not be suitable. On a recent walk I made outside London the public footpath ended up in the middle of a golf course in full swing and, although the sign indicated that ramblers were entitled to walk over the course directly across the flightpath of balls heading for hole 16, I doubt that many people were courageous or foolish enough to do so.

In London there are no trespassing problems as right of way is explicitly clear. For example, you could explore gigantic Richmond Park (2,470 acres) which is next to Wimbledon Common (1,140 acres). I mean, how much land do you require for a walk in London?

There are enjoyable waterside walks, the rivers and canals providing some refuge for London's wildlife. The 180-mile **Thames Path** links the source of the river in the Cotswolds with the Thames Barrier at Woolwich. Paths are almost continuous, from Docklands in the east to Kingston in the west, on both north and south banks of the Thames. The southern side is generally quieter and less interrupted. **The Thames Path National Trail Office (01865 810224)** has more details.

In the centre of town, a walk along the river from Tower Bridge to Parliament Square is to be recommended. So too is the river path within Battersea Park. Chelsea Harbour, SW10, is a modern riverside development with a marina, and a agreeable location for a riverside walk. Medieval and modern times merge around the Thames at Wapping and Rotherhithe, while a stroll from the path on the southern side of Kew Bridge by Kew Green and ending up at Richmond Bridge is a lovely walk along a particularly pretty, peaceful stretch of river.

An exploration of the area bordered by the Thames from Putney Bridge to Barnes Bridge can take in a couple of cemeteries, Barnes Common and over 80 acres of reservoir where numerous rare birds have been sighted. The Thames towpath here can in theory be followed as far as Inglesham in Wiltshire, although continuous walking along the river becomes impossible after a few miles, and diversions are necessary.

Although walking the 23-mile towpath of the River Lee takes you through some Hackney, Tottenham and Enfield industrial estates, there's a variety of countryside, wildlife and historic buildings and you can walk as far as Essex or Hertfordshire. Explore the Bow Back Rivers, starting at picturesque Three Mills, Three Mills Lane, E3 (Bromley-By-Bow underground) with a myriad of footpaths, towpaths and river channels. **The Lower Lea Project (8983 1121)** has details and leaflets.

You could meet up with the Grand Union Canal at, for example, the towpath underneath Wharf Road in Islington, by The Narrow Boat pub, walking past painted canal boats and not particularly talkative anglers, or alternatively join the canal at Regent's Park or Camden Lock. By following the towpath from pretty Little Venice to the countryside in miniature that is Kensal Green All Souls' Cemetery, you soon reach the 200-acre Wormwood Scrubs, the largest area of greenery in the district. A leaflet, 'Explore London's Canals', is available from **British Waterways Toll House, Delamere Terrace, Little Venice, W2 6ND.** *Enclose an SAE.*

Or why not go underwater? An amble past the space-age architecture of Docklands contrasts sharply with a stroll the quarter of a mile through Greenwich Foot Tunnel near Island Gardens station, a murky old subway built at the turn of the century for dockers working in the West India docks. It goes 60 feet down under the Thames, emerging at the other end at Greenwich (see Greenwich walk that follows). Be sure to take in the magnificent sight of Greenwich, which Wren believed to be the best view in Europe, before entering the tunnel on the eastern side.

London's charm is simpler to understand if the metropolis is thought of as a cluster of villages. Walking around districts such as Whitehall, Bloomsbury and Chelsea or the villages of Hampstead, Wimbledon or Dulwich reveals different sides of the character of this great city.

Culture-rich walks are possible in the grander locations such as Mayfair, Old Chelsea, Covent Garden, Monument and Blackfriars, or the less grand but possibly more lively such as New Cross, Notting Hill and Stepney. Conveniently, many of London's famous sights evolved near each other and therefore even the shortest walk can take many of these in.

There are many organised guided walks on specialist subjects (such as Dickens' London or Legal London) typically meeting at underground stations. One firm, **Original London Walks (7624 3978)**, offers over 80 consistently good walks each week. They cost £5 per adult. Further details concerning specific walks are in *Organised Walks and Tours* page 146.

There follows a few suggested walks around London, but for more insight, anecdotes and historical detail visit your library to consult one of a number of books that are available on the subject. Some unfortunately are little more than traipses around the same old places – almost always including the likes of Hampstead and 'poor man's Hampstead', i.e. Greenwich and Blackheath, as well as the obvious tourist trail routes, such as Westminster and the City. Invariably, these books shove into the introduction Dr Samuel Johnson's remark: 'When a man is tired of London he is tired of life; for there is in London all that life can afford.' (He obviously never used the Circle line in the rush hour.) Bored of their theme, such books are prone to include walks around Windsor, Oxford, Cambridge and Stratford-upon-Avon and then slap £12.99 on the back cover, if you please.

They vary from the lively, briefly informative *London Walks* by Tiffany Daneff (published by Michael Joseph); a rather more detailed tome like *London Walks* by Anton Powell (Robson); the entertaining, such as *A Walk Round London's Parks* by Hunter Davies (Hamish Hamilton), or the rather more pedestrian *Country Walks Around London* by Leigh Hatts (David and Charles). *Walking London* and *Secret London*, both by Andrew Duncan (New Holland), are packed with interest.

Other books include *Slow Walks in London* by Michael Leich (Hodder and Stoughton), *3-D London* (Nicholson), Susan Owen's *Discovering Country Walks in South London* (Shire), *Waterside Walks in West London* by P. and C. Scott (Spurbooks), *London Walks* by Guy Williams (Constable), *Frommes's Walking Tours* (Frommes) and *London Theme Walks*, by Frank Duerdon (Cicorone), *Haggerston Press's London Guides* by Rodger Hudson each deal with a neighbourhood thoroughly.

With such a wealth of walks possible, if you are in the right frame of mind for it, walking in London can be as rewarding as any transcontinental explorer's grand and expensive leisure plans.

A CITY WALK

Leave Monument underground station at the Fish Street Hill exit and then turn right to observe Wren's 67-metre-high great fluted Doric pillar, the Monument, the City's memorial to the Great Fire of 1666. The panel at its base tells its history. To walk its 311 steps up to a great view of London, costs £1. Those suffering from vertigo will be glad to know that in 1842 the authorities caged in the viewing platform to stop people falling off it.

By the Monument, in Monument Street, and many other places around the City, are brown signs pointing towards places of interest. At this spot alone they indicate routes to the Tower of London, a riverside walk, Leadenhall Market, London Bridge and one of the City's 42 churches, so there are clearly endless things to do.

To continue the walk, turn left, down Monument Street past a wall plaque on the left explaining how the Great Fire was started, and go left again up Botolph Lane. Halfway up the lane on the right is Botolph Alley. Go up this to Wren's St Mary-at-Hill Church in Lovat Lane. The passage next to the church on the right (which a notice erected by the rector deems to be 'no right of way' although hordes use it shamefully) leads after another right and left into cobbled St Dunstan's Lane, where there's a Wren church tower and a beautiful public garden. At the other end of the garden turn left, up St Dunstan Hill, cross Great Tower Street and go up Mincing Lane, an historic trading street. On the right is Minster Court, a new development that is impressive if you like overgrown greenhouses, peculiar architecture and overblown statues of horses. At the end of the lane turn left down Fenchurch Street (making a detour to St Margaret Pattens Church in Rood Lane on the left) then up Lime Street on the right where you come to Lloyd's of London, the world's leading insurance market. The new Lloyd's tower, with its pipes and protrusions, is clearly a plumber's or air-conditioning duct salesman's ultimate fantasy.

At the end of Lime Street is a possible detour – directly over the road is the Church of St Andrew Undershaft. If it's closed at least you've got a better view of Lloyd's. Returning to the end of Lime Street take a left turn into Leadenhall Street and you come to an enclosed market of iron and glass arcades, Leadenhall. Although Victorian, a market has been here since the 1300s. Return to and continue along Leadenhall Street, which becomes Cornhill and is home to St Peter upon Cornhill Church. This is not open to the public except by prior arrangement although there's a quiet churchyard dedicated to the art of crazy paving, accessible via St Peter's Alley. At St Michael's Alley, also off Cornhill, is St Michael's Cornhill Church and further down the alley can be found Jamaica Wine House, an *olde worlde* characterful pub on the site of London's first coffee house (1692) – jeans not allowed. Returning to Cornhill, further down is perfect spot for statue aficionados – three are on the right at a walkway known as Royal Exchange Buildings, and more are around the magnificent pillared Royal Exchange building itself at the end of Cornhill. (Here another detour could be made to the Mayor's and City of London Court up Threadneedle Street.)

By the Duke of Wellington monument (at the entrance of the Royal Exchange), a metal Silver Jubilee Walkway guidepost explains the view, which includes the Bank of England (windowless for security reasons) and its museum, and the Mansion House, home of the Lord Mayor of London, built in 1753 – tours by appointment. Here there are markers on the pavement for the City's Heritage Walk.

Go up Princes Street, which is between Threadneedle Street and Poultry, and left into Lothbury and then Gresham Street to see Guildhall and on the right St Lawrence Jewry Church, which was rebuilt by Wren after the Great Fire in 1666, but was subsequently gutted in World War II. Opposite the church, across Gresham Street is King Street. Go down it, then down Queen Street where you can detour to St Paul's Cathedral and St Mary Aldermay Church at the junction with Queen Victoria Street, or go left down Cannon Street at the end of Queen Street, where on the left Salters Hall Court houses peaceful St Swithin's Gardens and Abchurch Lane is graced by St Mary Abchurch Church. Continue along Cannon Street and you are back at Monument tube station.

A WESTMINSTER WALK

Starting at Westminster tube station, a walk around adjacent Parliament Square reveals the Houses of Parliament, the stunning Westminster Abbey and splendid St Margaret's Church plus statues, including ones of Churchill, Disraeli, Palmerston and Tony Blair. Sorry, wrong about the last one.

Leave the square, going down Parliament Street, passing the Cenotaph war memorial in the centre of the road, more statues and Downing Street, which has housed the Prime Minister's London address since 1731. Moving further on, walk up Whitehall past the Horse Guards (the Changing of the Guard ceremony is at 11.15am April–Aug daily, and alternative days Sept–May) and go down Horse Guards Avenue on the right, pausing to admire its magnificent architecture.

Turn left into part of restful Victoria Embankment Gardens or left further down the avenue onto Victoria Embankment to be beside the Thames. Before you reach Hungerford Bridge (which is shared by pedestrians as well as trains if you wish to look up or down river) turn left into Northumberland Avenue and then right into Northumberland Street. The Sherlock Holmes pub, despite a tendency for displaying pavement signs saying the likes of 'Watson the menu', houses author Conan Doyle memorabilia and on the first floor an interesting recreation of Sherlock Holmes' study. Further on up the street is Trafalgar Square, one of London's most famous landmarks, with its centrepiece, the 56-metre-high Nelson's Column (which took three years to build), and the National Gallery. The square was dedicated to Lord Nelson and named after his great victory, the Battle of Trafalgar.

Pass through the three huge arches ahead, Admiralty Arch,

to The Mall, both national memorials to Queen Victoria. St James's, one of the most beautiful of the Royal parks, is on your left as you pass Horse Guards Road, opposite the Institute of Contemporary Arts and a statue of the Duke of York, a cut-price Nelson's Column.

Here you could make a detour further down the Mall to St James's Palace, which was the main Royal residence until George III moved to Buckingham Palace. Next to the Palace is a large house with a stuccoed facade. It is Clarence House, Queen Elizabeth II's sort of granny flat, the home of the Queen Mother. Beyond this is another impressive building, Lancaster House, now used for state receptions. At the end of The Mall, behind the gilded memorial to Queen Victoria in the centre of the round-about, is the Queen's London home, Buckingham Palace, which is much bigger than it looks, with state rooms stretching far back from the frontage.

Returning to Horse Guards Road, walk across the park to the lake in the centre. The park is also the most royal of the Royal parks – demonstrated by the view of Bucking-ham Palace from the bridge over the lake. Walk on through the thin park to the other side and you will come to Birdcage Walk. Turn left along it. Birdcage Walk becomes Great George Street, Parliament Square and Bridge Street and you are back at Westminster under-ground station.

A WALK AROUND BLACKHEATH AND GREENWICH

Beginning at Blackheath railway station (where regular trains from Charing Cross stop) turn left as you leave the station, going up Tranquil Vale, passing various interesting shops that help to give Blackheath its village atmosphere — although there seem to be more than a fair share of delicatessens, cafes, restaurants and estate agents. When you reach the heath, there is some beautiful 18th- and 19th-century architecture to your left and the 1857 Gothic All Saints Church to your right. Blackheath stretches out past the church, and Canary Wharf Tower is in the distance.

Walk to the end of Tranquil Vale to the small roundabout, as far as the pond just before the Hare and Billet pub. Turn right, going down Duke Humphrey Road, across the heath (which is often busy with fairs, circuses, kite festivals and sports). At the end of this road, where there is a second pond, you can enter the oldest (1433) Royal Park, Greenwich Park. Through the gates turn right, away from the tree-lined avenue, into the attractive fenced gardens, walking by the duck-stocked lake. At the other end of the lake, when you reach the expanse of lawn dotted with trees and flowerbeds, turn left and walk through the gate. Head past the bandstand (summer music on Sundays) to the cafeteria and turn right to the end of the tree-lined avenue to enjoy a magnificent view by the statue of James Wolfe. To your left is Wren's Old Royal Observatory. Walk down the great slope Wolfe is looking towards (the majestic buildings just past the park's boundaries are the National Maritime Museum, including the central building, and Inigo Jones' 1615 Queen's House. A walk around the complex is a worthwhile detour). At the bottom turn left and you will come to the lower main gates of the park. Leave these, walking straight on, down King William Walk, passing the Royal Naval College on the right and a weekend covered market on your left. You end up at the pier next to the *Cutty Sark*, the world's only surviving wool and tea clipper, built in 1869, and in its shadow the tiny vessel Francis Chichester achieved the first solo circumnavigation of the world in, the *Gipsy Moth IV* (although the latter is set to move in the near future). Here you can follow a riverside path, or take a Thames boat to Westminster (around £5 adult single, although the invariably wildly inaccurate commentary provided by a crew member is free), or you could go to the domed entrance to the atmospheric foot tunnel opened in 1902 and walk under the Thames, emerging at the Isle of Dogs.

Wildlife Activities

See *Parks and Open Spaces* (page 149) which also lists some ancient woodland and other wildlife-rich areas.

London is extremely lucky that a number of nature reserves (FREE admission) and open spaces of particular wildlife interest exist within its boundaries despite all the damage humans have heaped upon the region. Lucky for us, but also very fortunate for the surprising variety of wildlife able to take refuge at these places.

Although London would not seem an obvious choice for wildlife to flock, it has some advantages over the countryside. Cities are on the whole warmer than the surrounding areas, the concentration of people means that there is more opportunity for wildlife to scavenge food and there is far less use of pesticides. In fact large numbers of birds now visit London's reservoirs and gravel pits, a huge variety of plant species abound, fish are tentatively returning to a purer Thames, and rural animals such as foxes live here in profusion.

There are a number of wholly artificial nature reserves, such as the William Curtis Ecological Park and Lavender Pond Nature Park. These are an attempt to make up for the open space lost each year to such things as new estates, motorways and roads.

Of course, every open space in London not blessed with the title 'nature reserve' is also home to some wildlife, so a few of the better of these sites are included too.

A word of warning: if the last time you picked up a nature book was as a child, and you can't tell a hedgehog from a wart hog, it may be a good idea to read up on the subject again before visiting one of the reserves. If you don't know exactly what to look for and the best time of year to do it, some of the reserves – especially the smaller ones – can be disappointing at first glance.

If you want further information about nature reserves, contact **The London Wildlife Trust (7261 0447)**. They organise 600 FREE activities each year including woodland bat walks, glow-worm rambles, wildlife gardening talks and courses and a full programme of 'Wildlife Watch' activities for children. Events take place at over 50 nature reserves in the capital. Ring for a free events guide. They also require volunteers to help with conservation tasks, which could be anything from reed, tree and hedge planting to the creation of wildflower meadows.

The Lower Lea Project (8983 1121), the Tower Hamlets Environment Trust (7264 4660) and **The British Trust for Conservation Volunteers (7278 4293)** also need volunteers for conservation work. Refreshments may be provided, and it may be possible for volunteers' expenses to be paid.

Alexandra Park Wood Green, N22 *Alexandra Palace rail*. There's woodland, dense scrub, meadow grassland and a pond sustaining plants, insects and wildfowl. From Alexandra Palace to both Highgate and Queen's Woods at Cranley Gardens, N10 runs The Parkland Walk, with woodland, grassland and scrub at a disused railway line. There's another section from Highgate underground station (Holmesdale Road, N6) to Finsbury Park, N4.

Barnes Common Rocks Lane, Barnes SW13 *Barnes rail*. Plants, insects, mammals and birds.

Battersea Park Nature Reserve Carriage Drive East, SW8 *Battersea Park rail*. Nature trails in 'The Meadow' and 'The Wilderness'.

Beckenham Place Park Beckenham Hill Road, SE6 *Beckenham Hill rail*. 60 acres of ancient woodland, a swamp, river and pond.

Benhill Road Nature Garden Camberwell SE5 *Denmark Hill rail*. This former prefab site of grass and trees has wild plants, insects including moths and butterflies and pondlife.

Bramley Bank entrance off Broadcombe, Croydon *South Croydon* *rail*. Impressive woodland with big pond, heath and grassland.

Brent Reservoir Welsh Harp, The Hyde, West Hendon, NW9 *Hendon rail*. Open water with beds of reed and bulrush.

Camley Street Natural Park 12 Camley Street, NW1 *Usually open Sat—Thurs, ring 7833 2311 for further details. King's Cross underground/Camden Road rail*. A former canalside coal depot with a variety of habitats that has been internationally acclaimed. Despite being just a couple of acres, there's a pond, flowerbeds, woodland, meadows, a wildlife garden and marshland. Summer playscheme for children.

Cannon Hill Common Cannon Hill Lane, SW20 *Access restricted, ring 7261 0447 for details. South Merton rail*. A section of woodland in the centre of the common that is a haven for woodland birds.

The Chase Dagenham Road, Dagenham *Dagenham East underground*. Of their many sites, this is the London Wildlife Trust's largest reserve.

Chislehurst Common *Chislehurst/Petts Wood rail*. Woodland here houses bats, weasels, rabbits and foxes.

Coldfall Wood Crichton Avenue, N10 *East Finchley underground*. 35 acres of ancient woodland.

Coombe Wood between Robin Hood Way and Henley Drive, SW15 *Ring for details of access (7261 0447). Raynes Park rail*. Copious woodland flowers and butterflies.

Covert Way Field Covert Way, Hadley Wood, Barnet *Hadley Wood rail*. Scrub, grassland and coppice.

Crane Park Island Crane Park, Twickenham, Middlesex *Witton rail*. A 4-acre island reached by bridge with three nature trails including one suitable for the disabled.

Devonshire Road Nature Reserve Devonshire Road, SE23 *Open Sat 2–4pm. Forest Hill rail*. Nature trail.

Dot Hill Dot Hill Road, Plumstead, SE18 *Plumstead rail*. Woodland and meadow.

Dulwich Upper Wood Nature Park Farquar Road, SE19 *Crystal Palace rail*.

East Ham Nature Reserve Norman Road, E6 (8470 4525) *Open Mon–Fri 9am–5pm; Sat and Sun 2pm–5pm (closes at dusk in winter). Visitor centre Sat and Sun 2pm–5pm. East Ham underground.* Ten acres of derelict Norman churchyard provide a home for nearly 50 types of wild birds, a number of plants and animals including foxes, owls, kestrels and pheasants, and more than 20 butterfly species which can be explored via several nature trails with coloured marker posts. The visitor centre has a small display and staff to answer questions. Occasional workshops, open days and other events. An excellent guide (also in Braille) to the trails and the wildlife, complete with map and identification chart, is available.

Epping Forest Chingford Plain, Rangers Road, Chingford, Essex *Chingford rail, Epping/Loughton underground.* 6,000 acres of ancient wood with 150 ponds and rich grassland, many bird species, a herd of black fallow deer and a 12-mile crescent of trees and grass.

Fox Wood Fox Lane, off Hillcrest Road, W5. *Hangar Lane under-*

ground. Woodland and small wildflower meadows by Hangar Hill Park, with trail.

Fryent Country Park Fryent Way, Kingsbury, NW9 *Wembley Park underground*. Get back to nature by helping the Friends of Fryent Country Park and Barn Hill Conservation Group with a variety of conservation projects. Call 8206 0492 for details.

Gillespie Road Open Space Gillespie Road, Highbury, N5 *Arsenal underground*. A nature park on old railway sidings with grassland, scrub and a pond.

Greville Place Greville Place, NW6. For access call 7261 0447. *Kilburn Park underground*. A large garden built in the 1920s, this woodland is rich in plant life with breeding birds.

Gunnersbury Triangle Nature Reserve Bollo Lane, W3 *Open most days, ring 8747 3881 for details. Chiswick Park underground*. Six acres containing a wood, pond, marsh and meadow, with a programme of FREE events in the school summer holidays.

Hainault Forest Country Park Fox Burrows, Romford Road, Chigwell *Chadwell Heath rail*. There's woodland, scrub and grassland within this former royal hunting forest.

Hampstead Heath NW1 and NW3. *Hampstead underground* Around Kenwood is woodland, a wild flower meadow, grassland and scrub. Areas of Hampstead Heath have been designated Sites of Special Scientific Interest by English Nature because of their outstanding natural history and geological interest.

Hanwell Springs Church Road, W7 *Access by arrangement, ring*

7261 0447 for details. Hanwell rail. Situated near some of the best of Ealing's open spaces, there are lots of birds.

Hyde Park W1, W2, SW7 *Hyde Park Corner/Marble Arch underground.* Woodland, waterfowl on the Serpentine, and The Meadow, a haven for butterflies, as well as a bird sanctuary.

Joyden's Wood Cocksure Lane, Sidcup *Bexley rail.* The wood has a nature trail.

Knight's Hill Wood Knight's Hill, SE27 *Access by arrangement, ring 7261 0447 for details. West Norwood rail.* Ancient woodland, the remnant of the Great North Wood.

Lamerton Street Deptford, SE8 *Deptford rail.* Shrubs, a butterfly garden and pond.

Lavender Pond Nature Park Lavender Road, off Rotherhithe Street, SE16 *Rotherhithe underground.* Nature trails through an orchard and herb garden and there's a pond, which is home to various fish, dragonfly and water birds.

Lesnes Abbey Wood Abbey Road, Belvedere *Abbey Wood rail.* A Victorian pond, fossil pit, and lots of wild flowers, weasels, fungi and birds.

Litten Nature Reserve Oldfield Lane South, Greenford *Greenford underground/rail.* Ponds, woodland, thickets and grassland are home to various plants and animals.

Mill Hill Dean's Lane, Edgeware, Middlesex *Telephone 7261 0447 for access details.* An old railway line now a wildlife corridor for woodland birds.

New Cross Gate Cuttings Vesta Road, New Cross, SE14 *Open*

Sun 2–5pm. New Cross Gate rail. Good birdwatching on this woodland, grass and scrub.

Nunhead Cemetery Linden Grove, Peckham, SE15 *Nunhead rail.* There are over 100 plant species among the wood and grassland of this 19th-century cemetery.

Old Ford Island off Wick Lane, E3 *Access by arrangement, telephone 7261 0447. Hackney Wick rail.* An open grassland reserve surrounded by scrub on the River Lee.

Oxleas Woods Shooters Hill, SE18 *Falconwood rail.* 8,000-year-old woodland with voles, shrews, foxes, badgers, over 30 species of breeding birds, over 100 species of flowering plants and over 200 species of beetles and wild fungi. The perfect spot to site a motorway, as was recently proposed.

Richmond Park Surrey, TW10 *Kingston rail.* The varied landscape of hills, woodland, and grassland abounds in wildlife, including over 600 red and fallow deer.

Selsdon Wood Court Wood Lane, Selsdon, Croydon *Hayes rail.* Woodland, wetland, grassland pasture and bird sanctuary.

Staines Reservoir Stanwell Moor Road, Staines, Middlesex TW18. *Hampton rail.* Visitors must keep to the public footpath through the central causeway. The reservoir is a site of Special Scientific Interest and a must for birdwatchers: a winter count recorded a massive 4,000 tufted duck.

Stave Hill Ecological Park Timber Road, Rotherhithe, SE16 *Rotherhithe rail.* A variety of natural environments encourage the rich wildlife.

Sydenham Hill Wood entrance on Crescent Wood Road, off

Sydenham Hill, SE26 *Sydenham Hill rail*. Ancient and recent woodland with rich birdlife, unusual grasses and flowers.

Ten Acre Wood Charville Lane, North Hayes, UB4 *Ruislip Gardens underground*. Oak woodland with flower-rich meadows and scrub.

Thameside River Road, Creekmouth, Barking. *Upney underground*. A lagoon, dykes and grassland.

Tower Hamlets Cemetery Park Southern Grove, E3 *Mile End underground*. An overgrown Victorian cemetery transformed into a nature reserve (complete with tombs). Tree trail.

Trent Country Park Cockfosters Road, Barnet, Herts *Cockfosters underground*. This country park has over 400 acres with nature trails and an abundance of small wildlife in the woods. There's also a large farm. At the entrance opposite Cockfosters underground station there's a woodland trail for blind people with messages in Braille. Why can't this be commonplace?

Tump 53, Bentham Road, Thamesmead, SE28. *Abbey Wood rail*. Water, reedbeds, meadow and scrub.

Walthamstow Marshes Spring Hill, Clapton, E5. *Clapton rail*. The only remaining ancient grassland in the Lea Valley, with nearly 400 plant species recorded.

The Warren Crockenhill Road, Orpington. *St Mary Cray rail*. Woodland, pond and marsh.

William Curtis Ecological Park 16 Vine Lane, Tooley Street, SE1. *London Bridge rail/underground*. A wealth of plants, birds and pondlife.

Wimbledon Common Parkside, Wimbledon, SW19. *Southfields underground*. Animals here include badgers, lizards, grass snakes and butterflies and rich birdlife on the ponds.

Working London

Admission is *free* unless otherwise specified.

Auctions

Bonhams and Brooke Montpelier Street, SW7 (7393 3900) *Open Mon–Fri 9am–4.30pm. Knightsbridge underground;* **Christie's** 8 King Street, SW1 (7839 9060) *Open Mon 9am–4.45pm; Tues 9am–8pm; Wed–Fri 9am–4.45pm; Sun 2–4.30pm. Green Park underground;* **Phillips** 101 New Bond Street, W1 (7629 6602) *Open Mon–Fri 8.30am–5pm. Bond Street underground;* **Sotheby's** 34 New Bond Street, W1 (7293 5000) *Open Mon–Fri 9am–4.30pm. Bond Street underground.* With thousands of pounds rapidly changing hands during a sale, auction houses can be particularly exciting places. Just don't nod your head at the wrong moment. Sales vary enormously and could be for anything from costumes to clocks, coins to carpets.

BEER

Young's Ram Brewery Tap Visitors' Centre, Ram Street, SW18 (8875 7005) *Open Mon–Sat 10am–6pm; tours 10am, noon, 2pm, 4pm. Adults £3.50, children 14–18 £2, children under 14 not admitted. Wandsworth Town rail.* See how that pint gets in your glass.

CARS

Ford Motor Company Thames Avenue, Dagenham, Essex (7526 4570) *Tours by appointment only Mon—Fri 9.30am, 1.15pm. Dagenham Heathway underground/Dagenham Dock rail (over-10s only).* Ring or write to Factory Tours, Room 3/001, at the above address to go on a 40-minute tour of part of the famous Dagenham works, which is 10 per cent larger than the City's square mile and is Europe's biggest engine plant. You get to see part of the manufacturing process of a car including an engine being fitted with components on the production line.

CIVIL LAW

Royal Courts of Justice Strand, WC2 (7947 6000) *Open Mon—Fri 9.30am—1pm; 2—4.30pm. No court cases Aug—Sept. Under-16s not admitted. No cameras, radios, food, drink, large bags, mobile phones. Temple underground.* Also known as 'the law courts', or the 'High Court', this massive neo-Gothic building holds the country's principal civil cases – those that are too serious for the county courts. Visit one of the 88 court rooms, during a fraud trial perhaps, or instead the small legal museum and small exhibition of judges' robes. The main hall is worth a visit on its own, to admire its huge mosaic floor.

CRIMINAL LAW

Old Bailey (the Central Criminal Court) Newgate Street, EC4 (7248 3277) *Open Mon—Fri 10.30am—1pm; 2—4pm. Under-14s not admitted. No cameras, radios, food, drink, large bags, mobile phones. St Paul's underground.* Magistrates' courts, for dealing with more minor offences, and crown courts, for more serious ones, are scattered around London (consult the telephone directory) but the Old Bailey's 19 courts are where the country's chief criminal cases are tried. It can be fascinating to watch an interesting trial from one of the public galleries although, if you're unlucky, you may find you've looked in on a dull one. The most gripping section of the trial is usually when a witness is being cross-examined by the opposing side's counsel. The oldest courts, numbers one, two and three, usually hold the best trials. When I visited, the murder case in court number one was conducted by two witty barristers convinced they were treading the boards of the National, an under-intelligent self-incriminating defendant who'd been caught red-handed when attempting to get a 32-inch safe through a 30-inch door frame, and a judge who fell asleep through it all. Court number one is where Crippen was sentenced to death in 1910 and the Great Train Robbers were sent down for 30 years. Who knows, if you get summoned to do jury service here, you can visit and get paid for it too.

FISH

Billingsgate Market 87 West India Dock Road, Isle of Dogs, E14 *Open Tues–Sat 5–9am. West India Quay DLR*. A huge wholesale fish market with plenty of activity, a large variety of fish, and water spilling everywhere.

FLOWERS

New Covent Garden Market Nine Elms Lane, SW8 *Open Mon–Fri 3.30–10am. Vauxhall underground*. Although there is a fruit and vegetable market here, casual visitors are not encouraged and it's not incredibly interesting anyway. On the other hand a visit to the wide-awake wholesale flower and plant market in the middle of the night on the way back from a nightclub or after a dose of insomnia can be quite surreal. The scents of the thousands of flowers can combine to make a potent perfume.

FRUIT AND VEGETABLES

Borough Market Borough High Street and Stoney Street, SE1 *Open Mon–Fri 5.30–10am. London Bridge underground/rail.* A wholesale market with great atmosphere. From the 13th century the market was held on London Bridge, moving to this site in 1756.

GOVERNMENT

The Houses of Parliament Parliament Square, SW1 *Commons (7219 4272), Lords (7219 3107). Westminster underground.* There has been a royal palace here since the 11th century but after an extensive fire in 1834 this famous sight, the Palace of Westminster, home of our ancient democratic process, was rebuilt in the mid-19th century in a neo-Gothic style. It has about 1,000 rooms linked by two miles of corridors and employs nearly 1,800 people. The two chambers, the Commons and Lords, are either side of a central hall and corridor. The 104-metre high Westminster Clocktower on the north-west corner of the Palace of Westminster contains the 3-metre-diameter 13.5-ton bell, known as Big Ben. If you are lucky enough to visit the clocktower (334 steps to the belfry) you are able to walk behind the illuminated clock faces and watch the clock ticking and the bells being struck.

Tours: Book a £3.50 guided tour of both Houses in advance through Ticketmaster (7344 9966).

'Line of route' tour: During the recess, parties can take a tour at any time on weekdays. When the Houses are sitting, hourly official tours are available weekdays before noon and on Friday afternoons. Groups must be sponsored by a Member of Parliament or peer or, if not a UK citizen, apply to your Embassy or High Commission or by writing to The Public Information Office of the House of Commons. Groups should be no larger than 16 people. Tickets are not required but guides expect a gratuity of around £25 per party.

'Big Ben' tour: Contact your MP, Embassy or High Commission to book the FREE 45-minute tours Mon–Fri at 10.30am, 11.30am and 2.30pm. Over-11s only. You climb the 334 steps of the belfry and walk behind the illuminated clock faces and watch the clock ticking and the bell being struck.

'Lord Chancellor's apartments' tour: FREE tours on Tues/Thurs mornings but long waiting list. Phone 7219 2184 for cancellations.

Strangers' Gallery, House of Commons. FREE admission. Open when the House is sitting from 2.30pm Mon–Wed, 11.30am Thurs and sometimes 9.30am Fri (phone 7219 5532 to check times). UK residents can apply to an MP or peer; if not a UK citizen, apply to your Embassy or High Commission in advance for tickets otherwise queue at the St Stephen's entrance. You could be waiting an hour or two at popular periods, such as Prime Minister's Questions, 3pm Wed.

Strangers' Gallery, House of Lords: FREE admission. Open when the House is sitting, from 2.30pm Mon–Wed, 3pm Thurs and occasionally 11am Fri. Queue at the St Stephen's entrance.

GLASS

London Glassblowing Workshop 7 Leather Market, Weston Street, SE1 (7403 2800) *Open Mon–Fri 10am–5pm. London Bridge underground/rail.* Visitors get to see molten glass being blown and moulded into colourful creations.

MANUFACTURING

Royal British Legion Poppy Factory 20 Petersham Road, Richmond, Surrey (8940 3305) *Open by appointment for tours Mon–Thurs 10.15am and 1.15pm. Richmond underground/rail.* Take a two-hour tour of the factory where over 30 million poppies are made each year as well as the wreath the Queen lays by the Cenotaph on Remembrance Sunday.

MEAT

Smithfield Market London Central Markets, West Smithfield, EC1. *Open Mon–Fri 5–10.30am. Farringdon underground.* With carcasses and bins everywhere full of livers and hearts, and porters wearing blood-stained white overalls, this wholesale meat market is not a place for the squeamish.

METAL

London Metal Exchange 56 Leadenhall Street, EC3 (7264 5555) *Monument underground.* Telephone the marketing department to arrange a visit to the exchange (Mon–Fri noon–

1.30pm) to see this unusual City market at work. The traders sit in a circle quietly to start with but a few minutes later the pace accelerates into frenzied shouting and gesticulating, only to cease at the sound of a bell. Then the process repeats with a different metal being traded on the floor. There's also a 17-minute video presentation providing background information.

MAIL

Mount Pleasant Post Office Farringdon Road, EC1 (7239 2311) *Tours are by prior arrangement, and bookings must be confirmed in writing at least 14 days before visit. Children under 9 not admitted. Farringdon underground/rail.* Follow the journey of a letter in Europe's biggest sorting office, including seeing the mechanical sorting equipment in action and a look at the underground Mail Rail installed in 1927 which carries 10 million sacks of mail around London on automatic trains. It's best to visit at around 2pm, which is when the Mail Rail starts.

SILVER

London Silver Vaults Chancery House, 53–64 Chancery Lane, WC2 (7242 3844) *Open Mon–Fri 9am–5.30pm; Sat 9am–12.30pm. Chancery Lane underground.* Enter the 35 vaults below ground level and discover the biggest collection of silver in the world, antique and modern. The traders are happy to talk about their wares, hallmarks and history. It's surprising how much money a tiny, unexciting-looking item can command. Guided tours by arrangement.

WATER

Thames Water Utilities *Telephone customer services (0845 920 0800) to arrange a tour of one of their London water or sewage treatment works to see the processes involved in treating water to make it drinkable.* According to Thames Water, visitors are usually taken aback at the vast scale of the operation, the immense amount of work and engineering required to do this. Water treatment works include Ashford and Hampton (serving south and west London), Copper Mills (north London), and New Riverhead, a recently installed site for the London Ringmain, which is a water pipeline around London that is so large you could fit a London cab in it. Sewage treatment works include Abbey Mills (serving north and east London), Beckton (north-east London), Beddington (south London and Croydon), Crossness (south-east London), Esher (Surrey and south-west London), Mogdon and Hogs Mill (south-west London) and Riverside and Nags Head, both serving Essex.

Some Suggested Itineraries for the Financially Famished

East End Family Day Out *Bethnal Green underground.* Two of London's best free museums suitable for the whole family, Bethnal Green Museum of Childhood and the Geffrye Museum, are just a road apart, with Hackney City Farm in between. The three combined make an excellent family day out, and it's all FREE.

City Churches Tour *Bank/St Paul's/Monument underground.* The City contains some of Britain's most beautiful historic churches and you can walk from one to another with ease. Be sure to visit in the middle of the day on a weekday, and take in one of the many FREE regular lunchtime music recitals.

Greenwich and Blackheath *Greenwich/Blackheath rail, Greenwich DLR.* For a trip out from the centre of the capital, you can't beat Greenwich and Blackheath. They are rich in open space – beautiful Greenwich Park, the oldest royal park, huge Blackheath Common, and if you have the time, ancient Oxleas Woods. Excellent architecture abounds and the National Maritime Museum, Royal Naval College and Old Royal Observatory are among the capital's top attractions. Children love to walk through Greenwich foot tunnel to the Isle of Dogs.

British Museum *Russell Square underground.* Many children can find the British Museum vast, so break up the visit with a trip to nearby Coram's Fields to see the animals. And near to that is Dickens' House Museum.

Art Days *Charing Cross rail/underground.* If you are an art lover, keep to WC1 and W1 for an almost endless supply of galleries: the National Gallery, National Portrait Gallery, Photographers' Gallery are by or near Trafalgar Square while Mayfair boasts many commercial galleries.

Covent Garden *Covent Garden underground.* Not only will children love the street theatre, but a trip to the Theatre Museum, the Cabaret Mechanical Theatre exhibition and the London Doll's House Company opposite will make the visit even more fun. Cross Kingsway to Lincoln's Inn Fields to see one of London's best, yet surprisingly little-known museums, the eccentric Sir John Soane Museum.

Area Index of Selected Attractions by Postcode

EAST

E1

E2

NORTH

N16

N17

NW1

NW3

NW4

NW5

NW6

SE23

SW1

SW3